# The Cherokee Cases

## The Confrontation of Law and Politics

Jill Norgren

*John Jay College of Criminal Justice*

and

*The University Graduate Center of The City University of New York*

McGraw-Hill, Inc.

New York   St. Louis   San Francisco   Auckland   Bogotá   Caracas   Lisbon
London   Madrid   Mexico City   Milan   Montreal   New Delhi
San Juan   Singapore   Sydney   Tokyo   Toronto

This book was set in Palatino by ComCom, Inc.
The editors were Peter Labella, Lyn Uhl, and Diane Schadoff;
the production supervisor was Diane Ficarra.
The cover was designed by Tippit-Woolworth Design.
Maps were rendered by Mapping Specialists, Limited.
R. R. Donnelley & Sons Company was printer and binder.

THE CHEROKEE CASES
The Confrontation of Law and Politics

This book is printed on recycled, acid-free paper
containing 10% postconsumer waste.

1 2 3 4 5 6 7 8 9 0 DOC DOC 9 0 9 8 7 6 5

ISBN 0-07-047191-6

Library of Congress Cataloging-in-Publication Data

Norgren, Jill.
    The Cherokee cases: the confrontation of law and politics / Jill
Norgren.
        p.    cm. — (McGraw-Hill case studies in constitutional
history)
    Includes bibliographical references and index.
    ISBN 0-07-047191-6
        1. Cherokee Indians—Claims.        2. Cherokee Indians—Land tenure.
    3. Indians of North America—Georgia—Claims.        4. Indians of North
    America—Georgia—Land tenure.        5. Georgia—Trials, litigation, etc.
    I. Title.        II. Series.
    KF8208.N67        1996
    346.7304′32′089975—dc20
    [347.306432089975]

                                                        95-13761

# *About the Author*

JILL NORGREN is professor of political science at John Jay College of Criminal Justice and the University Graduate Center of The City University of New York, where she teaches courses in law and politics. She has published widely in academic and political opinion journals and is co-author of *American Cultural Pluralism and Law* (Praeger/Greenwood, 1988) and *Partial Justice: Federal Indian Law in a Liberal Constitutional System* (Berg, 1991).

*In Memory of Petra T. Shattuck,*
*with Whom I Traveled the Maze*
*of United States Indian Law*

# Contents

# Foreword

We usually think of the Supreme Court as a legal institution, and certainly it is that. The high court and its justices however, have performed a far greater task than merely settling law cases and enunciating constitutional principles. Chief Justice Charles Evans Hughes for example, once declared the Court to be "distinctly American in concept and function" because its impact was felt far beyond the courtroom. Alexis de Tocqueville, the great pre-Civil War commentator on American democracy, concluded that "I am unaware that any nation on the globe has hitherto organized a judicial power in the same manner as the Americans." He went on to observe that in America "scarcely any political question arises . . . that is not resolved, sooner or later, into a judicial question."

Many important political questions have come to be settled by the Supreme Court because of the incapacity of the political system to come to terms with them. The docket of the high court, as a result, reads something like a social, political, and economic history of the nation, reflecting back through the disputes brought to it the major controversies of American history, ranging from state-nation relations, property rights, and slavery in the pre-Civil War era, to issues of economic regulation and the impact of urbanization and industrialization in the period up to World War II, and finally to matters of individual rights and liberty in our own time. By looking at what the Court has decided and how it has decided it we can come to terms with not just the institution, but with the major themes of American history.

The books in this volume are designed to tell more than the story of great constitutional battles. They are meant, as well, to shed light on important moments and movements in the nation's history and, in so doing, to reveal broad trends in our social, political, and economic history. Jill Norgren's insightful analysis of the famous *Cherokee Cases* more than meets this challenge by revealing much about the fate of Native Americans in the early nineteenth century. The cases evolved out of attempts by Georgia to assert jurisdiction over Cherokee lands within the state that were protected by a federal treaty.

In *Cherokee Nation v. Georgia in 1831*, Chief Justice John Marshall held that the Supreme Court had no jurisdiction to hear a Cherokee request to enjoin Georgia's effort. He defined the Cherokee people as a "domestic, dependent nation," rather than a sovereign nation for purposes of Article III of the Constitution. His decision effectively made the Cherokees wards of the United States government. One year later the Court modified this position in *Worcester v. Georgia*. In this case a congregational missionary had been convicted of failure to have a license that Georgia required to live in the Cherokee country. This time Chief Justice Marshall's opinion held the Georgia laws void because they violated federal treaties, the contract and commerce clauses of the Constitution, and the sovereign authority of the Cherokee nation. He found that the Cherokees were a distinct people with the right to retain independent political communities. Georgia refused to acknowledge the proceeding.

These cases are landmarks in the history of the interaction of the white and Native American peoples. Norgren's study of them reveals the deep conflicts that have divided the nation over the fate of the Indian peoples and their lands since its founding. The cases are a moment in both our constitutional and our social-political history. Like other volumes in this series, Jill Norgren's study makes it possible for us to understand who we are and what we have become, by explaining the rich history of our constitutional disputes.

Kermit L. Hall
*The Ohio State University*

Melvin I. Urofsky
*Virginia Commonwealth University*

# Preface

*The Cherokee Cases* is a legal history that examines two seminal Supreme Court cases of the early 1830s—*Cherokee Nation* v. *Georgia* and *Worcester* v. *Georgia*. Including this study in a series devoted to landmark Supreme Court decisions acknowledges the importance of these two cases in establishing the legal doctrine of the United States. My objective was to illuminate their role not only in legal doctrine, but also in the political development of the Cherokee Republic and the United States of America. As such, the study should be of interest to students of legal history, United States constitutional law, and political development, as well as to those with a more general interest in Native American and American studies.

The book opens with a brief introduction to early Cherokee and Georgia history, followed by an examination of the political role of the United States government in the expanding conflict between the Cherokee Republic and the State of Georgia. The second chapter, dealing with the earliest of the Cherokee cases, *State* v. *Tassels*, explores the relationship between the Cherokee leaders and their lawyers in the development of a court strategy. Next comes a discussion of Andrew Jackson and the age of politics that he created. Subsequent chapters examine the *Cherokee Nation* and *Worcester* decisions in some detail, set them in the context of other relevant Supreme Court actions, and document the failure of the United States to carry out the high court rulings in the *Worcester* case. A concluding chapter provides a brief survey of the impact of Cherokee decisions on Native American–United States legal relations in subsequent history. The decisions in the three Cherokee cases—*State* v. *Tassels, Cherokee Nation* v. *Georgia,* and *Worcester* v. *Georgia*—are reprinted in appendices.

This book draws upon twenty years of research and writing on federal Indian law. I began that enterprise with my colleague, Petra T. Shattuck. We read, learned, and wrote together for many years until her death. Much of the direction and wisdom in this book belongs to Petra.

Many individuals lent encouragement and intellectual guidance to this undertaking. For this I give warm thanks to Milner Ball, Curtis Berkey, Sheila Cole, Robert T. Coulter, Representative Bill Dover (Georgia), Sidney Harring, Charles Hudson, Sheila Mahoney, Serena Nanda, Anneka Norgren, Philippa Strum, Steven M. Tullberg, Melvin Urofsky, Mary Young, and Jean Zorn. I owe a particular debt to the following reviewers who gave this manuscript a careful reading and who have guided me in numerous, important ways: M. Browning Carrott, Southern Illinois University at Carbondale; David Edmunds, Indiana University; William Gienapp, Harvard University; Kermit Hall, University of Tulsa; Peter Iverson, Arizona State University; Yan Li, Grand Valley State University; Thomas Morris, Portland State University; Kent Newmyer, University of Connecticut; Roger Nichols, University of Arizona; Phillip Paludan, University of Kansas; Donald Roper, State University of New York College at New Paltz; Ronald Satz, University of Wisconsin–Eau Claire; and John Wunder, University of Nebraska–Lincoln. Christiana Norgren demonstrated considerable filial devotion by reading and providing a critique of the entire manuscript—with an eye to the needs of undergraduate readers—despite the demands of her own doctoral thesis work. Her vision was strong and her pen firm.

It is a special pleasure when the much-loved projects of a professor engage a student-colleague. Maureen Milici developed a deep interest in federal Indian law and took on much of the research of this book's concluding chapter as independent study. She is a gifted student of law and I happily acknowledge the legal research note she contributed for the concluding chapter.

Various grants and fellowships have supported my research on the Cherokee Republic and federal Indian law. I am greatly indebted to The City University of New York PSC-CUNY Research Foundation for repeated awards; to the National Endowment for the Humanities for travel to collection, summer seminar, and summer stipend fellowships; to the American Council of Learned Societies for a research grant; and to John Jay College of Criminal Justice for a research release-time award.

Ralph Norgren supported the writing of this book with humor and loving commitment. As I have said before, he is made of more than the right stuff.

Jill Norgren

# Introduction

## STATE OF GEORGIA "PARDON"

*The Cherokee people farmed, built homes and communities, and evolved a high order of civilization long before any English colonists arrived to begin their lives in Georgia. For so long as English and other European settlers did not much covet the property of the Cherokee, tolerant coexistence between the different peoples in Georgia peacefully occurred. Recognized formally as a sovereign nation, the Cherokee people administered their own lives and regulated for themselves commerce and visitation with non-native Americans residing in Georgia.*

*On December 22, 1830, the Georgia legislature passed an act requiring all white men to obtain special permits from the State of Georgia to live within the Cherokee Nation. Many educators and religious figures were the targets of this new law.*

*Two missionaries who had been active in recording and preserving Cherokee culture refused to submit to the new law. On July 15, 1831, Reverend Samuel Austin Worcester and Reverend Elihu Butler were arrested by Georgia authorities and charged with "Residing in the Cherokee Nation without License." Both clergymen were put on trial in Gwinnett Superior Court on September 15, 1831, found guilty, and sentenced to four years in prison.*

*The Cherokees stood by their devoted friends. While the two clergymen were held in the state prison at Milledgeville, the Cherokees hired lawyer William Wirt, who had been United States Attorney General under Presidents Monroe and Adams, to appeal the convictions to the U.S. Supreme Court. During*

1

*January, 1832, in an important opinion written by Chief Justice John Marshall, the Supreme Court ruled the State of Georgia had violated the sovereignty of the Cherokee Nation, and that Georgia had no right of any kind to impose its laws on the Cherokee people. The Supreme Court ordered the State of Georgia to vacate their criminal convictions and set free Reverend Worcester and Reverend Butler.*

*Officials of the State of Georgia refused to obey the U.S. Supreme Court, and the clergymen were kept in prison. President Andrew Jackson refused to use federal troops to enforce the order of the U.S. Supreme Court. Finally, during 1833, a new governor, Wilson Lumpkin, discharged both clergymen from the state prison.*

*Today, the State Board of Pardons and Paroles acts to remove a stain on the history of criminal justice in Georgia. The U.S. Supreme Court did what it could 160 years ago to reverse the wrong committed against Reverend Worcester and Reverend Butler. Believing justice ought to be denied no longer, by this Order the State Board of Pardons and Paroles unconditionally and fully pardons Samuel Austin Worcester and Elihu Butler.*

—Given under the hand and seal of the [Georgia] State Board of
Pardons and Paroles upon this 15th day of September 1992

In November 1992 newspapers throughout the United States announced an extraordinary event: the full and unconditional pardon by the state of Georgia of two northern missionaries, long dead, who had been imprisoned in *1831* for defying Georgia law and supporting Cherokee national sovereignty. In a ceremony, Governor Zell Miller presented the posthumous pardons to state representative Bill Dover, chief executive officer of the Georgia Tribe of Eastern Cherokee. According to the governor's press release, the unusual occasion of a pardon ceremony signified the state's effort to "correct this 161-year old miscarriage of justice" and "mend a painful period in Georgia and Cherokee history."[1]

In one way the pardon, which had been put into motion at Dover's suggestion, closed a chapter in the celebrated 1832 United States Supreme Court case of *Worcester* v. *Georgia*. In granting the pardons, the state of Georgia acknowledged that the missionaries had been innocent of the crime for which they had been convicted.

The statement accompanying the pardons conceded that Georgia had refused to obey the decision of the Supreme Court, holding that the missionaries had been wrongly convicted under an unconstitutional state law that also violated treaties guaranteeing Cherokee sovereignty.

But the pardons also open the way for a reexamination of *Worcester* and the events that resulted in both the illegal seizure of the lands of the Cherokee Nation and the forced removal of Cherokee citizens by the governments of Georgia and the United States. This new admission of guilt leads one to ask why Cherokee sovereignty was violated and why the missionaries were wrongfully imprisoned. A governor's earnest effort to mend relations in 1992 impels one to consider why his predecessor in the 1830s refused, with considerable vitriol, to obey a Supreme Court decision. And a pardon granted long after the parties have died raises the question of what happened to those convicted in this legal action while they were alive and forced to live with the consequences of the state's illegal actions.

This book tells the story of how, beginning in 1830, the leaders of the Cherokee Republic, having internalized the ideals of American law, hired lawyers to litigate in American courts. The lawyers they hired were Americans; the goal was to protect the Cherokee Nation's internationally recognized political rights, including national boundaries and national sovereignty. The Cherokee sought protection from the actions of the people and government of the state of Georgia. Georgians were neighbors of the Cherokee. Early Georgia-bound colonists had come from England to North America beginning in the 1730s. As their numbers grew, the colonists came into increasing conflict with the Cherokee and the other original inhabitants of the region over land and its use. The European colonists, whose standard of living was not necessarily superior to that of the Cherokee, had certain advantages in their pursuit of land. First, their numbers grew quickly, fed by an increasingly overcrowded England. Their weapons were superior. They brought trade and capital that permitted the creation of economic and social networks helpful to expansion. Finally, the eighteenth-century colonists had, in written language, a more efficient system of communication in their far-flung ventures than did the Cherokee, who did not have a written form of their language until the early nineteenth century.

But most critically, the Cherokee and the Georgia colonists were separated by different world views. The colonists came out of a tradition that honored individual effort and acquisitiveness. Individual rights—however limited by gender, race, and class—was an emerging theme in British colonial culture. The Cherokee, in contrast, lived by more communal norms. Among the Cherokee, for example, land was not held individually and was not considered a commodity subject to individual commercial transactions. Very different understandings of the universe also separated Cherokee and Georgian. The colonists, drawing on Western religious ideas, believed nature to be God's gift to humankind, for people to rule over. The colonist was both permitted and expected to tame nature and develop it in ways appropriate to the growth of empire and the enhancement of individual status. For the Cherokee, however, nature, and thus the land and its resources, had "sacred primacy." Human beings, according to the Cherokee, were only a part of the natural world and were required to respect its workings rather than manipulate them for selfish gain. As time passed, the clash of cultures also reflected the increasingly strong racial views of the colonists, who believed that the Cherokee, along with other Native Americans, were inferior to them.

By the early nineteenth century the Cherokee and their Georgia neighbors were in constant conflict. The Georgians pressed in on Cherokee land and made it clear that they wished to be rid of the Cherokee Republic. The Cherokee and the Georgians were not, of course, the only people locked in this struggle. Throughout the United States there was agitation to move Native Americans westward. In the first decades of the nineteenth century, the southeastern portion of North America became a central arena of American aggression and Native American resistance. As the U.S. government and local state governments pursued an Indian removal policy, the Native American nations of the Southeast—the Choctaw, Chickasaw, Creek, Seminole, and Cherokee—simultaneously promulgated their own policies and vied with the Americans for control of the region. Officials visited one another's governments and negotiated diplomatic agreements. Their people traded and sometimes intermarried. The early Europeans brought disease and death; this was unintentional, but nevertheless it reduced the Native American population and weakened its social structures. The Europeans also brought alcohol and quickly discovered that it too could be an effective and silent tool of conquest. Nations battled on the killing fields. And then, in the United States–Cherokee conflict, the Cherokee changed strategy: They decided to contest the aggression of the government and people of Georgia in courts of the United States, using laws of the Americans' own making.

The Cherokee made this decision in 1830 specifically in response to the draconian actions of the Georgia legislature in the last years of the 1820s. Impatient with the results of warfare, treaties, and national policies of trade and assimilation, Georgia representatives had committed themselves to the destruction of Cherokee society and government and the seizure of Cherokee lands through state legislation backed by police action. Their laws called for the extension of state jurisdiction over the people of the Cherokee Nation. This legislation set out to nullify all Cherokee law, make Cherokees second-class citizens of color under Georgia law, and claim and redistribute the lands of the Cherokee to Georgians. To block opposition to this plan to denationalize the Cherokee Republic, Georgia officials decreed that the state would arrest any Cherokee national leader who tried to convene a meeting of the Cherokee government and any American living among the Cherokee who did not swear an oath signaling approval of Georgia's jurisdiction laws.

The Cherokee fought back by appealing to the United States Supreme Court. In three landmark cases—*State* v. *Tassels* (1830), *Cherokee Nation* v. *Georgia* (1831), and *Worcester* v. *Georgia* (1832)— the Cherokee Republic argued that the actions of the state of Georgia violated fundamental legal agreements between the Cherokee and the United States acknowledging Cherokee sovereignty. Defeated in their first two efforts, the Cherokee finally succeeded when, in *Worcester*, the Court concluded that Georgia's jurisdiction laws were "repugnant to the constitution, laws, and treaties of the United States" and had violated the political rights of the Cherokee Republic.

These three cases have lasting importance for Cherokee and American political and legal history and fall into a category scholars have designated "landmark." Like many landmark Supreme Court cases, the conflict behind the Cherokee litigation was many years in the making. And like many such cases, these appeals represented a planned, sustained effort in the courtroom to resolve fundamental issues of power and rights, contentious issues that had not lent themselves to resolution in other forums—private or public. In common with other important appeals to the nation's highest court in the first decades of the nineteenth century, the Cherokee cases presented questions of state versus federal power. The openly anti-Cherokee position of the newly elected President of the United States, Andrew Jackson, gave the dispute an intensely political character, also not an uncommon characteristic of landmark litigation. Not surprisingly, given the brief existence of the United States, the legal doctrine relevant to Native American–American relations was underdeveloped and ambiguous and thus in need of clarification. In short, in a number of ways, the Cherokee cases followed a pattern typical of landmark litigation.

But the landmark Cherokee appeals were anything but typical. It is neither inaccurate nor overly dramatic to argue that these cases posed transcendent questions specific to the colonialist origins of the United States. The United States was still a young nation in 1830, when the first Cherokee appeal was filed. At that time it was acknowledged that the decisions of the Supreme Court would become part of the text establishing—or limiting—American claims to the continent. In these appeals the Cherokee Republic asked the members of the Supreme Court in the starkest terms to choose between the rights of the original inhabitants of the continent and the power of the colonizers, now the United States.

As a matter of patriotism and politics, the Supreme Court should have ruled openly and unequivocally for the United States. The Court operated, after all, under the authority of the United States. But this did not happen—exactly. Rather, using complex, obfuscating, and sometimes incorrect interpretations of history and treaties as well as English and international law, the Court attempted to forge a compromise that would permit the United States to view itself as a nation under the rule of law while continuing its quest to control the continent. This effort, begun in the earlier Supreme Court cases of *Fletcher* v. *Peck* (1810) and *Johnson* v. *M'Intosh* (1823) and completed in the Cherokee cases, saw the creation of an Americanized law of international relations and an American law of continental real estate that favored the United States while diminishing the rights of Native American sovereignties.

According to law, it appeared that the United States had little basis for its claims. Native Americans had ancient possession of the lands of North America. Binding international treaties between the United States and the Cherokee (and other Native American governments) recognized Indian sovereignty and national land boundaries. American legal and political ideals, as expressed in the U.S. Constitution, committed the United States to fairness in government proceedings and respect for what Americans considered the sacred, inalienable right to property. Nevertheless, in spite of these constraints, between 1810 and 1832 the members of the Supreme Court constructed a jurisprudence that emphasized American interests. In these efforts, the Court was led by Chief Justice John Marshall.

Marshall had presided over the U.S. Supreme Court since 1801. A bold, assertive jurist, he used the authoritative decisions of the Court to support his Federalist vision of a powerful central government and national economy. Marshall also was strongly committed to increasing the stature of the United States in the international community. The nation was barely a decade old when Marshall joined the Court; the nation was politically and economically vulnerable. Skillfully, Marshall began to mold the law. Part of his success lay in his understanding that despite the respected legal traditions of natural law, English common law, colonial law, and commentaries on international law, the United States had to have an *American* law developed by American jurists attending to American needs. Although the depth of Marshall's concern for the Cherokee remains open to question, there is no contesting the fact that as chief justice he used the Cherokee appeals to establish the legal doctrine, the jurisprudence, of an American law of United States–Native American relations. In the United States, this jurisprudence is called federal Indian law, a bland term that masks the intense politics and polemics associated with court decisions involving questions of Native American rights.

An American law that addressed the issues of United States–Indian relations could not be constructed without confronting the legacy of the Western legal traditions. The Marshall Court had to contend with the idea of inalienable human rights expressed in natural law, the concept of national sovereignty promoted in commentaries on international law, and the rules governing the acquisition and transfer of property embedded in the English law of property. The concept of natural law grew out of early Western philosophy and religious ideas. At the time of the Marshall Court, natural law referred to a set of abstract unwritten principles concerning "justice, humanity, tolerance and 'civilized' living that were 'beyond dispute' in any culture which considered itself enlightened."[2] In the late eighteenth century principles of natural rights—the inalienable rights of life, liberty, and property—became part of the American philosophy of natural law. Natural law as it was fused with natural rights represented a high—a revolutionary—human achievement. It symbolized the rejection of monarchy, corruption, and ascribed status and the establishment of a theoretical commitment to human equality. As a structure of universal moral and legal principles, natural law, natural rights, and international law logically posed the question of the status of Native Americans under Western law.

The Marshall Court might have approached the question of whether "Indians had any rights the white man was bound to respect" simply by acknowledging the common humanity and therefore the natural law rights of the Cherokee with respect to both their national sovereignty and their lands. Given the Indians' prior possession of these lands, the English concept of fee simple title (complete land title conveying the right to keep, use, sell, and will), and international law, the Court might have confirmed that Native American nations such as the Cherokee had a complete, unencumbered title to their land. In short, the judges might easily have cited existing legal principles, cases, and treaties to come to the conclusion that Native Americans had broad rights that the United States was bound to respect. But the Court did not do this.

If patriotism and politics did not direct the Court to rule unequivocally for the United States, neither did legal tradition guide it to rule completely for the Cherokee Republic and other Native American nations. Rather, the Court drew selectively on existing Western legal traditions to create a federal Indian law that was consonant with many of the political and economic goals of the United States. Where it served the Court's purposes, its members built a case on familiar rules. But where this approach worked against the interests of the United States, the judges rejected or manipulated older legal traditions, arguing that the United States was a new nation and that such rules were foreign to it. In the Cherokee cases, the Marshall Court shaped the legal tools that helped define the future of United States–Native American relations. Building on *Fletcher* and *Johnson*, the Marshall Court used the Cherokee cases to create a law of American continental real estate. In addition, by employing a cultural interpretation that argued that Native Americans did not have the traits needed to possess natural rights, members of the Marshall Court helped to establish the view that Indians were inferior and thus could be appropriately denied the full legal regard of the United States that otherwise would be demanded by natural law.

This book sketches the complex events and decisions involved in these landmark Supreme Court cases. It focuses on how the Cherokee sought to use the law to defend their sovereignty and how the United States responded to this pursuit of justice. It is a political history of neither the early Cherokee Republic nor the United States in the Age of Jackson. Fortunately, rich, textured studies abound on each of these topics, as do worthy biographies of the important actors, including Cherokee principals John Ross and Major Ridge, President Andrew Jackson, and Chief Justice John Marshall (see Suggested Readings).

The use of the courts by the Cherokee was part of a deliberate strategy to avoid dispossession and maintain political control of their republic. The people of the Cherokee Nation were not the first Native Americans to use the colonial or, later, state courts of the European-Americans. These three Cherokee cases, however, were the first brought by Native Americans to the U.S. Supreme Court. They are worthy of study for their political and jurisprudential importance, but they are also important because literate Cherokee left documents that express the Cherokee viewpoint of events. These documents include the extensive correspondence of the Cherokee national leader, John Ross, as well as articles published in the *Cherokee Phoenix*, the newspaper of the Cherokee Republic.

This book also explores the response of the United States to the Cherokee pursuit of justice in American courts. It analyzes the doctrine developed by the Supreme Court both as a response to the claims of the Cherokee and as a statement about national development. The role of the states, the President, and the Congress are highlighted, but the primary focus is on the Supreme Court. The Court is considered in its several capacities: political actor, moral arbiter, and legal interpreter. Much has been written about the contribution of the Marshall Court to the building of a pronational rather than a states' rights jurisprudence. Less attention has been directed to the impact of the early Supreme Court as an institution capable of searing the conscience of the American people. The opinions of the justices in the Cherokee cases, amplified by their correspondence, suggest that for several members of the Court the moral dimension of their work was never far from their minds.

This book narrates a tale that on the one hand is illuminated by reliable written documents but that on the other hand is shadowed by the limiting prism of time and culturally varying perspectives. It reconstructs many of the relevant facts and some of the motivations of the key leaders in this legal and political drama. It explains these events but in some ways prompts more questions than it answers. This is so because all studies are limited factually. But more important, questions arise because of the varying perspectives of readers. As legal scholar David M. Engel has written, the "role of law in everyday life can . . . be read in dramatically different ways, depending on the extent to which it is assimilated to the purposes or persons within a domain. . . . Perceptions of the role of law in everyday life are closely linked to understandings of social order and disorder and to the processes by which the identities and fates of human beings . . . are determined."[3] This book certainly will be read in different ways. However, it is the author's hope that each reader will appreciate the significance of the issues put before the Supreme Court by the leadership of the Cherokee Republic. These issues involved nothing less than the future control of a continent.

## CHAPTER 1

# Who Came First Was Not All That Mattered

*The Cherokee say that Someone Powerful made man and his sister after creating plants and animals. They also say that once man and his sister were made, man poked sister with a fish and told her to give birth. She did, many times, and the humans increased so quickly that Someone Powerful, fearing that there would shortly be no more room on earth, arranged that a woman could have only one child every year.*

*—Cherokee story of creation*[1]

## INTRODUCTION: SETTING THE SCENE

Cherokee legend describes creation. Much later, non-Cherokee scientists described the migration of Paleoindians across the land bridge that once joined Siberia and Alaska and the eventual arrival of the people known today as the Cherokee of the southeastern region of North America.[2] Anthropologists say that the Paleoindians, who came to this region at least 10,000 years ago, lived by gathering naturally occurring foods and hunting game. Archaeological evidence indicates that by 2500 B.C. these people were domesticating seeds and vegetables and producing cultivated foods. Corn first appeared in about A.D. 200. Its extensive cultivation in cleared fields by A.D. 1000 was a critical factor in the expansion of the Cherokee population.[3] In turn, an increased population led to modifications of the kinship system that governed social relations. Using the kinship principle of ranking by birth order, the earliest inhabitants of the Southeast slowly developed a complex, stratified social order that is now called the *chiefdom*.

Simple chiefdoms integrated a small number of towns and

clans, while complex chiefdoms brought numerous social and kin groups together under the centralized political rule of a paramount leader and his supporters.[4] The great southeastern chiefdoms, such as Ocute, were populous and included hundreds of villages and hamlets.[5] The population of the great southeastern chiefdom of Coosa is estimated to have been as high as 30,000 or even 50,000 people.[6] A paramount chief derived power from his kin group and exerted economic control over the everyday lives of the members of the chiefdom. Members of the chiefdom recognized the authority of the chief and his kinsmen through deferential behavior and payments in the form of tribute, labor, and military service.[7] This authority was legitimated by a divine right to rule, most commonly a cult of chiefly ancestors in which the chief's kin line was held to descend directly from the sun deity. As in many other parts of the world, politics and religion among the southeastern Indians met in the temple.

Contrary to later European myth, the first European explorers of North America's eastern coast did not encounter a whispering, empty wilderness but instead found a populated landscape "modified for more than 10,000 years by the activities of earlier immigrants."[8] In the early sixteenth century the southern Indian population was larger than it had been in the century after the arrival of Europeans. These Indian groups had complex, sophisticated societies: Contemporary records from the expeditions of Hernando de Soto (1539–1543), Tristán de Luna (1559–1561), and Juan Pardo (1566–1568) and archaeological artifacts indicate that there were dozens of interconnected but economically and politically independent kin-based Native American societies that exchanged goods and information and formed military and political alliances. The Spanish would have come upon both small hamlets with only a few households and far larger ones consisting of many households clustered into good-sized towns. The differing patterns reflected the quality of agricultural land, the cost of moving food within a kinship network, and the demands of military defense.

Southeastern people, including the forebears of the modern Cherokee, first encountered Europeans early in the sixteenth century, when Spanish sailors and explorers—some sailing from the Bahama Islands—anchored at several sites on the coast of the lower South. These early forays carried out by adventurers and slave raiders between 1514 and 1516 and in 1521 were grim portents of the future: The Europeans brought foreign diseases and at their departure abducted small groups of local people.

Beginning in the early 1520s, expeditions from the West Indies carried ever larger numbers of Spanish adventurers to the waters and coastal lands of the lower South. Between 1521 and 1526, for example, Lucas Vásquez de Ayllón, an official in Santo Domingo licensed by Emperor Charles V, came to the region several times on missions for slave raiding and colonization. For his 1526 expedition, Ayllón sailed with a fleet of six ships and more than 500 people. After disembarking in several places, Ayllón established San Miguel de Gualdape, the first—albeit short-lived—European colonial settlement in the region. Expedition members initiated trade and missionary work. Writers place the location of this village at the mouth of the South Santee River and relate that after 300 settlers were lost in the first months, the remaining 150 ill and starving colonists abandoned the site and returned to Santo Domingo.[9] Ayllón's expedition was followed two years later by another doomed colonial effort led by Pánfilo de Narváez. Sobered by these failures, the Spanish curtailed their activity in North America until Hernando de Soto organized his famous expedition to southeastern North America in 1539 in search of gold.

Unlike the English, who came later to colonize and to trade, the Spanish explored North America intent on finding riches and making religious converts. Hernando de Soto exemplified those ambitions. Made wealthy by his earlier explorations and plundering of Panama and Nicaragua as well as his conquest of the Incas, de Soto returned to North America with an *asiento* (royal papers of permission) from the Spanish king to conquer and settle *La Florida*—eastern North America. He left Spain on April 7, 1538, with more than 600 people, 250 horses, and a fleet of several ships. After a stay of several months in Cuba, his fleet left Havana on May 18, 1539, and cast anchor a week later south of Tampa Bay. Working their way into the bay, de Soto's ships landed near the mouth of the Little Manatee River at the Indian town of Uzita. This marked the beginning of a four-year, 3,500-mile march of exploration, warfare, and pillage that claimed the lives of thousands of Indians and eventually that of de Soto and half his men.[10]

It is difficult today to comprehend the rapidity of the change caused by the arrival of Europeans in these regions. The members of the de Soto expedition, for example, were the first but also virtually the last Europeans to observe the large and powerful chiefdoms of the interior Southeast. In a matter of decades—perhaps less than seventy years—epidemic disease, warfare, and famine resulted in a catastrophic population loss that in turn led to a complete change in the social and human landscape.[11] The disease carried by European expeditionary members was a particularly important reason for this change. In reports, de Soto and other Spaniards noted the impact of disease on local populations. Today it is known that the original inhabitants had no immunity to these diseases. At southeastern chiefdoms such as Cofitachequi, de Soto found and reported deserted towns and buildings piled with corpses.[12] Such reports were not uncommon. In 1587 an Englishman described the deadly effect of European disease on the coastal Indians of present-day North Carolina: "Within a few days after our departure from everies such townes, that people began to die very fast, and many in short space."[13] Spanish missionaries later estimated that the 25,000 to 30,000 Apalachees living near the English in the decade 1608–1617 were by 1638 reduced by disease to 16,000.[14]

As a result of war, disease, and famine, by the end of the seventeenth century the complex, centralized southeastern chiefdoms at Coosa, Ocute, and Ichisis described by members of the de Soto and Pardo expeditions had collapsed. Political continuity was destroyed within chiefdoms, and political decentralization occurred throughout the region.[15] People fled from diseased communities. Remnant bands moved across the landscape. The survivors came together to form new communities, some at the sites of older villages and others on vacated land. These villages, however, were much smaller than their predecessors.

Contact with Europeans created circumstances that irrevocably transformed these southeastern societies and the map of the Southeast. As Indian societies affected by adversity migrated from the site of their sixteenth-century homelands, a good part of what today is called northwestern Georgia and eastern Tennessee was depopulated. In this transformation, however, there was reconstruction. Members of small Indian towns, for example, began to band together for mutual protection against the increasing numbers of Europeans. From these alliances sprang new Indian confederacies, including that of the Creek. It is here that the Cherokee enter the story directly as, late in the seventeenth century, they expanded out

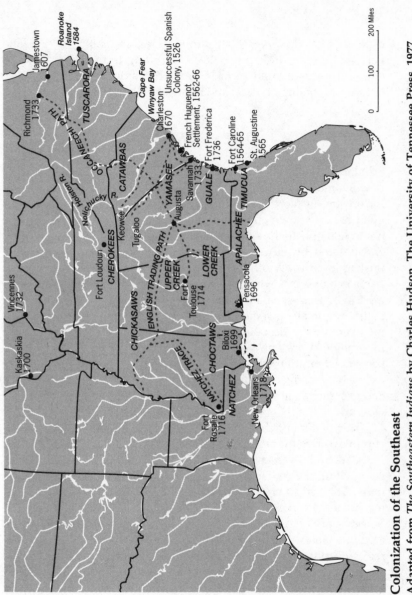

**Colonization of the Southeast**

Adapted from *The Southeastern Indians* by Charles Hudson, The University of Tennessee Press, 1977

of their isolated Appalachian communities, apparently taking land vacated by other Indian societies. According to their oral histories and European written records, from this point on the Cherokee became a growing physical and political presence in the Southeast.[16]

## THE CHEROKEE

Scholars do not believe that the Cherokee wielded a great deal of power among southeastern peoples at the time of the arrival of Europeans in North America in the sixteenth century, but not a great deal is known about the Cherokee in that century. They were not long native to the Appalachian Mountains where they were first encountered by Europeans. They came from the north, probably pushed south by other tribes, and may have settled in the Appalachians only when confronted by the boundaries of the existing Muskogean-speaking nations of the southeast.[17] They were originally Iroquoian-speaking. There is evidence, but not certainty, that members of the de Soto expedition encountered Cherokee in the mountains of present-day North Carolina. Regardless of the Cherokee's exact location when the Spanish came, scholars argue that they might have arrived in the region as early as the eleventh century and in transitional stages moved and expanded their territory to the west and south.[18]

This pattern of changing and expanding location makes it difficult to describe the size of the settlement area of the Cherokee in the sixteenth and seventeenth centuries. The land claimed by the Cherokee early in the contact period has been estimated at 40,000 square miles. This settlement area, which was rich in fish and game, covered most of the southern Appalachian Mountains and parts of the central portions of the Appalachian valleys and ridges and the Piedmont plateau. Other, less-used Cherokee land radiated out from this region, making the area claimed by the Cherokee more than 124,000 square miles, an area that eventually was converted into several states of the United States.[19] By the eighteenth century the Cherokee lived in as many as sixty-four mountain towns and villages. These settlements, home to 350 to 600 people each, were scattered over a large, rugged, and often inaccessible terrain that did not encourage the development of a centralized government. The existence of three dialects also limited communication among the towns. While this mountain homeland may have discouraged greater political activity, for some years the winding, narrow, and dangerous trails also insulated the Cherokee from European traders, settlers, and diseases.

Were the Cherokee a nation in this period? The Cherokee did not have a large state apparatus—that is, a strong central government with the power to make and enforce laws or a strong bureaucracy—before the late eighteenth century. They did, however, constitute an identifiable ethnic group in a specific territory recognized by others. Joined by ties of blood, the Cherokee regulated their lives in accordance with common cultural traditions. The norms and values of this culture stressed mutual defense, discouraged conflict within the extensive community, and bound the Cherokee together through a tradition of unwritten clan law.[20] When the new republic of the United States established diplomatic relations with the Cherokee after the War of Independence, the relations—for example, treaties—were explicitly described as relations between nations. In other words, the Cherokee, like the Americans, developed institutions of national government in response to both internal and external factors over a period of time.

The sixty-odd towns of what became the Cherokee Nation were clustered in several regions: the so-called Lower towns in the valleys and foothills of present-day western South Carolina, the Middle settlements along the Tuckasegee River and on the headwaters of the Little Tennessee, the Valley towns west of the Middle settlements on the Hiwassee River, and the Overhill towns below the Cumberland Mountains on the Tellico River and on the lower reaches of the Little Tennessee.[21] From the southern reaches of the Lower settlements to the northern towns of the Overhills, Cherokee territory stretched 150 miles on local trails. As with any large group of people living in a vast and varied landscape, the local life of the Cherokee differed with the location. The Lower Cherokee towns lay on the fertile headwaters land of the Savannah. The Cherokee there—closest to Charles Town—were the first to profit from trade with the new Carolina colonists. They formed the first line of defense against the Creeks and were the first to take action against European attempts to acquire their land. To the north, in the mountains and secluded valleys beneath the Great Smokies, were the oldest Cherokee towns, including Kittuwa. These settlements were remote from the main trading routes and the everyday politics of the greater Cherokee people. In contrast, to the northwest in today's

Monroe County, Tennessee, the Upper or Overhill Cherokee pursued a life centered on the cultivation of the fertile valley lands of the Little Tennessee and Tellico rivers; the Overhill Cherokee were drawn outward in military conflict with the French Indians.

Before the late eighteenth century the Cherokee governed themselves through clan law and town councils. Factionalism, difficulties of communication, and tradition discouraged the Cherokee from building the grand machinery of a central government. Nonetheless, at times of crisis and in matters of foreign diplomacy, large councils were held and leaders would emerge who, using methods accepted by the Cherokee—conference, discussion, and consensus—helped establish the broad outlines of policy.

Clan law and township norms shaped everyday life. Cherokee clan law established individual and collective rights and duties; it governed the behavior of households and joined the Cherokee into a single people. Clan law regulated marriage, established who educated children, and determined sanctions for murder. Through clans, social order was maintained and the next generation was socialized.[22]

Decisions that fell outside the authority of the clans became the work of town governing councils. A town council was an assembly of all the men and women of the community, any of whom had the right to speak. As town populations averaged only a few hundred adults and children, it was possible to meet in such councils nightly. With their members sitting together by clan, the councils probably dealt with issues of mutual protection, such as the hours to be spent cultivating fields vulnerable to attack. The council may also have assigned fields and land for homes and maintained a communal granary. The town council neither legislated nor judged. Rather, it was the place where formal community decisions were made through consensus, with the objective of town harmony. Persuasive speakers emerged as leaders to head the council. On occasion those leaders spoke for the town in its dealings with other Cherokee towns and foreign governments.

## THE NEWCOMERS

In the century after de Soto's march through the Southeast, boatloads of Spanish, French, and British explorers, soldiers, missionaries, traders, and finally settlers found their way onto the lands of the

Cherokee and neighboring southeastern tribes, including the Choctaw, Chickasaw, Creek, and Yamassee. Where they could, the European newcomers built missionary stations, established trade relations, and wooed tribes with which they sought political, economic, and military alliances. The Spanish were the first to send soldiers, traders, and missionaries northward, up the Atlantic coast, in the late sixteenth century. The English established a permanent foothold on the Atlantic coast with the founding of the small, swampy river peninsula settlement at Jamestown in 1607. In time the French, who in the 1560s had failed in their efforts to colonize Florida, worked their way south into the western lands of the Cherokee from the Great Lakes and the northern Mississippi Valley.

If one looks at a map of the southeastern region of North America at the beginning of the seventeenth century, the names of a dozen major tribes and political confederacies illuminate it. In contrast, English Jamestown is a shadowy mark. Various European missionary settlements exist but are too insignificant to be represented on the map, as are the crude dwellings of itinerant English, French, and Spanish traders. The region is home to Native American nations, and they dominate its economy and politics. The Europeans venture off their boats and find themselves dependent on Indian tolerance of their presence. The English travelers are particularly vulnerable. Unlike the Spanish and French, who for the most part send male soldiers, traders, and missionaries, ordinary English women and men have risked the Atlantic crossing. They plan to settle in North America and establish agricultural communities, but they know little about North American crops or the farming techniques appropriate to the region. They receive surplus food from nearby Indians, some of whom teach them local horticulture.

The arrival of settlers has a very different effect on members of Indian nations compared with the arrival of earlier traders and missionaries. Christian missionaries bring new ideas and the possibility of altering indigenous cultures spiritually; traders exploit natural wealth, carry manufactured goods that quickly find favor, and transform the economy. But the impact of the settlers is distinct and perhaps the most shattering. They demand land and the right to farm it. The principle of private ownership of land is integral to their concept of homesteading. This concept and the Anglo-American legal system from which it flows are at odds with the culture of the Cherokee.

In the seventeenth century 200,000 English women and men come to colonize North America. With their arrival, the map begins to change, but more important, the fabric of Indian life is altered as a result of the proximity of the Europeans and the enslaved Africans they bring to clear and plant the land. The English settlers come with the encouragement of their government. They are religious dissenters, opportunists, and common people fleeing the social and economic disruptions of seventeenth-century England. They come to Jamestown and start the colony they call Virginia. Next they establish Carolina. This colony was chartered in 1663, when Charles II, further testing the possibilities of empire and profit in North America, "awarded" eight Englishmen a vast tract of Indian land stretching from the southern border of present-day Virginia to Spanish Florida. The king intended Carolina to be a buffer zone if the Spanish tried to move north.

The extension of the English Carolina settlements onto lands long held by several Indian nations, including the Cherokee, and also claimed by the Spanish provoked a long period of military and political struggle among the Europeans and nearby Native American groups. Indian nations, whose support was critical to the well-being of the colonies, were constantly courted by European and colonial governments. Fluid regional politics shaped and reshaped Indian-European alliances throughout the seventeenth and early eighteenth centuries. Historians have written that by the early eighteenth century the realities of regional politics made it impossible for the British to ignore the Cherokee. The Cherokee Nation had become too great in size not to be wooed and too strategic in location—sitting astride what came to be called the "western waters"—not to be coveted. Travelers who were permitted to wander through Cherokee towns could imagine a bright future for themselves among the rich fields and woodlands or could find a watercourse heading almost anywhere in eastern North America.[23]

The Cherokee kept no written records until the early nineteenth century. The absence of written chronicles limits our ability to know reliably what the Cherokee thought about the early-arriving Europeans and their plans. One can, however, reconstruct the effect of the Europeans on the Cherokee and the other peoples of the region. The impact of the diseases brought to North America by Europeans and Africans has already been described. The deadly microbes devastated Indian communities, sometimes before the victims saw the faces of the Europeans who carried the illnesses. Wave after wave of infection followed the sixteenth-century pandemics and continued to kill entire Indian communities in the region well into the eighteenth century.

Trade initiated by the Europeans also changed Cherokee society. The Cherokee became important trading partners of the Europeans, conducting a mutually profitable commerce in high-quality deerskins. Trade in deerskin brought interior Indians, including the Cherokee, into world economic markets for the first time. This trade also introduced the Cherokee to European technology and European consumer goods, which quickly found favor. In a short time this exchange of goods created balance of trade problems for the Cherokee and other southeastern Indians. For the most part, deerskins were the means of payment for imported European goods among southeastern Indians. Overhunting, however, quickly diminished the deer population. With insufficient deer but a steadily increasing appetite for European products, Indians fell into debt, and debt from trade ultimately led to additional pressure for land cessions.

Competition among the Europeans for trading advantage and political alliance forestalled these debt problems for a few decades for some of the Indian nations. The competition between the French and English for the political favors of the Choctaw and the Creek, for example, permitted those Indians to obtain manufactured goods for a time as diplomatic gifts without having to overhunt or cede land. This was not an advantage shared by the less centrally located Cherokee.[24] By the second half of the eighteenth century, after the defeat of the French in the "Great War for Empire," all the southeastern Indian nations had come to rely on the English for goods, and the English prepared themselves to make strategic use of accumulated trade debts.

Paramount among the goods that created a dependency on European trade was the "river of liquor" brought to the Indians. Itinerant traders lugged rum far into the interior of the Southeast, making enormous profits. More critically, however, after causing physical and social addiction and creating trade deficits, the rum traders positioned themselves to exploit the debt and the addiction by demanding payment in land. Important traders and merchants became self-appointed officials, setting prices and negotiating debt settlements with various tribes. Historians write that in the second half of the eighteenth century it was the "Augusta rum traders" who insisted that the Cherokee and Creek make land cessions to settle trade debts. For their part, the southeastern Indian societies were trapped by their inability to adapt quickly when deer became scarce. In contrast to the English merchants of Carolina with whom they traded, who diversified their capital by investing profits made in the deerskin trade in plantation slavery and cash crops, most southeastern Indians possessed neither the capital nor the credit to take up new forms of work quickly and thus retool their economies.[25]

## THE CHEROKEE AND THE GEORGIA COLONISTS

This story has raced ahead quickly, introducing the Augusta, Georgia, rum traders before introducing the colony and the people of Georgia. In June 1732 a small group of prominent Englishmen received a royal charter making them trustees of the colony to be called Georgia. The government offered the charter in the belief that the new settlement would absorb unemployed Englishmen and provide sources of wealth, including raw materials, for England. The charter marked out a sea-to-sea grant of Native American land between the Savannah and Altamaha rivers, inland to their headwaters, and "westward to the South Seas."

The trustees who took on the task of organizing and governing Georgia envisioned the colony as a special venture. Guided by one of their group, James Oglethorpe, and his belief in the power of a good environment and second chances, the trustees represented Georgia as a place where philanthropic, religious, and imperial goals would be joined. These governors offered passage, land, and initial expenses to refugee Protestants and Jews, small farmers, shopkeepers, debtors, and other "unfortunates" in search of work, whose physical presence would create a buffer zone against the Creek and Yamassee as well as the Spanish and French.[26]

The trustees' intent was to create a yeoman farmer society consisting of disciplined, hardworking families. The earliest rules of the colony provided land grants of no more than fifty acres to settlers who crossed at the expense of the Georgia Trust. Colonists who paid their own passage were eligible for larger grants of land, but no grant could exceed five hundred acres. These policies were

intended both to discourage the development of a landed aristocracy (as had occurred in Carolina) and to encourage a yeoman
farmer frontier population willing and physically able to defend the
vulnerable border colony.[27] The trustees attempted to reinforce this
vision in 1735 by barring African slaves from the colony, reasoning
that without such labor, farmers would be constrained to till their
own soil or hire free white labor.[28]

Accompanied on ship by the trustee Oglethorpe, an initial
group of 120 carefully picked would-be colonists made "a very
favourable passage" across the Atlantic in seven weeks, landing in
January 1733 at Charles Town, Carolina. Oglethorpe lost no time
searching for a settlement site. With the intercession of local people,
he won permission from the Yamacraw leader, Tomochichi, to
establish a community at Yamacraw Bluff, which the colonists
renamed Savannah. The Yamacraw welcomed the new English
colonists as trading partners and allies against the stronger inland
Indian nations.[29] In the following years, as more boatloads of
colonists arrived, the small compact communities of farmers envisioned by the trustees spread outward from Savannah. The utopian
vision of prosperous yeoman families faded quickly, however, as
Georgians discovered that the products of their small tracts of land
could not compete with the agricultural output of the large Carolina
plantations. As a result of the poor economy, backward conditions
and dissatisfaction marked the first years of the Georgia experiment. Nevertheless, by the early 1750s there were 3,000 English settlers in Georgia.[30]

Although ultimately not successful in creating an innovative
colonial model, the early Georgia trustees did develop a successful
policy of establishing relations with the most important Indian
groups in the area—the Chickasaw, the Choctaw, and in particular
the Creek and the Cherokee. Oglethorpe was a practical and level-
headed diplomat who in the 1730s and 1740s keenly appreciated the
strategic power of those nations. The issues of colonial diplomatic
policy were straightforward: Small in number and possessing a
fragile economy, the Georgia colonists needed peace with Native
Americans as well as military alliances that could be invoked to protect their towns and villages from the threat of Spanish or French
attack. (Spain and England did in fact go to war in 1739 in a dispute
over the Florida–Georgia border.) Persuading through his charm
and arguments concerning mutual interest as well as through mate-

rial incentives such as the distribution of powder and shot, Oglethorpe won the cooperation of the Indians.[31] A biographer has written that unlike "the French officials, who went into Indian country only when escorted by guards and attended by pomp and circumstance, Oglethorpe . . . 'relied entirely on the good Faith of the *Indians*' . . . and 'unravelled' the cloth of deceit that the Spanish and French had been so laboriously weaving. Largely as a result of Oglethorpe's policies Georgia was spared, almost alone among southern colonies, a major internal Indian war during the formative years."[32]

Fierce competition for the trade goods of the southeastern Indian nations—eagerly sought by the other English colonies as well as by the Spanish and the French—demanded that the Georgia colony trustees also develop policies that would make Georgia an appealing trading partner for Native Americans. Oglethorpe was constantly importuning the Trustee Council in London for operating funds. The economic self-sufficiency of the colony depended on a successful trade policy. Partially because Oglethorpe was blind to some of Georgia's marketable commodities—lumber, for instance—trade with Native Americans was particularly important in the early decades of the colony. Thus, in 1735 the Georgia trustees sought to stabilize Indian relations with the passage of regulatory economic legislation that was binding on the colonists. "An Act for Maintaining Peace with the Indians in the Province of Georgia" authorized the trustees to regulate British traders in the colony who wanted to do business within nearby Indian communities. The legislation required that those traders purchase a license from colonial officials and post a bond indicating that they would observe the rules and regulations of the colony.[33] Related action requested by Indian leaders and by Oglethorpe made the importation and sale of rum, brandy, and other strong liquors in Indian communities an offense, with violators running the risk of losing not only their bonds but their trade licenses. Both acts were intended to foster "standards of fairness and morality with the natives who, upon benefiting from just policies, would show their thankfulness not only by rendering aid if war broke out but also by converting to the Christian religion."[34]

This trade, which was essential to the well-being of the colonists, brought marked change in the Indians' way of life. Among the Cherokee, extensive trading began with representatives of Charles Town sometime after 1710. Once this trade began, the impact was "swift and startling," launching a transformation of Cherokee society over the course of a hundred years in which one-time hunters and simple agricultural people became by 1810 the owners of substantial animal stock, farm equipment, and domestic goods; several grist, saw, and powder mills; and some slaves.[35] But trade also brought about the loss of land as settlement for debt and subsequently the displacement of Cherokee farmers and hunters.

The debt that resulted from dependence on European goods led the Cherokee to suffer a particularly significant loss of land in the two Treaties of Augusta. In those treaties, signed in 1763 and 1773, Georgia received great cessions of land from the Cherokee and the nearby Creek. As a result of the first treaty, new lands were opened to white settlers above the town of Augusta as far north as the Little River and west to the Ogeechee. Ten years later the second Treaty of Augusta opened several million acres above the Little River to new settlers.[36] The impact of these treaties on the Cherokee and the Creek cannot be underestimated. Waves of newcomers from England and from the backcountry of Virginia and Carolina poured into the expanded Georgia colony. The population of the colony, which was thought to be about 6,000 whites and 3,000 slaves in 1760, rose by 1773 to more than 30,000.[37]

The effects of the Augusta treaties extended far beyond the loss of land and the increase in the non-Indian population. The thousands who came to the colony as a result of the treaties moved to the backcountry on the northern frontier, near Cherokee and Creek land. These new settlers were not traders; their economic future lay in the land. In 1763 Georgia's colonial governor, James Wright, observed that many of the newcomers were drifters, or *crackers*—people without families or property. The governor disliked them because he wanted to populate the newly opened lands with a "better sort" of folk—people who could afford to purchase land grants for the benefit of the state treasury. The Indians disliked the crackers because they ignored legal boundaries and settled on Cherokee and Creek land that had not been signed over in the Augusta treaties.

The older merchant class in Georgia had allied itself with the Cherokee because there was profit in trade. In contrast, the new settlers saw colonial officials and merchants, as well as the Cherokee and the Creek, as barriers to their aspirations. A 1776 backcountry petition against Indian trade blamed merchants and Indians for violence: "Whilst an Indian trade is carried on it tends to bring those savages down into the settlements, and they seldom return without either committing murder or robbery and generally both upon white people."[38] Quick to perceive and protect common interests, the new settlers joined together, organizing an aggressive lobby on behalf of local policies that would push the Cherokee and the Creek out of their way. In less than twenty years in the late eighteenth century, these settlers restructured Georgia's politics, destroying the political monopoly of the merchant class. The new settlers ended the British policy of trading with the Cherokee and the Creek and focused instead on policies that would lead to the removal of southeastern Indian nations to the west.

A critical moment in this refashioning of Georgia politics occurred immediately after the 1773 Augusta Treaty. As a result of Creek reservations about the treaty, violence flared late that year on the Creek–Cherokee–Georgia border. For British colonists in Georgia this event set the course by which some—merchants and members of the upper class—remained loyal to England in the coming War for Independence, while poorer backcountry citizens renounced the mother country *and* used the cry for freedom to pursue Indian land. In Georgia the Revolutionary War began in 1773, not 1776. For a decade there was brutal fighting among those who wished to control Georgia's destiny.

The Cherokee had no choice but to ally themselves with the pro-British faction against the backcountry insurrectionists. As a result, anti-British militia from Virginia, Carolina, and Georgia invaded the Cherokee Nation from three directions with large armies and inflicted substantial damage. For their part, the British provided the Cherokee with little aid during the war and betrayed them at its end. In the 1783 treaty of peace, British negotiators recognized unconditional American sovereignty and granted the former colonies land—much of it Cherokee and Creek—extending west to the Mississippi River.[39] The Cherokee and the newly independent United States formally established peace with the 1785 Treaty of Hopewell. The United States recognized Cherokee sovereignty and, after exacting a cession of land, guaranteed the integrity of the remaining Cherokee lands.[40]

In this period Georgia officials moved the capital inland from

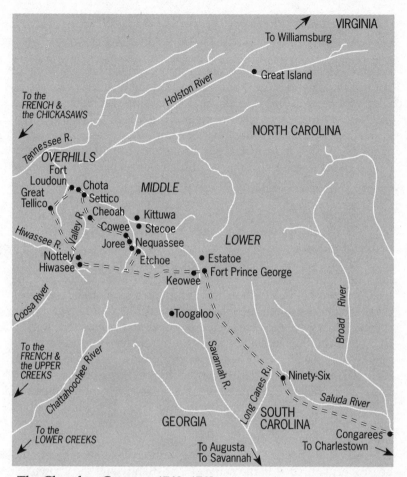

**The Cherokee Country, 1740–1762**
**Adapted from *The Cherokees* by Grace Steele Woodward, University of Oklahoma Press, 1963**

coastal Savannah to Augusta. This was a symbolic and practical change signifying the territorial growth of the state and the increased importance of the upcountry region to the state's economy and politics. Like much of the United States, Georgia faced west, ready to heed the call of manifest destiny.

## LAW: A BASIS FOR RELATIONS—
## BUT WHOSE LAW?

When the United States of America came into existence, a body of law was already in place that incorporated many of the premises on which the new nation built its legal and political relationship with the Native American governments of the continent. The use of law in dealings with tribes was inherited from European colonial governments. It was, however, law thoroughly grounded in the Europeans' belief in the preeminence of their values even though some founders of the republic were familiar with principles of Native American law, including the Iroquois Great Law, and might have incorporated them into the developing Anglo-American legal system.[41] This legal system, some argue, provided a legal facade for the denial of Indian rights.[42]

The Europeans' use of law as a principle of foreign relations with non-Christians dates at least to the medieval period and the legal theories of Pope Innocent IV. Innocent, a scholar-cleric, offered persuasive ideas about the legal status and rights of non-Christian societies that later influenced the political and military actions of Catholic heads of state after contact with Native Americans in the new world. In the early years of exploration, the papacy both assigned lands and spelled out a theological law of relations with indigenous people. Beginning in the sixteenth century, Spanish rulers convened formal boards of inquiry, often composed of church scholars, to consider what, if any, rights they thought were due the indigenous people of the new world. These inquiries focused on the actions, including war and enslavement, that could be properly pursued in the name of Christianity and the Crown.

Two broad points of view developed from these inquiries. One school argued that the Indians were inferior or even inhuman and thus were marked from birth for subjugation. Another group, led by Francisco de Vitoria and Bartolomé de Las Casas, while characterizing the Indian as a primitive nonbeliever in need of conversion, asserted that the Indian was a rational human being possessing rights of territory and sovereignty that had to be acknowledged by Europeans.[43] According to Vitoria, war should be declared only for a just cause (failure to allow foreigners to travel across native lands, engage in trade, or preach the gospel), and only defeat in a just war could lead to forfeiture of sovereignty and land.

Vitoria's work provided an early law of nations that embraced Native Americans in a framework of human rights informed by a Christian theological perspective. In codifying international law in the seventeenth century, the Dutch jurist Hugo Grotius drew on the theories of his predecessor but transposed Vitoria's law of nations into a secular framework. Grotius asserted that religion was not grounds for a just war and that all people held the right to enter into treaty relationships, a right "that does not admit of a distinction arising from religion." A century later, the Swiss diplomat Emmerich von Vattel expanded this theory of international law by classifying political communities of indigenous people as sovereign nation-states entitled to the respect of other nations.[44]

As a result of the work of these legal theorists, as well as practical considerations, several basic tenets of international law had emerged by the early eighteenth century that formed the basis of treaty relationships between European governments and North American Indian nations such as the Cherokee. The first principle acknowledged the sovereignty of Indian nations. The second tenet established the idea that the tribes held a transferable title to their land. The third principle held that the acquisition of Indian lands could not be left to individual colonists but must be controlled by the colonial government or the Crown.[45] As a result, the diplomatic example of colonial Europeans, in particular the British, imparted to the new political community of the United States what one observer has described as "a substantial legacy of legal thought, political experience, and jurisprudential assumptions about the management of Indian affairs."[46] The United States decided to draw on this earlier law and establish legal relations with the Indian nations.

The decision to use law indicated the Americans' appreciation of the power of the large North American tribes and the limited powers of the new United States. Physically exhausted from the war with England, lacking a national treasury, and still facing competition from Europe, the American republic in its early decades was characterized by a pragmatic understanding of the utility—and necessity—of lawful and diplomatic relations with tribal governments. Yet the focus was on Western law. The United States ignored Native American systems of law and what those systems might have contributed to an international law of jurisdiction and property for the North American continent.

Shortly after its declaration of separation from England, the newly independent United States, through the Continental Congress, began charting the course of its diplomacy, seeking treaties of peace and friendship with neighboring Indian nations. In Article IX of the Articles of Confederation (1777), in the Proclamation of 1783, and in Article III of the Northwest Ordinance (1787), the members of the Continental Congress set out to limit the power of state governments over Indian affairs by requiring a nationally directed diplomacy with Indian nations and to define the broad legal principles to be followed by the United States in those relations:

> The utmost good faith shall always be observed towards the Indians, their lands and property shall never be taken from them without their consent; and in their property, rights and liberty, they never shall be invaded or disturbed, unless in just and lawful wars authorised by Congress; but laws founded in justice and humanity shall from time to time be made, for preventing wrongs being done to them, and preserving peace and friendship with them.[47]

The designation of a national authority under the Articles of Confederation to direct the diplomacy of the United States with Indian nations met with opposition from many of the states. Not infrequently, when the national government attempted to implement policies guaranteeing tribal land rights and regulated trade, states such as New York, North Carolina, and Georgia protested and attempted their own initiatives. In 1784, for example, New York officials, intent on disrupting negotiations at Fort Stanwix, ordered the arrest of federal treaty commissioners. In the same period, Georgia provoked violence on the part of the Indian nations when state officials pursued a land-cession treaty without authorization from the U.S. government. A committee of the Continental Congress characterized the problem as follows: "An avaricious disposition in some of our people to acquire large tracts of land and often by unfair means, appears to be the principal source of difficulties with the Indians."[48]

The commitment to a national Indian policy was reaffirmed by the men who met in Philadelphia to write the U.S. Constitution. Article I, Section 10, barred states from entering into treaties, while the Indian commerce clause, Article I, Section 8, asserted the responsibility of the federal government alone to negotiate with Indian nations. (The Indian commerce clause eliminated the two reservations of state authority included in Article IX of the Articles of Confederation. Article VI of the U.S. Constitution, the "supremacy clause," underscores this distribution of responsibility and author-ity.) But transfer of complete or plenary power to the U.S. govern-ment was not conceded by states such as Georgia even though they ratified the Constitution. While federal officials sought to stand behind U.S. guarantees of Indian sovereignty and land title, pro-mote peace on the frontier, and conduct all diplomacy with Indian nations through federal representatives, states from Massachusetts to Georgia continued to negotiate with Indian delegations—legiti-mate and otherwise—without federal permission and to take Indian land without anyone's consent. The motive was a simple and straightforward desire to increase the size and prosperity of each state.

At the end of the Revolutionary War, Georgia, for example, claimed the rights to a hundred million acres of public land, includ-ing the entire territory of present-day Alabama and Mississippi. Much of this land was claimed by various Indian nations and, more recently, by Spain; it was also of interest to the Confederation Con-gress, which wished to enlarge the United States through the cre-ation of new states. It is not difficult to understand why the Geor-gians wanted this land. It was valuable for agriculture and for the profits to be made in speculative investment. The land could be used to make state land grants to new settlers, whose homesteads would serve as buffers against the Spanish as well as the Cherokee and the Creek. Moreover, as a larger state, Georgia might command more influence in the Union.

The Georgia ratification convention unanimously approved the U.S. Constitution in 1788 despite the assignment of power over Indian affairs to the national government and the national govern-ment's recognition of Indian sovereignty and land rights. Georgians felt satisfied that practically all their demands had been met by the delegates at Philadelphia: certainty of law and order between the states, possible central government assumption of state war debts, guarantees of political and military support against the Spanish and Indians in case of war, noninterference in local affairs and in slavery and the slave trade, and full representation in the new national leg-islature.[49] When affirming the national constitution, state conven-tion representatives undoubtedly believed that the new U.S. gov-ernment would be concerned about Georgia's exposed frontier and that ultimately the state would have no trouble making a case in

Washington for dispossessing the Cherokee and the Creek from Georgia's "western" lands.

Whatever their hopes or illusions, the people of Georgia were stunned when, soon after taking office, President Washington negotiated a treaty that affirmed Creek land rights. The 1790 Treaty of New York (named for the site of the meeting) negotiated by the President and the Creek leader Alexander McGillivray was an early diplomatic venture in which the new federal government took charge fully and did not consult with affected states such as Georgia. By the treaty, Creek land was both ceded and returned, but most critically, President Washington guaranteed to the Creek contested lands to the south and west of the boundaries established by the treaty, thus blocking Georgia's opportunity to expand. The guarantee of those boundaries by Washington pledged the United States to defend the Creek Nation against any further encroachments by Georgia.[50] A hue and cry arose from upcountry Georgians and land speculators, all of whom disavowed the actions of the Washington administration.[51] As the decade proceeded, little changed in federal Indian policy. The eighteenth century ended with Georgians mistrustful of a national government committed to a federal Indian policy that on its face seemed incompatible with the interests of Georgia.

## *TRANSITIONS*

We now have three parties to the events that will bring our principals to the U.S. Supreme Court: the Cherokee Nation, the state of Georgia, and the United States of America. At the beginning of the nineteenth century, each group and its government was in transition, and each was trying to determine how to strengthen itself and deal with rapid change.

Scholars describe the last quarter of the eighteenth century as one of the most difficult periods in Cherokee history. The necessity of becoming allies of the British during the Revolutionary War cost the Cherokee dearly and led to twenty years of suffering during and after the war. During those decades, Cherokee economic life was shattered, and there was constant bloodshed and razing of Cherokee villages by the colonists who were shortly to become the victorious Americans.[52] By 1800 non-Indians virtually surrounded the considerably diminished Cherokee land base. Increasingly, missionaries and agents of the U.S. government traveled with and lived among the Cherokee, seeking both to control their external relations and to transform Cherokee culture through a so-called American civilization program.

Remarkably, however, the Cherokee sustained themselves culturally and politically in those years by taking control of, rather than yielding to, the process of transformation. Through the selective incorporation and adaptation of non-Cherokee ideas and institutions, the Cherokee fashioned a course that allowed them to sustain many of their traditions and beliefs. In stages, in the first three decades of the nineteenth century, the Cherokee reorganized their economy and political structure. Farming and animal husbandry replaced fur trading as the most important economic activities. A mixed-blood elite emerged that profited from owning slaves and developed commercial ventures such as mills, trading stores, taverns, ferry services, and turnpikes. Political authority was centralized under the direction of certain traditional leaders in combination with the newly powerful mixed-blood leadership. By 1827 the Cherokee had adopted a republican style of government with a bicameral legislature, a court system, and a legal code responsive to the growing market and contract economy. These changes, which were accompanied by a shift from a matrilineal, exogamous clan system to one of the patriarchal nuclear family, were not, however, accomplished without dissension and factionalism.[53] Differences reflected regional alliances (Upper and Lower towns), old and new leadership, class, and heritage (full-blood versus mixed-blood elites). Some Cherokee, discouraged about prospects for their future east of the Mississippi River, accepted offers from the United States to move across the river to Arkansas. The vast majority of Cherokee, however, rejected hard-sell pitches from U.S. agents urging their removal west and instead supported the changes needed for political centralization. In this transition period the emerging mixed-blood leadership was increasingly permitted to pursue a balanced policy of national development and acculturation, and the people of the Cherokee Nation exhibited a resilience in the face of disruption that was repeatedly underestimated by the outsiders with whom they dealt.

The Revolutionary War had also been difficult for the people of Georgia. At the end of the war the state was in a sadly disorganized condition with regard to finance and industry and faced critical decisions about its future.[54] As a colony, Georgia had been quite dependent. Victory over Great Britain left Georgia an isolated out-post against the Spanish, who were now in possession of Florida, and the nearby Creek and Cherokee. However, the state had two key assets: a fast-growing population and the most extensive terri-tory in the Union.

Like the Cherokee, the people of Georgia proved bold in taking hold of their future. Soon after the treaty of peace with England, private investors and Georgia officials marked out a determined policy of territorial expansion and land speculation. Elected officials quickly committed the state to a strong states' rights position in political and economic issues. Early in the 1790s, for example, Geor-gia officials made a forceful showing of states' rights by refusing to acknowledge the jurisdiction of the U.S. Supreme Court in the case of *Chisholm* v. *Georgia*, defiantly instructing state attorneys not to participate in arguing the case before the high court.[55]

By the beginning of the nineteenth century white Georgians had made another decision. Most agreed that their prosperity lay in "white cotton" produced "with black labor" on land to be taken from Native Americans.[56] This committed a majority of Georgians to continue their support of slavery. It also required Georgians to develop a state Indian policy that would both prod and react to fed-eral Indian policy on questions of Native American sovereignty and land rights. As a result, the first two decades of the nineteenth cen-tury became a political test: To what length would the people of the state go to obtain the Creek and Cherokee land they desired for set-tlement, cotton, and the development of roads and canals? In this test, Georgia had to contend not only with the Creek and Cherokee but also with the third party to this conflict, the government of the United States.

In 1800 the United States was a nation of sixteen states with a total population just under 5.5 million people. Two administra-tions—those of George Washington and John Adams—had directed the United States along a course of increasingly centralized national power. Washington's administration, led by Secretary of the Trea-sury Alexander Hamilton, founded a national bank and established a workable scheme for dealing with state and national debt that relied in part on the exchange of western (Indian) land for debt cer-tificates. Efforts had been made through the 1795 Jay Treaty with England and another treaty with Spain to stabilize foreign relations and facilitate foreign commerce. By the end of John Adams's term in

1801 even the stormy relations with France, whose earlier radical-ism the President disdained, was on the mend.

Thomas Jefferson took the oath of office on March 4, 1801, amid continuing signs of transition. Only months earlier the national cap-ital had been moved from Philadelphia to Washington. Unfinished buildings stood everywhere. More critically, every day political divisions were intensifying between the Federalists, who supported the growth of a strong national economy built on manufacturing, commerce, and agriculture, and the Republicans, who favored the interests of the yeoman farmer over those of the hereditary squire and championed democratic national government meant to be effective but not to overshadow the states. From these and other political visions, early nineteenth-century Americans sought to divine their best individual future and define further the shape of the growing republic.

In this political debate one point was clear: Virtually all Ameri-cans believed that westward expansion was essential to the nation's future. The land already possessed by the United States was not thought to be adequate. Certainly the people of Georgia were not alone in the pressure they directed toward members of Congress and the President to establish national policies that would facilitate territorial expansion. But for Georgians, expansion could occur only through the destruction of Cherokee and Creek political sovereignty and land rights. The people of Georgia wanted those Indian nations removed or destroyed but were obliged under the Constitution to let the federal government negotiate all questions of Indian land cession and sovereignty. Georgians lobbied strenuously for a larger Georgia that would include the lands of the Creek and Cherokee, aware that as they did so, the government in Washington was sign-ing solemn and binding diplomatic documents with Indian nations, including the Cherokee, that recognized Indian sovereignty and national territories.

## *POLICY OPTIONS: COEXISTENCE, WAR, ASSIMILATION, OR REMOVAL?*

The officials who signed those treaties for the Cherokee Nation and the United States at the beginning of the nineteenth century did not rejoice in the idea of a shared continent. Yet each nation had practical political, military, and economic reasons for accepting coexistence. Even in Georgia there were people who urged caution. While not necessarily respectful of Native Americans, these Georgians were respectful of property rights and worried about the economic implications, particularly in the area of land titles, of the breakdown of law.[57] Georgians also prided themselves on being a Christian people. Their religious scriptures admonished them to care for others and warned of the judgment of a wrathful God if they failed to fulfill their Christian obligations. Thus, early in the nineteenth century, while the members of the Cherokee Nation struggled with solutions to the proximity of their American neighbors, the people of Georgia weighed policies by which they might, in their minds, legally obtain the nearby rich domain that belonged to the Cherokee and the Creek.

A few Georgians counseled a wait-and-see policy of coexistence, probably believing that the rapidly growing non-Indian population would inevitably drive Native Americans west. Others, in agreement with the Indian assimilation policy of President Washington's administration, urged that the Cherokee and other Indian peoples abandon their ways and accept the culture of the people of the United States. Through agents of the American government and missionaries, the President promoted a program of "civilization" in which Native Americans were given the promise of full and equal citizenship in the United States if they abandoned common ownership of land for ownership "in severalty"—that is, as individuals— and successfully adapted to the use of the English language, farming, and Christianity. This plan envisioned the denationalization of the tribes, with tribal land not under cultivation—"surplus land"— being ceded to federal or state governments. President Washington expected that all the Native Americans east of the Mississippi River (approximately 125,000 people in eighty-five different tribes) would be acculturated within fifty years.[58] A third, very different approach supported by a larger number of Georgians contemplated the removal of Native Americans, such as the Cherokee, across the Mississippi as soon as possible after a legal transfer of land title. Members of this group argued that neither coexistence nor assimilation was a desirable or workable policy.

While Washington's strategy of assimilation continued to dominate federal Indian policy, by 1800 officials and citizens in Georgia had grown more sympathetic to the idea of Indian removal. Thus,

when Georgia and congressional representatives sat down to negotiate a cession of western lands to the United States that Georgia
claimed under the 1783 Treaty of Paris, the state officials made a
critical demand. In return for the state's cession of those millions of
acres—of dubious legal title—Congress must promise that "as soon
as possible" it would oversee the extinguishment, on "reasonable
and peaceful" terms, of Cherokee and Creek title to land Georgia
wanted, land the United States had guaranteed by treaty to those
tribes as recently as 1791 and 1798.[59] On April 24, 1802, Washington
agreed to this condition and federal and state officials signed the
"Article of Agreement and Cession," popularly called the Compact
of 1802.[60]

   In an adroit move, Georgia had trumped the federal government. The Indian commerce clause barred state officials from dealing with the Creek and the Cherokee. Understanding this, Georgia
had obtained formal agreement that federal officials would acquire
the rich, contiguous Cherokee and Creek land that the people of
Georgia fancied, and at national expense. Georgia had rejected a
policy of coexistence with neighboring Indian nations and had won
federal approval of and assistance for an Indian extinguishment
program.

   A critical policy question faced the U.S. government after the
signing of the 1802 compact. If officials in Washington succeeded in
obtaining eastern tribal lands, should the government urge the dis-
placed Native Americans to move westward, or should they be
given individual family allotments on ceded land and be aided in
becoming citizens of the United States? When emissaries of President Jefferson stumbled into the Louisiana Purchase, a deal by
which France transferred title to 827,000 square miles of land west
of the Mississippi to the United States in 1803 for $15 million, the
policy pendulum swung toward Indian removal.

   Jefferson had grabbed at the offer of the Louisiana Purchase. He
bought the title from France, unconcerned with the land rights of
Indians long established in this western territory. He used untested
constitutional powers in this expansion and obtained what the
United States deemed legal land title. With the Louisiana Purchase,
the U.S. government felt certain that it had enough western land to
absorb generations of new immigrants *and* implement an Indian
removal policy by which eastern Indian nations could be persuaded
to cede all their land to the United States and be relocated on the

new Louisiana Purchase lands. Jefferson made a commitment to this new policy, and only months later U.S. agents made their first—unsuccessful—effort to persuade the Cherokee to leave the Southeast.[61]

While U.S. Indian policy in the late eighteenth and early nineteenth centuries vacillated between acculturation and removal, the leadership of the Cherokee Nation increasingly settled on a policy of coexistence and resistance to removal. Small groups of discouraged Cherokee did accept the removal offers made by the United States in 1809 and 1819. The majority of the Cherokee, however, firmly rejected the pressure of U.S. removal diplomacy. Instead, they supported the twin strategies of a stronger, centralized Cherokee government and controlled cultural change as essential to the achievement of international coexistence. The Cherokee leadership believed that controlled acculturation would further Cherokee participation in the growing North American market economy. It also calculated that controlled acculturation would provide a defense against the growing use of negative stereotypes of Native Americans (red savage, imbecile, child) and encourage Americans to accept the positive nature of Indian nationhood. It is a tragic irony of this period that the Cherokee underestimated the extent to which a Native American, acculturated or not, would be an *other* to Euro-Americans, while those promoting the "civilization program" in the United States failed to foresee how acculturation would make the Cherokee more determined to hold on to their national lands and more capable of mounting a sophisticated political and legal campaign to combat removal.[62]

In the early 1800s an increasing number of factors began to work against the Cherokee's policy of coexistence. Little more than a decade after the Louisiana Purchase, the victory of the United States in the War of 1812 produced a spirit of nationalistic expansionism among Americans unlike anything seen before. The war was a dramatic turning point in American history. Andrew Jackson's smashing victory at New Orleans ended the European presence in the Mississippi Valley. The destruction of Tecumseh's old northwestern Indian alliance and the defeat of the Creek Nation removed other international threats to the security of the United States.[63] Each of these military victories validated the Americans' political enterprise, the experiment in republican government. The new sense of physical security also triggered increased white migration into the Southeast. And while soldiers from the Cherokee Nation had joined American troops in the 1812 war against the British, the Creek, and Tecumseh, their service brought the Cherokee Nation neither respect nor fair treatment in the postwar treaties. To the detriment of the Cherokee's political position after the War of 1812, American frontiersmen proved unwilling to differentiate one Native American nation from another. They wished to dispossess both the defeated Creek *and* the partisan Cherokee of land made more valuable by the invention of the cotton gin.

Equally important although not immediately apparent to the Cherokee leadership was the growing political influence after the War of 1812 of General Jackson and the frontier voter. The eastern political establishment and the new President, James Monroe, found it increasingly difficult to ignore frontier factions that clamored for the removal of the Cherokee, Creek, Chickasaw, and others. By 1818 the Monroe administration was increasingly undecided about programs encouraging Indian acculturation. Monroe, following the policies of earlier presidents, believed that his representatives could continue to negotiate land-cession agreements with Indian governments. He pressed the southeastern Indian nations for more land and instituted a complementary removal policy despite evidence that most Cherokee and Creek, for example, opposed both policies. When the President finally acknowledged that he had miscalculated and that the Cherokee, the Creek, and other governments would not give the consent necessary for lawful treaties of land exchange and resettlement, the Monroe administration shifted its tactics. From 1818 through 1825, Monroe's Secretary of War, John Calhoun, "encouraged the use of ruse, subterfuge, circumvention, and outright fraud to achieve through chicanery, under cloak of voluntary cooperation, a continued stream of land cessions. . . ."[64]

The stark contrast between the firm Cherokee policy of coexistence and the American flirtation with a policy of removal sharpened during the Monroe administration. The Cherokee committed themselves to a multiracial continent populated by different nations. But the people of the United States, who had been uncomfortable with the idea of Indian separateness, now began to criticize the possibility of Indian acculturation. Content neither to honor Native American national status nor to respect the Indian as an equal, Americans seized on the policy of removal in the 1820s as the desired course of action.

Many historians have argued that the U.S. policy of removal represented the single-minded impulse of a land-hungry people. Other scholars have written that the quest for Indian land and thus Indian removal expressed the more complex interest of Americans in programs of internal development—connecting canals and roads—critical to the growth of a market economy.[65] Still others have asserted that the elevation of the removal policy signified the transition from an eighteenth-century Enlightenment world view in which all men—including Indians—were equal to the world view of the nineteenth-century romantics, in which the Indian became an inferior, savage "other," incapable of participating in the social and civic culture of the United States and so appropriately taken to the wilderness of the West.[66] Whatever the cause, the years in which this American policy shift occurred (1817–1830) became the crucible of Cherokee resistance and survival. These were years of preparation and resolution for the Cherokee, and the events of this period help explain why the Cherokee Nation turned so readily and with so much faith in the 1830s to the use of litigation in courts of the United States to defend its sovereignty and property rights.

## CHAPTER 2

# Prelude to Litigation

In the years after the signing of the Compact of 1802, two diplomatic positions developed with respect to the land specified in the agreement. Realizing that their formerly vast tracts were being reduced, the Cherokee became increasingly adamant in their refusal to sign further treaties of land cession with the United States.[1] However, with equal certainty and tenacity, Georgia citizens continued to press the government in Washington to carry out the provisions of the Compact so that Georgians could obtain what they were now calling "Georgia lands." As political and physical aggression by Georgians toward the Cherokee increased, the Cherokee leadership responded by setting in motion national policies of resistance and survival. Three actions were of particular importance: the centralization of Cherokee government powers, the initiation of a sophisticated campaign of public relations asserting Cherokee rights, and the continuation of a Cherokee-controlled strategy of acculturation. Through these policies, which were taken up over a period of years, the Cherokee's national leaders consciously set a course against Georgians and others who were determined to deny Cherokee sovereignty and land rights. Although the leadership did not have litigation in mind in the early years of these policies, political centralization, improved communications, and acculturation ultimately provided the impetus and resources to pursue Georgia in American courts. The success of these Cherokee policies led to litigation that echoes through Cherokee and U.S. history.

## CHEROKEE RESISTANCE

The development of a modern, centralized Cherokee political system began with the secularization of the Cherokee government, a process by which, throughout the eighteenth century, medicine men and priests became less important in giving advice on problems caused by political and economic change and a secular political leadership emerged. In the 1750s the Cherokee began to experiment with national councils modeled on their traditional town councils. By the end of the century the national council had evolved into a formal, if ad hoc, institution of governance by all "headmen and warriors." In addition to negotiating several important treaties with the United States in the 1790s, the Cherokee national councils established a national police force in 1808, abolished clan blood revenge, and created new legal norms. This system of large, ad hoc governing councils proved ineffective for day-to-day administrative tasks, and so in 1809 the Cherokee empowered a fixed executive group called the National Committee to look after the general welfare on a daily basis. Composed initially of thirteen representative and experienced leaders, the Committee represented an important step toward centralized national government. In 1817 a political reform law fixed the Committee at thirteen members, established two-year terms of office, and required written records, in English, of its resolutions.

The 1817 law declared that all acts of the National Committee had to be presented to the members of the National Council "for their acceptance or dissent." Treaties, often involving land, had to be affirmed by the National Committee because they involved "our common property." It was anticipated that the mixed-ancestry Cherokee would dominate the Committee, while the full bloods would control the National Council. Historians have commented that in effect the 1817 law created a bicameral legislative system in which the National Committee initiated the laws and the National Council of headmen from the towns concurred in or rejected them.[2] Scholars have further argued that with its additional clearly defined statements on land tenure, citizenship, and national identity, the 1817 law, although not having the name, may properly be thought of as the first Cherokee national constitution.

The replacement of the traditional Cherokee political system that relied on unwritten custom, oral law, ad hoc councils, and decentralized town autonomy with these national institutions of government forged a critical structure for both adaptation to internal change and resistance to foreign threat. The final step in this political process was completed in July 1827 when a Cherokee convention met and wrote a national constitution. The new document was in many respects modeled after the constitutions of neighboring American states and that of the United States. It established the familiar three branches of national government, with the significant difference that the primary executive office, that of Principal Chief, was to be filled by the legislature.[3] The new political charter committed the Cherokee to a republican form of government, a decision that occasioned praise in many newspapers and political salons in the northern American states. Among Georgians, however, the 1827 constitution created a renewed sense of threat as they realized that the acculturation and assimilation urged from the time of George Washington might succeed and make it possible for the Cherokee to defend their lands against Georgia. State legislators condemned the Cherokee Constitution and the failure of the United States to fulfill the terms of the Compact of 1802: "If the United States will not redeem her pledged honor; and if the Indians continue to turn a deaf ear to the voice of reason and of friendship; we now solemnly warn them of the consequences."[4] A furious Governor George Troup demanded that President Adams denounce the document, while members of the Georgia congressional delegation renewed pressure on the U.S. War Department to remove the "red savages" who were "wasting" lands that could be put to a higher use by "noble" white Georgia frontiersmen.[5]

It is ironic that from the late 1700s the Cherokee Nation and the United States pursued similar tasks of nation building. From the time of the American Revolution, citizens of the United States sorted through the common law of England and the political philosophy of England and the Continent to find a workable system of law and government for their new state. The people of the Cherokee Nation aspired to do the same. And while the Cherokee drew on the Anglo-American system, the constitution of the Cherokee Nation shows that the Cherokee maintained the core values of their culture. Chief among these was the commitment to communal land ownership. Article I, Section 2, of the 1827 Cherokee Constitution spelled this out: "The sovereignty and Jurisdiction of this Government shall extend over the country within the boundaries above described, and the lands therein are, and shall remain, the common property of the Nation. . . ." The Cherokee knew that foreigners wanted to acquire Indian land by any means possible. Their constitutional decree served as a statement of resistance to Americans and any assimilation-minded Cherokee that the Cherokee would control the fate of their nation. By the 1820s most Cherokee citizens had come to realize that communal ownership of the land was the key to their survival as a people.

Besides the prize of land or perhaps as a way to obtain land, people from the United States also sought to win the mind and soul of the Cherokee. Indian acculturation was an American policy goal. By 1800 both U.S. government agents and missionaries (receiving financial aid from the U.S. War Department) were traveling to Cherokee towns and villages, hoping to change the world view and lifestyle of the Cherokee. They brought Christianity as well as Western notions of enlightened self-interest and competitive individualism. The Cherokee, of course, had their own highly developed spiritual system and a firmly held, and very different, belief that social order prevailed when men and women were in harmony with one another and with all other aspects of nature.

American agents and missionaries made little effort to understand the beliefs of the Cherokee, while the Cherokee had difficulty appreciating the isolating individualism and competitive disharmony of the Euro-American way of life. It was the genius of the Cherokee people that led them neither to resist nor to accede totally to the westernizing efforts of the Americans. Instead, the Cherokee leadership sought to deal with the American outsiders through a conscious policy of Cherokee-controlled adaptation. In the first decades of the nineteenth century Cherokee of various backgrounds and leadership positions came together to consider what aspects of Western economic and political life had positive value for their society. In formal and informal meetings they planned the selective incorporation of those ideas into Cherokee life. This determined effort to oversee foreign influences contributed significantly to the specific course of Cherokee resistance to Georgia. And while not remaining the people they had been before the late eighteenth century, the Cherokee who wrote and approved the 1827 constitution continued to lay claim to a specifically Cherokee identity.

It was this identity and the land base on which Cherokee culture rested that the Cherokee leadership sought to protect with a sophisticated campaign of public relations. The Cherokee had long traveled to the U.S. capital on diplomatic missions. Not infrequently, memorials were presented to the U.S. Congress on matters of trade, the need for U.S. military patrols on the common border, and broken treaties. These visits multiplied as friction with Georgia increased. In 1826 the Cherokee expanded this public relations effort, striking out in a new direction. In that year they sent a young bilingual Cherokee, Elias Boudinot, on a speaking tour of the northeastern United States, where, while lecturing on the violation of the international rights of the Cherokee at sympathetic religious congregations, he was to undertake a subscription drive to raise the funds needed to purchase a printing press.

A publication in the Cherokee language had not been possible until Sequoyah's 1821 invention of a Cherokee syllabary. The new syllabary provided the impetus for obtaining a printing press. While the primary selling point to American subscribers was the idea of producing the New Testament in Cherokee, the idea of a national newspaper was never far from the mind of Cherokee political leaders, who understood that it would be a permanent tool of public education and opinion making and an instrument of nation building.[6] After succeeding in raising the money, Boudinot ordered a press in Boston with Cherokee and English fonts and arranged for it to be delivered to the Cherokee national capital at New Echota.

In February 1828 the first issue of the bilingual newspaper, the *Cherokee Phoenix*, made its appearance with Boudinot as editor. The Cherokee national government provided the operating funds for the *Phoenix*, its official paper, and distributed it free of charge. Boudinot described the paper's political objectives in the February 21, 1828, issue, writing that the staff "will invariably state the will of the majority of our people on the subject of the present controversy with Georgia, and the present removal policy of the United States Government."

Until the seizure of the printing press by the Georgia militia in 1835, the *Phoenix* was the political instrument the Cherokee government intended it to be. Important statements of Cherokee policy and political resistance were published in it. Lengthy documents, manifestos, and legal opinions solicited from attorneys by the Cherokee Nation were also reprinted.[7] With a wide circulation in the Cherokee Nation, the United States, and even parts of Europe, the newspaper quickly became a vehicle for educating both Cherokee and American citizens about the Nation's fight to protect itself against the militancy of Georgians and the failure of the United States to honor its treaty obligations.

The publication of the *Phoenix* began just in time for the presentation of the Cherokee's case. In November 1828 Andrew Jackson won the United States presidency. Jackson was known to be a friend of states' rights and an opponent of Indian national sovereignty. Free of the neighboring Creek, encouraged by Jackson's election, and in a frenzy over the discovery of gold on Cherokee land, Georgians pressed forward with an increasingly aggressive legal, political, and military offensive.

## GEORGIA ON THE OFFENSIVE WITH ANTI-INDIAN JURISDICTION LAWS

For the first two decades of the nineteenth century Georgia had maintained relative quiet on the subject of states' rights. As late as 1821 state senators had refused to take sides on the explosive question of the Bank of the United States.[8] As the 1820s proceeded, however, the national politics of protective tariffs and slavery and the failure of the Adams administration to provide unequivocal support for Indian removal revived the fortunes of states' rights advocates in Georgia. In the matter of Indian affairs, Georgians despaired of finding a federal policy to their liking. More than two decades had passed since the state had signed the 1802 Compact with the federal government, and so the governor and the state legislators decided to try to end the standoff between Georgia and the Cherokee through state law. They began their effort knowing full well that the U.S. Constitution delegated relations with Indian nations only to the federal government.

The state began with an assault against the criminal jurisdiction of Cherokee courts. In 1827 it attempted to extend the jurisdiction of Georgia courts in counties near the Cherokee Nation over crimes by or against Georgia citizens committed in the Cherokee Nation. At the same time, the state legislature made the extraordinary declaration that the Cherokee, despite their international treaty guarantees, were mere tenants at will on land whose legal title, these officials said, lay with Georgia. It was no accident that Georgia increased its firepower in the same year that the Cherokee, in their 1827 constitution, declared themselves a republic. Georgia officials sent copies of these declarations to President Adams, who did little to disavow the law and the sentiments underlying it. In response, the Cherokee petitioned Washington officials to act against Georgia. While many members of Congress supported the Cherokee and branded the jurisdiction law a violation of American treaty agreements, the Cherokee could not persuade President Adams to take action against the state.

Andrew Jackson's election as President the following year had been much anticipated in Georgia and further emboldened Georgia legislators. Only weeks after the November election, state representatives threw out a new challenge to the Cherokee leadership. They enacted another jurisdiction law ("An Act to add the territory lying within the limits of this state, and occupied by the Cherokee Indians to the counties of . . . and to extend the laws of this state over the same"), through which the state intended immediately to make all white people living in the Cherokee Nation subject to the laws of Georgia. More threatening still, the legislation stated that Georgia would consider all Cherokee laws and customs null and void as of June 1, 1830. If successful, the law would have made all Indians living under the jurisdiction of the Cherokee Nation in 1830 subject to the laws of Georgia as second-class citizens of color lacking the political and legal rights of whites, including the right to testify against whites in a Georgia court.[9] (Neighboring states, including Alabama and Tennessee, passed similar laws.) The purpose of the Georgia legislature was straightforward: Through this and other laws, its members hoped to break the Cherokee Nation as a political and legal entity.

The Georgia politicians' ultimate hope was that these laws would make it impossible for the Cherokee to resist a treaty of removal. To pressure the Cherokee further, state officials turned loose the Georgia Guard—a volunteer militia authorized by state law—whose sustained harassment of and violence against the Cherokee stood in marked contrast to the passive resistance advocated by the national Cherokee leadership and followed by most of the Cherokee Nation's citizens. To enhance this climate of fear and specifically to stifle dissent among local missionaries and others who advocated Cherokee rights, Georgia officials enacted law late in 1829 that made it a criminal offense for anyone "to prevent . . . any Indian . . . from enrolling as an emigrant, or removing. . . ."[10] All these laws received the blessing of newly elected President Jackson, who thought them constitutional and who told the nation in his first annual message to Congress on December 8, 1829, that removal west was the logical choice for eastern Indians who did not wish to live under the rule of American states.[11]

The Cherokee, of course, would have none of this. Valid treaties with the United States guaranteed their sovereignty, which represented nothing if not the power to govern themselves. Georgia's proposed assertion of jurisdiction violated those treaties—treaties that according to Article VI of the U.S. Constitution were the supreme law of the land, superior to state law. John Ross, who was elected Principal Chief of the Cherokee Nation in October 1828, understood Georgia's intentions all too well. Ross, a mixed-heritage Cherokee businessman and farmer, had served in Cherokee government for more than a decade as clerk to earlier chiefs, member and president of the National Committee, liaison to the U.S. agent, and delegate to Washington.[12] A few months after the Georgia legislature passed the 1828 jurisdiction law, the newly elected Ross told the Cherokee: "The Georgians threatening to extend their laws over us is to scare us and to make our minds easier to go off and give up our lands. . . . Hold fast to the place where you were raised." Further encouraging the Cherokee, Ross argued that "if you all unite together and be of one mind there is no danger of our rights being taken away from us."[13]

From the perspective of the Cherokee, the time was long past for the United States to discipline delinquent states such as Georgia. In meetings with U.S. agents at the Cherokee capital of New Echota and through diplomatic missions and petitions sent to Washington, the Cherokee entreated the federal government to come out against the jurisdiction laws and curb the physical violence against the Cherokee.[14] Jackson, however, flatly refused to honor treaties signed with the Cherokee or quash Georgia's assertion of states' rights. Through Secretary of War John Eaton, Jackson indicated that the executive was not "disposed to question" the exercise of jurisdiction by Georgia. The President believed that sovereignty over the land was held by Georgia—title having passed from Great Britain to that state—and that the Cherokee had only the right of occupancy.[15] For more than a decade Andrew Jackson had been saying that the power relationship between eastern Indian nations and the United States had changed and that while the policy of treating with Indian nations had been the government's practice, it was now anachronistic.[16] That the Native Americans had been there first did not matter. He urged them to remove or denationalize.

## THE COMING OF THE LAWYERS

It was at this point, in 1829, that the leadership of the Cherokee Nation determined to use the federal courts of the United States as an additional point of pressure and for redress. They received encouragement from American supporters, several of whom were prominent churchmen and public officials. Many of these men, including Daniel Webster, Henry Clay, and U.S. Senator Theodore Frelinghuysen, were anti-Jacksonians who for partisan political reasons would have been pleased to see the President embarrassed by a Cherokee court victory. Discussions began concerning a suitable attorney and test case. Because no Cherokee were trained in Anglo-American law, the lawyer had to be a non-Cherokee.

Before the Cherokee leadership could hire an attorney, a self-appointed lawyer-spokesman stepped forward. His name was Jeremiah Evarts. Although he never litigated on behalf of the Nation (and never received a salary), the political brief written by Evarts on behalf of Cherokee national status significantly influenced the legal arguments made in court by lawyers subsequently retained by the Cherokee Nation. Evarts's tract, directed at the American public, appeared in 1829. Formally entitled *Essays on the Present Crisis*, it quickly became known as "the William Penn Essays" because Evarts had employed the pseudonym of the famous Quaker leader.[17]

Evarts was a pious northerner who, after practicing law for three years, spent the rest of his life doing religious work. For much of his career Evarts's efforts were on behalf of the well-known American Board of Commissioners of Foreign Missions (ABCFM), whose headquarters were in Boston. The American Board, like other northern evangelical and Bible and tract societies, was heir to John Calvin's admonition that the elect should carry on as moral stewards, "molding other men's lives through the use of both persuasion and governmental power."[18] The nineteenth-century men and women who formed these societies were influenced by Protestant ideas of individual perfectibility and social reform. They acted out of the optimistic belief that everything from personal behavior to national politics could be affected by the application of a perfectionist moral code. Ending slavery, drinking, vice, and desecration of the Sabbath became the work of religious society members. As the first half of the nineteenth century unfolded, Unitarians, Quakers,

Transcendentalists, and Evangelicals extended this vision of a more perfect America to include Native Americans. Weaving concern for legal principles with theology, interdenominational and nondenominational organizations became influential advocates for reform of Indian policy. With their concern for conversion and constitutionalism, religious society members argued that the dealings of the United States with Native Americans had to be governed by the higher law of liberal constitutionalism and the higher purpose of a secular "city on the Hill."

Through assignments for the American Board, Evarts had become familiar with the Cherokee and the other southeastern Indian nations. He traveled among them, met their leaders, and listened—with the ear of a lawyer and a moralist—to them describe deteriorating relations with the United States. Separate from local attorneys who did occasional work for Native American clients, Evarts was in the vanguard of lawyers who understood national politics and used their legal skills in the high-stakes game played by those who opposed and those who supported Indian removal.

Evarts's commitment to the Cherokee fight against the abrogation of treaty guarantees and removal began at least as early as 1819. In February of that year Evarts wrote to the American Board to draw attention to a congressional plan to remove the Cherokee. He urged that the ABCFM oppose this policy of removal.[19] The position outlined by Evarts was legal and practical: He argued first that the lands and the sovereignty of the Cherokee Nation were guaranteed by legally binding treaties with the United States. Evarts held that removal would be futile and that the protection of a new Cherokee territory would be more difficult in the western regions. The prescient Evarts wrote that "if there is a great emigration of whites to the parts near the contemplated residence of the Cherokees, they will be immediately pressed harder than they are now. . . . [W]hy not protect them where they are? It can be done easier than on the river Arkansas. . . . For myself, I very much suspect, that the Cherokees after removing to their trans-Mississippi country, will find themselves hemmed in by a growing population. . . ."[20]

Throughout the early 1820s Evarts played a gentleman's game. He studied U.S. Indian policy closely, expressed himself politely in political memorandums, and traveled to Washington to follow congressional debates. But when Georgia pushed the Creek west and became intransigent about Cherokee removal, a change came over

Evarts. He became a relentless lobbyist against those who would break treaties in order to gain land: The volume of his correspondence on the Cherokee cause increased, he organized sympathizers to get up petitions and rallies and lobby influential American political figures, and he joined the small group of Americans offering direct advice to the Cherokee. Finally, Evarts produced the William Penn essays, a tract that many of his colleagues considered his most important effort on behalf of Native Americans. In this volume Evarts simultaneously made the specific case for Cherokee legal rights and put forward a more general argument for the maintenance of a just and Christian stance in U.S. Indian policy.

Extensively researched and coldly logical in its analysis, Evarts's brief reviewed the entire legal and political history of relations between the United States and the Cherokee Nation. He argued that the Cherokee held an "absolutely unincumbered" title to the land they occupied, rejecting Georgia's and Jackson's assertion that they were "merely permitted" to live on land whose title had passed at the conclusion of the Revolutionary War from Great Britain to Georgia.[21] It was a "plain case," Evarts wrote, of a more ancient people legally in possession of a land title and sovereignty that the United States had "repeatedly guaranteed to the Cherokees, as a nation . . . in treaties which are now binding on both parties."[22] Explicit in his argument was a challenge to the Jackson administration to assert the authority of the federal government over Georgia in matters of Indian affairs.

Evarts sent the essays, under thin veil of the William Penn pseudonym, to the *National Intelligencer,* a leading Washington periodical, which published them as a twenty-four-article series. To educate congressmen who were ignorant of the situation of the Cherokee, supporters of Evarts's work printed the articles as a book and in 1830 sent a copy to each member of the Twenty-first Congress, which had just begun debate on an Indian removal bill. This removal legislation was intended to create a legal commitment on the part of the United States to a policy of moving Indians across the Mississippi. President Jackson championed the bill. To offset the influence of the President and congressional partisans, Evarts and his local supporters also arranged for the essays to be reprinted in dozens of hometown newspapers.

It is impossible to know whether any votes on the removal bill in April and May 1830 changed as a result of Evarts's brief. Evarts's foes, the proponents of removal, won approval of the bill in a close vote. The essays, however, contributed to the considerable momentum achieved by the antiremoval lobby. They also provided the first publicly available, written legal argument, and as such, the Evarts brief became the definitive work on the legal claims of the Cherokee Nation. Chief Justice John Marshall, on completing a reading of the essays, pronounced them the "most conclusive argument that he ever read on any subject whatever."[23] Cherokee leader John Ross congratulated Evarts on the clear and correct "elucida[tion] of the rights of the Cherokee Nation."[24] The governor of Georgia commented archly that the Penn essays "have much more of the character of the politician and lawyer than that of an humble missionary."[25]

Evarts, the missionary, revealed his training in law both in the nature of the William Penn essays and in the general importance he placed on the public influence of attorneys and courts. During the campaign against the removal bill, for example, Evarts urged that a newly written statement on the rights of Indians be circulated among lawyers in major cities. He also wanted eminent lawyers in different parts of the United States to write legal opinions on the Indian question "with a view to publication."[26] The courts also were a critical part of the formula. In 1830, while Evarts lobbied unsuccessfully to block passage of the removal bill, he sought to convince the Cherokee of the utility of collateral support from the courts. The Supreme Court, he believed, was the proper forum for the interpretation of treaties.

Sometime late in 1829 Evarts had joined an American Board colleague, David Greene, in urging John Ross and the Cherokee National Council to consider an appeal to the U.S. Supreme Court as an additional part of the Nation's campaign to protect itself against Georgia. Evarts was optimistic about the impact of a favorable court decision. In a letter to a prominent New York businessman active in religious societies, Evarts described his hopes for Cherokee litigation: "I think that they should be encouraged to hold on, till the voice of the country and the decisions of the Supreme Court shall compel Georgia to do them justice."[27] Evarts trusted that with education and the imprimatur of a high court decision, a groundswell of public sentiment would arise to defeat Georgia and the Jacksonians. When the 1830 Indian Removal Act passed in Congress, the Cherokee had no choice but to rethink their legislative lobbying strategies. Repeal or modification of the legislation could be pursued, but both were uncertain possibilities. Realizing that at the moment the cause of the Cherokee Nation had neither the support of the American President nor a majority in the U.S. Congress and being disinclined to use a military strategy, Chief John Ross accepted Evarts's advice and agreed to initiate an aggressive legal strategy.

## THE CHEROKEE NATION HIRES AN ATTORNEY

There seemed to be no question that the counsel for the Cherokee in a great case testing international rights before the U.S. Supreme Court should be a litigator of considerable skill and prominence. Various men, most of them well-known anti-Jacksonians (National Republicans, shortly to be called Whigs), were considered. Early on, Evarts supported the well-known William Wirt and sent his name to the Cherokee leadership.

In deciding whether to hire Wirt, the Cherokee were presented with a dilemma: On the one hand, having no Cherokee attorneys trained to litigate in American courts, the Nation had to rely on foreign members of that profession; on the other hand, American lawyers' commitment to the social and political values of Cherokee society was generally untested or unreliable. Many American attorneys, even those who opposed the 1830 removal bill, had tarnished records of support for Indian sovereignty or, for that matter, the general worth of the Indian race. Henry Clay, a supporter of the Cherokee in the 1830s, was quoted in the 1820s memoirs of John Quincy Adams as having thought that Indians were "a race not worth preserving."[28] Another prominent Cherokee partisan of 1830, Judge Ambrose Spencer, had earlier written a decision in New York upholding the jurisdiction of that state over the Seneca Nation.[29]

Wirt also had a sullied record. In 1824, as U.S. Attorney General, he had issued an opinion denying the right of the Cherokee government to impose a revenue-producing licensing tax on American traders doing business in the Cherokee Nation.[30] Wirt wrote that it was "fallacious" to view the Cherokee Nation as having sovereignty equal to that of the United States. He argued that Congress could approve a Cherokee tax but that "by the treaties they have entered with us, they have placed themselves under the protection of the United States," giving the United States the sole and exclusive right of regulating affairs of trade between the two entities. In an aside Wirt did, however, urge that Congress treat Indians—at least those, like the Cherokee, whose government he found stable and sophisticated—more equally and legislate measures that would permit the Cherokee to raise revenue through licensing taxes. The Cherokee National Council flatly rejected Wirt's opinion and refused to repeal the tax. The United States stood behind the Wirt opinion. When the Cherokee refused to refund the tax to the traders, U.S. agents simply deducted the amount claimed from the annuity owed to the Cherokee. Forced in this way to capitulate, the Cherokee leadership petitioned Congress, using an argument that drew its logic from the petition on taxation, representation, and sovereignty sent in 1775 by the American colonists to the British Parliament.

It was not surprising that Samuel Worcester, an American Board missionary living with the Cherokee, sent a letter to Boston in November 1829 asking that Evarts be told of "prejudice in the minds of some against Mr. Writ, on account of his once having expressed an opinion against the right of the Cherokee to tax whites trading among them."[31] Perhaps because other prominent attorneys turned the Cherokee down or because in a later (1828) opinion as U.S. Attorney General Wirt had written that the Cherokee constituted an independent nation governed by their own laws, the Cherokee did hire him late in the spring of 1830.[32]

When the Cherokee Nation became his client, Wirt was fifty-eight and had lived in the East all his life. Orphaned as a young child, he had scrambled to provide for himself and to read law as an apprentice. At age twenty Wirt passed the Virginia bar and had the good fortune to marry into a gentlewoman's family, through which he gained access socially to Jefferson, Madison, Monroe, and other late eighteenth-century men of law, politics, and letters. Before he was thirty Wirt had been elected clerk of the Virginia House of Delegates and had served as counsel for James Callender in his sensational libel case testing the Alien and Sedition Act. Real prominence as a lawyer came after he joined in the prosecution of the case against Aaron Burr. In the twenty-odd years that preceded his becoming a lawyer for the Cherokee, Wirt had appeared frequently before the U.S. Supreme Court, participating in several suits— *McCulloch* v. *Maryland, Cohens* v. *Virginia, Dartmouth College* v. *Woodward,* and *Gibbons* v. *Ogden*—that tested the very fabric of the new American republic. In short, Wirt was a regular in a small circle of nationally prominent litigators, an attorney who favored his own superb oratory and reasoning to the use of black letter law, a man many considered Daniel Webster's equal as the greatest lawyer of the day.[33] Although he was not one of their own, on the basis of experience, skill, and reputation, the Cherokee did well to hire Wirt as their lawyer.

For his part, Wirt entered the service of the Cherokee Nation with caution. He and his large family lived entirely off the legal fees he commanded as a lawyer of great reputation. Jackson's implacable commitment to the removal of the Cherokee and increasingly solid political position would have given pause to any man about to rub the President's nose in constitutional principle. Indeed, a few weeks after he was hired by the Cherokee, Wirt wrote a close friend, Virginia judge Dabney Carr, that he was aware of the delicacy of his situation as the "instrument" to be used in thwarting a project on which the President and the state of Georgia were bent.[34] He told Carr that this delicacy had made him hesitate, but he was "impressed with the injustice about to be done to these people" and so had agreed to "examine their case and give them my opinion, and, if necessary, my professional services in the Supreme Court." Reflecting further on the predicament in which "I was about to place myself, and perhaps involve the Supreme Court of the United States," Wirt asked Carr to advise him "whether there is any thing exceptionable against me either as a lawyer or a citizen of the United States, in the part I am taking in this case."

Wirt's concerns did not keep him from plunging into detailed work for the Cherokee while waiting for Carr to respond. The legal strategy now adopted by the Cherokee replaced, at least temporarily, the political activity that had failed to block passage of Jackson's Indian removal bill. While an optimistic Jeremiah Evarts believed that the removal bill could be repealed when Congress reconvened in the autumn of 1830 or at least that the necessary appropriations could be blocked, Wirt went ahead and established a business relationship with the Nation. Days after accepting the position of national counsel for the Cherokee, Wirt wrote to Chief John Ross, making it clear that his service was conditional upon the Cherokee "keep[ing] peace and not tak[ing] the law into their own hands." The Baltimore lawyer also suggested the need for additional "eminent counsel" and an assistant to work with him as well as local lawyers to file papers and litigate for the Cherokee in county courthouses. All this, he wrote, would be expensive, and Ross had best decide not to proceed if he intended "an ill-timed parsimony."[35]

For their part, Ross and the Cherokee National Council were anything but passive clients, presenting Wirt with a specific list of legal questions addressing their situation. In reply, during June, Wirt prepared three lengthy memorandums. He sent them to the Cherokee government at the end of the month with the headings *Opinion on the Right of the State of Georgia to Extend Her Laws over the Cherokee Nation, Opinion on the Claims for Improvements, by the State of Georgia on the Cherokee Nation, Under the Treaties of 1817 & 1823,* and *Opinion on the Boundary between the Cherokees and Creeks in Georgia.* With an eye toward their political as well as legal importance, the Cherokee National Council ordered the printing of 1,000 copies to be used in a campaign of public education and political appeal. Reprints went out to President Jackson and former Presidents of the United States, to the governors of all the states and territories, and to "other distinguished personages." The pamphlets, while certainly an additional weapon in the Cherokee cause, excited the pro-Jacksonian press, which accused Wirt of acting against his country and indulging in a personal vendetta against the administration that had thrown him and his friends out of office.

At first glance, Wirt's opinions show full legal enthusiasm for Cherokee sovereignty and the right to resist removal. Opening his first essay, Wirt wrote, "[L]ong before the arrival of the Europeans on this continent, and from time immemorial, they have been a sovereign nation, rightfully under the sole and exclusive government of their own laws."[36] But Wirt quickly followed this assertion with statements revealing his facile acceptance of earlier Supreme Court doctrine attempting to diminish the ultimate legal title of the Indian nations to their land. Citing with approval Chief Justice John Marshall's 1823 opinion in *Johnson* v. *M'Intosh,* Wirt wrote that "the Europeans held that the *title of the Indians to their lands* underwent a change by force of discovery: that is to say, the particular power of Europe which made the first discovery acquired the right to purchase these lands of the Indians, in preference to and in exclusion of all other discoverers."[37]

With this statement, Wirt signaled his acceptance of the "doctrine of discovery." Discovery doctrine had been a convention of intra-European diplomacy that was intended to keep colonial powers from making overlapping land claims. Marshall's court, however, formally expanded the doctrine by describing the Native American, or *aboriginal*, title as one of occupancy and use, not a *fee simple* title carrying all rights of ownership and title conveyance. Fee simple title, Marshall had argued, resided with the United States (as successor to the discoverer nation, Great Britain), which according to doctrine was the only sovereign body to which the Indians could sell or surrender their lands or with which they could have political relations. In this first assignment, Wirt's work illustrates one of the limitations faced by the Cherokee as the client of a lawyer from another cultural and legal tradition: The law of discovery—a doctrine essential to the maintenance and expansion of U.S. territory— had not been accepted by the Indians, yet their lawyer had asserted the doctrine in essays that were broadly circulated in the United States.

There is no record, however, that the Cherokee were dissatisfied with the opinions. The general conclusions of the essays were what the Cherokee had hoped for: Georgia's jurisdictional laws were unconstitutional and therefore null and void because they violated Cherokee sovereignty and laws and treaties of the United States. Given this information, the Cherokee were eager to begin testing the power of U.S. courts to stop Georgia and by implication President Jackson. Wirt, however, moved cautiously. He wrote to the governor of Georgia, perhaps only as a formality, early in June that he did not wish to conceal his efforts on behalf of the Cherokee and suggested that a "decision might be expedited by making a case, by consent, if that course should suit the views of the State of Georgia."[38] The governor wrote back that he expected the Cherokee to move and that he would have no part in letting the federal courts sit in judgment of Georgia law. This settled formalities, eliminated the possibility of "friendly" litigation, and pushed Wirt to move ahead with the preparation of a case for the U.S. Supreme Court challenging Georgia's jurisdictional acts.

Despite his opinion that U.S. law considered the Cherokee a sovereign people governed by their own laws, Wirt was uncertain whether the Supreme Court would consider the Cherokee a nation. Wirt knew that the Court's decision on this matter would determine the kind of legal case he could fashion. If the Court accepted the idea that the Cherokee constituted a foreign nation, a case could be brought under the Supreme Court's seldom used original jurisdiction. This was an appealing strategy because his client could then avoid legal action in Georgia courts, where Wirt knew the Cherokee would face delay and harassment. He summed up his expectations of Georgia officials to Judge Carr: "They will probably refuse to receive and put upon their records any plea which will show that the construction of treaties was involved, so that the record will contain nothing to found the jurisdiction of the Supreme Court, under the 25th section."[39]

Eager to avoid a misstep in the selection of a legal strategy, Wirt took an unusual step. He implored Carr to speak to Chief Justice Marshall "as a brother judge," asking him for "his impressions of the political character of this people" in light of President Jackson's declaration that the Cherokee were not a sovereign people. Carr forwarded Wirt's letter to Marshall, who thought it best to refrain from giving a legal opinion, although he did write that he wished that the political branches had acted differently on the question of Indian removal.[40]

Still not content to rely on his own judgment, Wirt told the Cherokee through John Ross that he needed more advice on basic legal strategy. Letters went out to other nationally prominent lawyers—Daniel Webster, Ambrose Spencer, James Kent, Horace Binney, and John Sergeant—during the summer of 1830, asking whether the Supreme Court could be expected to respond to an original jurisdiction case. In the meantime, Wirt pressed Ross to get him the legal documents necessary to apply to Marshall during the summer recess for an injunction to prevent the enforcement of Georgia's Indian laws.[41]

At the same time, the search began for other "eminent counsel" to join Wirt on the case. Ross and Evarts corresponded about an offer made to Daniel Webster. Wirt was pleased at this prospect but wrote Ross that Samuel L. Southard had said that he would volunteer his services, a possibility that might have interested Ross because the cost to the Cherokee government of Wirt's services, those of the newly retained Georgia law firm of Underwood and Harris, and those of ad hoc advisers had begun to mount. In the late summer Wirt continued to consult with Ross on legal strategies, while Underwood and Harris began to represent Cherokee clients brought into legal proceedings, both civil and criminal, following Georgia's attempted extension of jurisdiction on June 1. Local legal actions were taken in response to alleged incidents of assault, Cherokee men digging in the Cherokee's gold mines (now claimed by Georgia), murder, debt actions, and the case of the Cherokee judge John Sanders, who had been indicted by Georgia for keeping his Cherokee courtroom open after the Nation had been "denationalized." Cases of this kind were to keep local Georgia attorneys busy for the next five years. Underwood and Harris were only two of the half dozen lawyers needed to defend the Cherokee citizens pulled into the web of Georgia's criminal justice system in the early 1830s.

Late in September 1830 Wirt wrote to Ross that Webster and Binney had declined to serve as co-counsel but that wealthy Philadelphia lawyer and congressman John Sergeant, known for his close association with the Second Bank of the United States and an ardent anti-Jacksonian, had accepted. The letter advised Ross to tell Sergeant about the financial problems caused by Jackson's refusal to pay U.S. annuities owed under treaty agreements to the Cherokee Nation. The Cherokee government used those annuities—payments for land cessions—as national revenue. "Prepare him not to expect a large retainer . . . send him two hundred dollars and promise a liberal fee in the event of success."[42]

In this letter Wirt also speculated about the possibility of professional sabotage. The number of local lawyers employed by the Cherokee Nation kept increasing, and Wirt was clearly nervous about them. He asked John Ross for all their names, since "tricks may be played to draw from your counsel the whole course of his defense in order to deflect it." Wirt further queried Chief Ross about whether he could be certain that the lawyers of the Underwood firm were not part of the opposition since they were Georgians. This long letter illustrates the sophisticated nature of the relationship between Wirt and his Cherokee client. It also contains a detailed outline of the several possible strategies for a legal case complete with intricate evaluations of each one. Ross demanded this kind of information from his lawyers and put it to use in his own public consultations. In this period, for example, Chief Ross met with U.S. Supreme Court Justice Johnson and discussed the Cherokee's legal problems.[43]

During early autumn 1830 Wirt and the Cherokee waited. The private counsel Wirt sought had not yet been received. Not ready to fashion a case for the Supreme Court, Wirt busied himself with responding to the continuing attacks made on him by the Jacksonian press and the governor of Georgia. In private correspondence, the lawyer argued vehemently against charges in the press that he had goaded the Cherokee into the controversy with Georgia for his own political motives. Wirt wrote that while his first letter to Ross contained the opinion that the Cherokee had the right to remain on their land, he had also told Ross that "if I could be assured that you would gain in exchange for your lands, others of equal value, where you would never again be disturbed by the approach of whites, and where you and your descendants w[oul]d be masters forever . . . *I for one would most [not legible] advise you to go and to give up this heartbreaking contest.*"[44]

## THE LEGAL TEST OF RIGHTS BEGINS

By November Wirt had received the expert opinions he had solicited over the summer. His friend Judge Carr had read the three briefs Wirt had written for the Cherokee and concurred in their analysis. Chancellor James Kent of New York also agreed with Wirt's earlier conclusions but went on to write his own formal opinion arguing that the Cherokee were an independent and sovereign nation and that the Supreme Court would thus acknowledge original jurisdiction in a case brought by the Cherokee government. Binney joined in those views, as did Daniel Webster, who had been arguing for an original jurisdiction suit all along. Ironically, Wirt's new co-counsel, John Sergeant, like Wirt himself earlier, nervously considered the possibility of the U.S. Supreme Court rejecting original jurisdiction.

In mid-November Wirt was on the move. He sent John Ross copies of a bill of injunction he had prepared for the Supreme Court, which if successful would enjoin Georgia from enforcing the new jurisdiction laws. Copies already had been sent to each of the justices. It was obligatory that sixty days' notice be given to Governor Gilmer and the state attorney general. Wirt instructed Ross that he and a Cherokee judge must sign the various papers and serve them on the state officials. In the same correspondence, Wirt also made it clear that he had not taken the Cherokee on as a pro bono client. Circling back, as he often did, to that "ungracious subject" of fees, Wirt reminded Chief Ross that so far he had received only a $500 retaining fee. Explaining the world of lawyering to the Cherokee leader, Wirt told Ross that this money did not apply to his actual services but merely stopped him from taking the opposite side. The Baltimore lawyer said that the briefs he had already written should be billed at not less than $500 and that arguing a case before the Supreme Court would cost the Cherokee at least $3,000. Conjecturing that his service for the Cherokee might "lose me business," Wirt said he must be paid at least $1,000 before he began arguing at the Supreme Court and "a further and most liberal compensation" if he succeeded. Wirt ended his letter by reminding Ross that the Cherokee also pay his postal account.[45]

Wirt had received professional encouragement for an original jurisdiction case and had initiated the process of filing a bill of injunction on behalf of the Cherokee against Georgia's new laws. But late in 1830 the attorney simultaneously gambled on the possible success of another sort of legal action after the dramatic kidnapping of a Cherokee citizen, within Cherokee territory, by Georgia state officials.

George Tassels, also known as Corn Tassels, stood accused of having "waylaid and killed" another Cherokee "within the territory in the occupancy of the Cherokee. . . ." Before the Cherokee could prosecute him, however, Georgia officials abducted Tassels, saying that the state was arresting him under its new jurisdiction law. Tassels was one of several Cherokee seized by state officials eager to press forward with a full test of its new laws and President Jackson's willingness to tolerate them. Georgia brought Tassels to trial at the Hall County Superior Court, where in September 1830 he was convicted and sentenced to be hanged.

The seizure of Tassels and other Cherokee citizens led Ross and the Cherokee leadership to assign several of their locally hired attorneys, including William Underwood from Underwood and Harris, to defense trials. Ross instructed Underwood to challenge the legality of Georgia's jurisdiction laws in court. Underwood did this, asserting in the Tassels case that treaties between the United States and the Cherokee Nation expressly recognized the Cherokee's right of self-government. He pointed to Article VIII of the 1785 Treaty of Hopewell, which acknowledged the right of the Cherokee to declare war against the United States, and described this article as providing unequivocal evidence that the United States recognized the Cherokee as a sovereign, foreign state. Underwood argued that Georgia's jurisdiction laws violated international law as well as the U.S. Constitution and that Tassels's arrest had been completely illegal.

Underwood's opponent, the solicitor general of the western Georgia circuit, replied that Indian tribes were considered "inferior, dependent, and in a state of pupilage to the whites." The state's attorney went on to argue that by the Compact of 1802 "the United States relinquishes to the State of Georgia all her rights to the land lying east of the tract ceded by the State of Georgia to the United States . . . and that the treaties were void, because the general government had no right to treat with Indians within the limits of the States, but upon the single subject of commerce, that being the only power granted them in the constitution."[46]

After making their arguments, the two lawyers sat back to await the decision of the court. By all reckoning, even this southern state court should have realized that it had no choice but to find that the state's jurisdiction laws ran contrary to the clear language of the many binding treaties acknowledging Cherokee sovereignty signed by the United States. That is not what happened, however. Despite the treaties of earlier years, Georgia felt that national law should be understood in new ways, and the Georgia justices did not shy from saying so. They were encouraged by the tendency of elected officials to ignore federal law. They were also emboldened by South Carolina's increasingly unguarded assertion of states' rights in opposing the national tariff, the passage of the Indian Removal Bill, and President Jackson's stated opposition to tribal governance. But political events were not the Georgia justices' only source of encouragement. Legal opinions of the U.S. Supreme Court in the earlier cases of *Fletcher* v. *Peck* (1810) and *Johnson* v. *M'Intosh* (1823) offered the jurists hope that their renunciation of international and national law would not result in severe penalties. How savvy these Georgia judges were in interpreting the interconnected fates of states' rights and national politics is best determined by turning to an examination of Washington in the Age of Jackson.

## CHAPTER 3

# The Age of Jackson

*The Cherokees are "established in the midst of a superior race and without appreciating the causes of their inferiority or seeking to control them, they must yield to the force of circumstances and ere long disappear."*

—PRESIDENT ANDREW JACKSON,
*Message to Congress, December 3, 1833*[1]

*. . . they must have strong excitements to leave the place of their nativity and the graves of their fathers."*

U.S. AGENT RETURN J. MEIGS[2]

## INTRODUCTION

In the early nineteenth century Washington, D.C., did not resemble the great capital cities of Europe. When President Andrew Jackson took office in March 1829, Washington was a picturesque but marshy expanse along the Potomac slowly being transformed into a national government center. National government personnel there numbered only 350.

The area had been home to the Algonquin and the Piscataway. Europeans came to the region shortly after 1700 and in various ways laid claim to the land. In 1790 the U.S. Congress selected a ten-square-mile area to be a federal district and the permanent home of the government of the United States. The Residence Act of 1790 delegated to President George Washington the power to erect public buildings in the district; on September 9, 1791, the city was named in his honor. The move from Philadelphia to the new capital was set for the year 1800. The rural land along the Potomac was chosen because of its proximity to the river, its accessible position, and the closeness of the river's headwaters to the Ohio River with its access to the inland region of North America.³ New Yorkers and Philadelphians had argued against building a new capital city but had lost the debate. Others believed in the practicality of a mid-Atlantic capital and saw the symbolic value of a new government metropolis built out of the Potomac dirt and swamp, just as many Americans imagined building an American empire out of the "whispering forests" and vast plains of the continent.

The President's house into which Andrew Jackson moved had first been occupied by John Adams in 1800. By the time of Jefferson's presidency people were calling the residence "the White House" because of its whitewashed sandstone exterior. The building at 1600 Pennsylvania Avenue was an elegant structure modeled after the home of Dublin's Duke of Leinster. The British burned the residence in August 1814 during the War of 1812, but the walls remained sound and the original structure was saved.

The Capitol was also badly damaged in the August 1814 fires. As conceived by President Washington and Thomas Jefferson, the Capitol was to be the most important architectural element in the district. They intended that in its placement and design, the home of the national legislature would convey the uniqueness of republican government. It is not accidental that the Capitol, not the White House, occupies Jenkin's Hill and commands a view from a site described by the eighteenth-century architect Pierre Charles L'Enfant as "a pedestal waiting for a monument."⁴

After the War of 1812, the Capitol was rebuilt, becoming an even more important symbol of national liberty and republican values. The building process required fourteen years. The completed Capitol had a low wooden dome over a central rotunda, north and south wings, and porticoes on the east and west. It housed the Senate and the House of Representatives as well as the Library of Congress and the U.S. Supreme Court. A grand building, it nonetheless did not have running water until 1832 or gaslights until the 1840s.

The plans for Washington had not included a building for the Supreme Court. Most Americans did not anticipate or desire that this national appeals court would play such a central role in their democratic experiment. In January 1801 the Supreme Court justices were assigned a small room in a corner of the original north wing of the Capitol in which to conduct the Court's business. The space was described as "a half-finished committee room meanly furnished and very inconvenient."[5] These were the physical circumstances in which John Marshall began his thirty-four-year tenure as chief justice. Eight years later the Court moved to another chamber in the Capitol specially fashioned for the jurists. This large room, with a dramatic vaulted ceiling designed by Capitol architect Benjamin Henry Latrobe, sat on the ground floor directly below the new second-story Senate chamber. The Court meeting room was damaged in the fire set by the British during the War of 1812. It too was rebuilt with an even more unique umbrella vault, a swirl of arches that some nineteenth-century visitors described as "half a pumpkin shell." Although the ceiling was a marvel, the first-floor location was criticized as a "dark, damp, low subterranean apartment"; it was thought to have contributed to the early deaths of some of the justices. Happily or not, the Court settled into the rebuilt chamber in February 1819 and continued to meet there until 1860.

Native Americans were no strangers to the new capital of the United States. Contemporary accounts repeatedly refer to lobbying carried out by representatives of different Indian nations in the halls of the House and the Senate. The personal presentation of petitions, called memorials, occurred with regularity. Oral arguments at the Supreme Court also attracted visiting tribal officials. In 1832 the noted British commentator Harriet Martineau described the presence of Cherokee visitors in John Marshall's Court. Twenty years earlier the writer Charles Ingersoll had observed that "when I went into the Court of Justice yesterday, one side . . . was occupied by a party of ladies. . . . On the opposite side was a group of Indians, who are here on a visit to the President. . . ."[6] Indeed, in the early nineteenth century great orators presenting a case before the Supreme Court attracted overflow crowds. When Daniel Webster was to argue a case, the galleries in the legislative chambers emptied and observers hurried to the Court on the floor below. "Rich men were said to have offered bribes in order to secure the best seats in the small room."[7]

The men who planned the Capitol intended that its relatively simple design reflect a plain, striving republican society in which the nation's people governed. Quickly, however, there were proposals to use the walls of the interior to celebrate the history of the developing nation and legitimate state-supported beliefs and values. Beginning in 1806, and particularly in the rebuilding period after 1815, portraits, reliefs, allegories, and historical paintings were installed in the Capitol. The first major commission in 1817 went to Connecticut artist John Trumbull "to compose and execute four paintings commemorative of the most important events of the American Revolution." Trumbull produced four epic-size canvases, hung in the Rotunda, depicting the signing of the Declaration of Independence, the surrenders of General Burgoyne and Lord Cornwallis, and the resignation of General Washington (signifying the end of war and a peaceful transition to civilian rule).[8]

When tribal representatives entered the Capitol Rotunda during the presidency of Andrew Jackson, they passed Trumbull's paintings; they also passed four newer commissions, each documenting a scene from the colonial period involving the meeting of Native American and European peoples. The large sandstone relief carvings entitled *Preservation of Captain Smith by Pocahontas, The Landing of the Pilgrims, William Penn's Treaty with the Indians,* and *Conflict of Daniel Boone and the Indians* highlight the interconnected fates of the two peoples while suggesting to nineteenth-century American visitors the superiority and likely triumph of the colonists in the struggle for control of the continent: Pocahontas, a convert to Christianity and European life through marriage to John Rolfe, pleads for John Smith's life and symbolizes the appeal of Western values and assimilation to the Native American; next, a small boatload of pilgrims makes a triumphal entry before the half-bent figure of an unresisting Indian man offering corn; farther along, William Penn shakes hands with an Indian in honor of their jointly signed treaty, an action that suggests peace as well as the preeminence of the Western system of law; and finally, in the last and most violent scene, an implacable Daniel Boone engages in combat with a fierce-faced Indian while standing on the corpse of another Indian.

No record exists to tell us how members of the Cherokee delegation responded to this selective and distorted historical narrative, but Cherokee officials were perceptive. Events at home gave them a contemporary context in which to interpret each tableau, and they undoubtedly understood these artworks as national propaganda. For Americans of the Jacksonian era, by contrast, the reliefs confirmed the deeply felt belief that their presence in North America, as well as the westward movement of their society, was the fulfillment of destiny and for some a providential mission.

# AMERICAN REPUBLICANISM TRANSFORMED INTO JACKSONIAN DEMOCRACY

Andrew Jackson took office as the seventh President of the United States forty years after the birth of the new republic. The American republic, born out of the Constitution of 1787, was a society radical in its rejection of monarchy and a hereditary governing elite. The War of Independence and the constitutional government established in 1789 envisioned a new social and political order, a republic. To the people of the revolutionary period, republicanism was an evolving idea. Initially, in England, it had meant a society with a reformed monarchy and governing institutions. In America, this notion quickly gave way to a more extreme ideology, one that challenged "the primary assumptions and practices of monarchy" and offered new conceptions of the individual, the family, and the state.[9] The men who wrote the U.S. Constitution endorsed new principles of individual political rights and civil liberties; they failed, however, to abolish slavery or address the use of law and social custom to subordinate women. Their concern for the protection of capital and their fear of popular majorities also led to a restricted system of representation with, for example, only members of the House of Representatives directly elected by the people (direct election of Senators began only with the ratification of the Seventeenth Amendment in 1913).

The idea of republicanism nevertheless reached deeply into American life. Republicanism represented a social as well as a political revolution. As shaped by the thinking and actions of ordinary Americans, republicanism increasingly came to signify a society of free, practical people who valued work and merit—as the aristocracy had not—and their right as citizens to design government policy that served their interests. Common people who were encouraged by the decentralized nature of colonial life and their perception of available land seized on the far-reaching possibilities of republicanism with its ideas of social and political equality. However, ordinary Americans interpreted republicanism less as a classical philosophy emphasizing selflessness and the common good and more as one permitting rational self-interest. They cast aside the older republican idea that elected officials should be virtuous, unsalaried men capable of making disinterested decisions in the common interest. Everyday Americans infused republicanism with newfangled democratic notions, sanctioning the election of officials with partisan and even personal interests. And they argued that the enhancement of private interests would benefit the entire nation. This was not what the early leaders of the American republic had had in mind.

The introduction of more democratic ideals at the beginning of the nineteenth century led to important changes in the American political system. The idea of the virtuous gentleman-citizen gave way. New states entered the Union with constitutions establishing—for the first time—universal white manhood suffrage. Older states abolished property qualifications for voting among white adult males. By 1825 only Louisiana, Virginia, and Rhode Island among the twenty-four states of the Union had not settled on universal white male suffrage.

At this time also, through the growing use of patronage, a new class of men received appointments to government bureaucracies. The expansion of patronage was an outgrowth of the development of modern political parties late in the second decade of the new century. Democratic-Republican parties emerged in the north. They differed from the older Federalist and Republican parties in that they had permanent and professional organizations committed to recruitment of candidates, mobilization of voters, and regular competition in elections. And in victory they rewarded loyal party members with government offices. Some called these rewards *spoils.*

Andrew Jackson's 1828 election to the presidency symbolized these democratic stirrings and inaugurated a new era in American politics. While late eighteenth-century American republicanism had loosened the bonds of monarchism and hereditary elites, it had not championed the unchecked power of the electorate. Jackson, however, never a member of the eastern social and political establishment and denied the presidency in 1824 because of rules that that establishment had promulgated, found it easy to support a new vision of the electorate that put majority rule at the center of the governing philosophy. Unlike the early Federalist leaders, Jackson did not fear the "turbulence and contention of democracy." In his speeches the President argued that the people should govern and that their will should direct the government.

Yet tragically, the democratic vision embraced in early nineteenth-century America was a narrow one. It was patriarchal and racist. Women were not included in the political community and were further disadvantaged by civil laws and practices that made them both domestic and economic dependents. Race matters were even worse. The political and intellectual currents that bore the new tide of democracy also introduced a more methodical racism. At the beginning of the nineteenth century African slaves and free African-Americans were thought of by whites as foreign and, in the minds of many, not likely to be assimilated. By 1830 these views had begun to harden into a "scientific" racism drawing on philosophical authority. Increasingly whites made arguments about the "innate moral and intellectual inferiority of the black race" that were based on what they believed to be facts of nature.[10] And in the same years that early nineteenth-century white men experienced an egalitarian revolution and began to exercise their new voting rights, their governments, in slave and free states, took steps to disenfranchise free African-Americans: New Jersey in 1807, Maryland in 1810, Connecticut in 1811, New York in 1821, Rhode Island in 1822. The American creed nurtured the abolitionist movement in this period, but it also bred an increasingly unrestrained contempt for people of other races. Not surprisingly, in those years American policies that had encouraged Native American acculturation shifted toward programs of exclusion and removal. At the national level no government official spoke more approvingly of this change in policy than Andrew Jackson.

Andrew Jackson was born in 1767 on a small farm in the Carolinas. Hard luck followed him until, still a teenager, he went to Charleston to claim a three-hundred-pound legacy from his Scotch-Irish grandfather in Ireland. The money was squandered during several months of fast living, after which the young man set himself the task of obtaining a rudimentary knowledge of law from country attorneys. At twenty-one Jackson moved to Tennessee, where over a period of years he used his legal skills and personal savvy to establish himself as a land speculator, slaveholder, local judicial officer, member of Congress, and major general of the militia. Well into middle age, in the closing days of the War of 1812, Jackson gained national acclaim as the "Hero of New Orleans." Two years later he faced national censure for violating military orders when he was sent to Florida by President Monroe. The ability to please and infuriate characterized Jackson's life and political actions. His politics, like his personality, ran to extremes. One biographer has offered this unsparing portrait:

. . . his cruelty, violence, and rage were as much a part of his character as his gallantry, gentleness, and kindness . . . his entire life as well as his political ideology included conflicting contrasts. A poor orphan boy with little appreciable education, he rose to hold the first office of the land and died a man of considerable wealth. Without military training or knowledge, he won the greatest military victory for American arms up to that time; a slave owner all his adult life, he regarded liberty as the priceless heritage of all men. A staunch advocate of equality, he thought only in terms of white adult males. Women, blacks, and Indians did not enter his thinking about liberty or equality, and his public statements to Congress invariably included the most racist ideas prevalent at the time. Jackson came into office with a promise that he would reform the bureaucracy and restore morality to government, yet his administration . . . set the stage for machine politics and boss rule.[11]

When Jackson took office in 1829, the United States was concluding a decade of unparalleled economic activity. The development of banking and credit institutions as well as commercial and constitutional law, a revolution in transportation and industrial technology, and the creation of the Wall Street Stock Exchange changed how people did business and the type of business they did. The foundations of capitalism were being built during this period, but there were profoundly felt differences about whether that would be good for America. Rural people content with local barter economies, limited public works, and low taxes decried the policies urged by city men who favored an expanded money supply, a national bank, and government-funded roads and canals. As one historian tells the story, the rural majority wanted government "weak, cheap, and close to home," while the mercantile gentry regarded strong central government as "an indispensable instrument of market growth" and would tolerate higher taxes and a national debt to achieve their goals.[12]

It was an ongoing struggle. In 1816, after much contention, the eastern business community prevailed and Congress chartered a national bank that would create a uniform and reliable paper currency and sound credit practices among state banks. Three years later the U.S. Supreme Court held that the establishment of this bank fell within the constitutional powers of the national government. The Court also gave its approval to other national policies favoring business, including internal development projects and protective tariffs, and upheld the power of business against local government in cases involving corporation charters and debt relief.

However, those who subscribed to Jefferson's early ideas of republican simplicity fought back. In the name of limited government and fiscal responsibility, they defeated national legislation to provide public financing for new roads and canals. And in the 1824, 1828, and 1832 presidential elections the same voters gave Andrew Jackson, a national military hero who lacked ties to the eastern business community and its ideas, more popular and electoral college votes than any other candidate. (The 1824 election was decided by the House of Representatives, which despite Jackson's plurality voted the presidency to John Quincy Adams.)

Jackson was a nationalist, although of a different school from Clay, Webster, and Calhoun. He believed in the Union as a source of protection for individual liberty. He also argued, however, that because an overly powerful central government could jeopardize freedom, state power should be supported. The national government should not overshadow state government, and the states should respect the integrity of the Union. Jackson took office in 1829 without a precisely defined economic program, although in principle he opposed paper money, federally financed public works, and a national debt. States' rights partisans claimed him as a friend. The new Democratic party had come of age.

Political events quickly cast Jackson into dramatic confrontations over the protective tariffs favored by business, the rechartering of the Bank of the United States, and congressional funds for a national turnpike. Creating drama of his own, by the end of his first term in office in 1832, the President had used his considerable popular support to corral national, or what Jackson called special privilege, capitalism: He blocked the development of a new national road system with his 1830 veto of the Maysville Road legislation, supported reduced tariffs and greater free trade when threatened with nullification of the 1828 federal tariff by the government of South Carolina, and vetoed the 1832 bill to recharter the Bank of the United States. Jackson led the parade of new Democrats who wanted development to be locally based. He rebuffed the old economic powers in his bank veto message, insisting that the "rich and powerful too often bend the acts of government to their selfish purposes."

Yet inexorably, the United States inched forward, even in the Jacksonian years, toward an ever-expanding regional and national market economy. Manufacturing grew, and with it wage labor. Urban communities increased in both size and number. Everywhere people wanted to pursue the opportunities afforded by new markets and test their entrepreneurial visions despite evidence of boom-bust cycles and rising inequality. While Jackson opposed the aspects of capitalist development that represented business privilege, he supported policies that would remove the barriers and restrictions in government practice—for example, government-granted corporate charters and tight credit—that affected private business efforts. Jackson and his followers were not revolutionaries. They were men of many backgrounds—planters, farmers, mechanics, laborers—who asserted the right to open the channels of commerce and compete without being limited by government actions, even those designed to keep order in the economy.

## JACKSON'S INDIAN POLICY

Removal of eastern Indian nations to the western side of the Mississippi River was the centerpiece of Andrew Jackson's Indian policy. He took the oath of office in March 1829, having long supported the absolute inevitability of removal. While Cherokee leaders such as John Ross believed in the possibility of a shared community, Jackson did not, and he played on the belief of like-minded Americans that the "voluntary" removal of Native Americans was an acceptable, even moral, policy. Americans supported removal for a variety of reasons. For some, the policy was part of a national movement that had begun with the War for Independence against England and had extended into a national expansion program that included expulsion of the Spanish from the South and the removal of Indians generally. Other Americans embraced Indian removal as consistent with a deeply internalized vision of the people of the United States as having a special mission to foster Western civilization in North America. Older Americans and new immigrants favored removal because they sought a place for their families to live. Racists advocated ventures that would homogenize communities. Land speculators and entrepreneurs saw profit and market opportunities in vacated Indian land.

Andrew Jackson became an adult on the Tennessee frontier, where settlers wanted to eliminate obstacles to westward expansion and foster economic opportunity. Intruders on the lands of the

Cherokee, the Creek, and other Indian nations, men like Jackson nevertheless saw Native Americans as "the problem." Jackson began fighting local Indians, probably the Creek, within months of his arrival in Tennessee in 1788. According to one biographer, by the 1790s Jackson "had emerged as a fire-breathing frontiersman obsessed with the Indian presence and the need to obliterate it." He criticized congressional Indian policy and the use of treaties: "I fear that their Peace Talks are only Delusions . . . why treat with them does not experience teach us that Treaties answer No other Purpose than opening an Easy door for the Indians to pass through to Butcher our Citizens. . . . What Motives Congress are governed by with Respect to their pacific Disposition towards Indians I know not; some say humanity dictates it; but Certainly she ought to Extend an Equal share of humanity to her own Citizens."[13]

Jackson the nationalist sought to secure territory for the United States. Any group, European or Indian, that opposed American expansion had to be defeated. In the years before becoming President, as an army general fighting the British and the Spanish, Jackson had committed himself wholeheartedly to this goal. He fought Europeans in the name of American expansionism, just as he had fought the southeastern Indian nations. And he was victorious. In the Creek War, Jackson salvaged months of disastrous campaigning and defeated the anti-assimilationist Red Stick (Creek) faction at the 1814 Battle of Horseshoe Bend. Although a sizable part of the Creek Nation fought with the United States, Jackson used the victory to dictate a symbolically and strategically important Creek land cession of 20 million acres. Jackson's insistence on wringing every possible concession from the Creek in the Treaty of Fort Jackson reveals his deep commitment to the demands of westerners for the destruction of the southern Indian nations. His success in negotiating this treaty, whose object was land seizure and the destruction of Indian sovereignty, put Jackson on the road to the presidency and put the United States on an ever more certain path to empire.

Jackson's success at Horseshoe Bend in 1814 and later against the British at the Battle of New Orleans led to his involvement in seven years of fighting against Spain, England, and the southern Indian nations. During those years, unflagging in action, outspoken and aggressive, Jackson gained recognition as the greatest hero of his time. He stopped the British at the Gulf of New Orleans when the men in Washington had not been able to prevent them from burning the capital, bullied Spain out of the Floridas, and pursued the Creek and Seminole with a single-minded mania. People were enthralled by the tall, gaunt "Iron General," wrote songs about him, and increasingly gave credence to what he had to say. He was no longer merely a private citizen lamenting congressional disinterest in the desires of western citizens. After 1814 Jackson was a hero whose popularity, many said, was greater than that of Washington, Franklin, or Jefferson. And the hero said that the United States should pursue its dreams of expansion and wealth. His policy advice as a general and his military actions from 1814 to 1821 prepared the way for the Indian policy he sanctioned and directed a decade later as President.

First, Jackson prevailed on the matter of the treaty with the Creek. He simply refused to accept the nullification of this treaty, as demanded by the British at the close of the War of 1812. He forced the British government to choose between continuing to fight the South and protecting its Canadian claims. The British chose Canada, and Jackson began the wholesale removal of the Creek from the ceded lands. Encouraged by his success with the Creek, Jackson engineered several new treaties, winning vast acreage—as the price for peaceful relations—from the Cherokee, Chickasaw, Choctaw, and Creek in present-day Tennessee, Mississippi, Alabama, Florida, Georgia, Kentucky, and North Carolina. Some of those tribes had fought the Red Sticks with Jackson, but he did not make allowances. Ally or foe, they were Indians and he would have their land. In 1816 Jackson wrote to the new Secretary of War, William H. Crawford, that "the people of the west will never suffer any Indian to inhabit this country again."[14] Frontiersmen worshiped him for respecting their dreams, cotton planters quickly began to reap profits from the rich soil of the treaty lands, and nationalists embraced Jackson's plans to establish roads for commercial and military use between inland areas and the Gulf of New Orleans.

The Treaty of Fort Jackson had extracted millions of acres of Creek land as the price of defeat. The treaties that followed were extraordinary, however, because Jackson won sizable additional cessions from other Indian nations with which the United States was not at war. These many successes emboldened Jackson and encouraged him to propose a new federal Indian policy to President Monroe in 1817. Jackson's program drew on his long-standing opposition to Indian sovereignty and his belief that the defeat of the Creek at Horseshoe Bend and of their British allies at New Orleans symbolized new power relationships that favored the United States.

He argued that Congress and the President should unilaterally refuse to recognize the sovereignty of Indian nations and discontinue the treaty system. Jackson supported the immediate extension of American jurisdiction over Indians "living within the territory of the United States" and the taking of Indian land through the exercise of eminent domain.[15]

Jackson's proposals were radical and did not win wide support. Jackson was authorized, however, in 1817 to initiate another policy that he favored: the removal of eastern Indian nations to territory west of the Mississippi. Although Jackson was successful in persuading only a fraction of the people of the Cherokee Nation to make the move between 1817 and 1819, this temporarily satisfied him. He felt that removal policy could be imposed on all the eastern Indian nations within a very few years. In his biographer's words, Jackson's experience with the Cherokee "convinced him of the inevitability, the practicality, and the workability of removal."[16]

While Jackson correctly prophesied a full-fledged American removal policy, he erred badly in predicting that the eastern Indian nations would voluntarily agree to move. Jackson and other treaty commissioners in the Monroe administration quickly learned that most tribal members did not intend to be forced from their land. At the same time, Indian governments such as the Cherokee refused to go to war. Lacking legal means to obtain the desired land cessions, during the first Monroe administration Secretary of War Calhoun gave federal agents the authority to use subterfuge and fraud to acquire Indian land. This represented a major shift from earlier federal Indian policies and was at odds with instructions from Congress. This conscious strategy of illegality marked the end of an era and forced the United States to confront the reality that in Indian policy the idea of expansion with honor had to be abandoned.[17] Americans had calculated that through tight federal control of Indian policy, order could be maintained over reckless frontiersmen and "civilization" could be exchanged for cheap land. By Monroe's time this naive dream had begun to fade, and Americans slowly came to acknowledge that empire could not be achieved with honor.

## Changing World Views and American Indian Policy

Ideas of destiny and mission seem always to have been at the center of how Americans have envisioned their place in North America and how they should relate to Native Americans. The Puritans imagined themselves a chosen people sent to establish a worldly Holy Commonwealth whose social contract included conversion and then incorporation of Native Americans. Religious attention to individual perfectibility and social concern was introduced into eighteenth-century America by the Quakers in particular. In William Penn's famous colony, theological and worldly goals intertwined with an optimistic belief that everything from personal behavior to national politics could be changed by means of a proper moral code. In New England too, acculturation of Indians found expression in liberal Protestantism. Dartmouth College was chartered in 1769 "for civilizing, and Christianizing, and instructing the Indian natives of this land."

In 1789 President Washington announced acculturation and eventual assimilation of Indians as the policy of the United States. The mission of the nation was to bring about the "civilization" of Native Americans. Along with many public officials and religious leaders, Washington believed that this could be done before the middle of the new century. Influenced by the ideas of the Enlightenment, Washington, Jefferson, and others offered a republican interpretation of human equality that accepted the possibility of reclaiming the Indian through social programs. Environment made the Native American only superficially different from the European; new environments—school, church, farm—could make the Indian an acceptable member of Western society. The first Congresses readily endorsed Washington's policy. Indians would be helped to learn English and take up farming. Communally held tribal land would be divided among them "in severalty" (individual ownership). Indians who agreed to abandon their destiny and acculturate were promised an eventual place in the republic as full and equal citizens. Tribal government would dissolve, no longer confronting the United States with competing sovereignties. Lands no longer used for "hunting and roaming" would become the property of the federal government or the state governments.

Educated men of Washington and Jefferson's time believed that Native Americans were part of the family of humanity in a genetic sense. The social changes they expected from their Indian neighbors were dictated, however, by a firm belief in the superiority of Western ideas and values. In the colonial period the American creed drew on religious explanations. Colonists, in particular the Puritans, believed themselves to have a unique covenant with God. They described themselves as part of a divine "errand into the wilderness."[18] Defining themselves as a chosen people, they and their descendants read the Bible and imagined the millennium—a "thousand-year" period during which Christ would rule untroubled by Satan's wiles—predicted in Revelation's (20:1–5) final message of redemption.

The millennial vision took hold. Free of Europe's evils, among them feudalism and religious persecution, and tested by an ocean voyage, the colonial mind merged biblical prophecy and worldly opportunity to create the idea of the *American* millennium. In North America all creation could be renewed, free from imperfections and transformed by the glory of God.[19] Redemption and conversion were emphasized. North America, the land of the millennium, could under no circumstances be abandoned, even though another people, Native Americans, asserted rights to the continent. To leave it was to abandon the ultimate promise of Christianity. The land of the millennium must be claimed, along with the hearts of new converts. This was the moral lesson imprinted on an American society by Puritan thought. Colonists everywhere responded to the idea even as they gave it different meanings. And so the idea of being a special people with a providential destiny to claim the continent was established.

American millennialism became secularized with the birth of the republic. George Washington was given the mantle of the new messiah and was asked to lead the fledgling nation on its providential course.[20] Already imbued with spiritual meaning, worldly millennialism now also embraced republicanism, with its promise of justice, personal freedom, and prosperity. Secularized millennialism continued to draw strength from the idea of a special destiny. It drove early nineteenth-century Americans to fight Britain and Spain and to make a relentless push against the Native American nations.

## Prelude to Removal Legislation

By 1817 Britain had conceded its interest in the southern part of the North American continent, electing instead to solidify its position in the north through the Anglo-American Convention of 1818, which established the forty-ninth parallel as the United States–Canada border. In 1819 Spain signed over its claims to the Floridas to the United States. The United States was ready to assert jurisdiction from the Atlantic coast to the western side of the Mississippi River. The presence of the eastern Native American nations made this impossible, although the international agreements that concluded the War of 1812 changed the international order in ways that were not to the advantage of the Indian nations.

By the 1820s the United States posed a greater threat to Native Americans than ever before. The old Native American alliances with Spain and Britain had disintegrated. Population pressure drove American citizens and newly arriving immigrants west into the territory of the Indian nations, their journey quickened by the advent of the steamboat and the building of roads and canals. Restless, confident, and greedy, Jacksonian Democrats and eastern moguls alike sought the economic development of the frontier. Still, from the settlers' point of view, the Native American was in the way. Moreover, the appeal of President Washington's vision of the assimilated Indian was fading. On the one hand, in many Native American communities resistance to acculturation persisted as Indian citizens held firmly to their own cultures. This made Americans skeptical that Washington's plan would be realized by the 1840s. On the other hand, in Cherokee society, for example, where conscious acculturation had been carried out by the leadership, Cherokee citizens quickly learned that their land and commercial resources had not only traditional but now market value and refused to surrender them.

The failing appeal of the old Indian policies coincided in the early decades of the nineteenth century with a revolution in how Americans thought about God, people's place in the world, and one another. Americans were democratizing government; now, it was said, they should do the same in their churches, and they did. "People were their own theologians . . . wholly free to examine for [themselves] what is truth, without being bound to a catechism, creed, confession of faith, discipline or any rule excepting the scriptures. There had been nothing before in America on such a scale quite like the evangelical defiance and democratic ferment of this Second Great Awakening."[21]

The rise of what has been called plebeian evangelicalism and the age of romanticism (that is, the validation of subjective experience) came at the expense of Calvinism and Enlightenment (empirical and rational) thought. In this profound cultural transformation, historian William McLoughlin has written, Americans developed a new national outlook that had a significant impact on the direction of federal Indian policy:

> The removal of the Indians to the west was not simply an incident in this cultural transformation; it was an integral part of it. . . . In redefining God during the Second Great Awakening, Americans also redefined how He worked, which is to say how they thought about man's place in the universe and America's role in human history. The shift from Calvinist . . . determinism included the belief that man had free will, that he and God were partners, and that God had chosen the Americans as a special people with a special mission to save the world and bring on the millennium. The nineteenth century missionary impulse to perfect the world by converting everyone in it became so ethnocentric that it embodied a patriotic zeal to exclude lesser breeds from more than spiritual salvation. In popular thought, God had chosen the white, Anglo-Saxon, Protestant Americans to save the world. As the voice of the people became the voice of God . . . Americans discovered who they were by deciding who they were not, and those who were deciding were not black Africans or red Indians; this was a white man's country led by special kinds of Europeans who had the innate potential to fit the mold now called "American."[22]

This new world view permitted white Americans to make their claim to the continent even more aggressively and with greater moral certitude than in past decades. Its intellectual and spiritual premises encouraged whites to feel they had the right to decide who should be part of the American community of men and under what circumstances. It is perhaps not coincidental that in the same year—1817—in which Jackson negotiated the first limited treaty of removal west with the Cherokee, a colonization movement began with the purpose of transporting free blacks to Africa. Members of the white-organized American Colonization Society contended with considerable sophistry (just as supporters of Indian removal would) that those who had been freed needed to be saved from themselves and from the bad influence of whites. Henry Clay, who supported colonization, saw manumission and resettlement as a way of avoiding the insurrection and race war certain to arise out of slavery.[23] Both the colonization and the removal program were expressions of the desire for a racially homogeneous America. Jacksonian Democ-

rats had succeeded in disassembling critical aspects of the class hier-
archy only to replace it with race thinking that willingly subordi-
nated Native Americans and African Americans.

## PASSAGE OF THE 1830 INDIAN REMOVAL ACT

Andrew Jackson took office with clearly stated views concerning
the future of federal Indian policy. In the South, on the western
frontier, and even in certain eastern communities, men had supported Jackson for President because of his opposition to Indian
sovereignty.

For two decades before becoming President and during the 1828
campaign, Jackson had openly insisted that Indians did not constitute sovereign nations and did not hold absolute legal title to their
land. He contended that only practical considerations had led the
post-Revolution American government to treat Indian communities
as foreign powers and negotiate international agreements with
them. The nineteenth century, he claimed, had brought changed
political circumstances that American policy should acknowledge.
Thus, in 1817 General Jackson told President Monroe in a letter that
"I have long viewed treaties with the Indians as an absurdity . . .
[they] are subjects of the United States inhabiting its territory and
acknowledging its sovereignty."[24] Jackson maintained that removal
should be voluntary, a conclusion that is difficult to reconcile with
the clear and stated intentions of southeastern Indian nations, made
in various diplomatic communications, throughout the early 1820s.

A backward glance at history shows that Jackson's Indian policy recommendations did not constitute an abrupt departure from
the policy direction taken by his predecessors, James Monroe
(1816–1824) and John Quincy Adams (1824–1828). Monroe and the
Senate had authorized the use of removal provisions in the 1817
treaty with the Cherokee and subsequent agreements, including the
1820 Treaty of Doak's Stand with the Choctaw. Adams adopted
ever harsher Indian policies and increasingly ignored binding obligations to them under international law. He ended his presidency by
dispatching American soldiers to intimidate the Creek, whom he
hoped to force to remove, and then by refusing to condemn Georgia's jurisdiction legislation. During the Adams presidency Congress had seriously considered a removal bill. A continentalist, as

President, Adams was not uncomfortable with policies of national expansion and empire.[25]

## The Removal Bill

Jackson announced his administration's Indian policy proposal on December 8, 1829, in an address to Congress:

> I suggest, for your consideration, the propriety of setting apart an ample district West of the Mississippi, and without the limits of any State or Territory, now formed, to be guarantied to the Indian tribes, as long as they shall occupy it: each tribe having a distinct control over the portion designated for its use. There they may be secured in the enjoyment of governments of their own choice, subject to no other control from the United States than such as may be necessary to preserve peace on the frontier, and between the several tribes. There the benevolent may endeavor to teach them the arts of civilization. . . . This emigration should be voluntary; for it would be as cruel [and] unjust to compel the aborigines to abandon the graves of their fathers, and seek a home in a distant land. But they should be distinctly informed that, if they remain within the limits of the States, they must be subject to their laws. . . . Submitting to the laws of the States, and receiving, like other citizens, protection in their persons and property, they will, ere long, become merged in the mass of our population.[26]

Increasingly obsessed with removal, Jackson lobbied for his policy despite months of futile negotiations with the southeastern Indian nations in 1829. The core of the removal proposal was emigration west, but Jackson also used the address to announce his administration's support for Georgia's jurisdiction laws and to argue that eastern Indians who elected not to migrate "must submit to [state] laws." Fighting to win over the religious societies that had already stated their opposition to removal, the President had made certain to signal continued government approval for their "civilizing" work in the West.

Jackson spoke pointedly of winning passage of the necessary congressional legislation by the spring. Georgians were buoyed by his speech. On the issues of Indian denationalization, state jurisdiction, and removal, Georgians and the President were of one mind. Jackson further solidified the relationship by selecting the proremoval Georgian John N. Berrien as his Attorney General. To the extent that the *Corn Tassel* judges worried about reaction to their decision in the nation's capital, they must have assumed that they could count on the approval of frontier lawyer and Indian fighter, now President, Andrew Jackson.

By the early spring of 1830 both the House and the Senate had written removal proposals and had reported them out of their respective committees on Indian affairs. Jackson felt optimistic about the likelihood of passage. In the 1828 congressional election candidates from Jackson's party (shortly to become the Democrats) had won 26 of the 48 seats in the Senate and 139 of the 213 places in the House of Representatives. Yet despite this support, the removal legislation provoked a firestorm of debate that polarized Washington and the nation. The content of the legislation raised profound questions of politics and morality. It squarely and starkly posed the question of whether national expansion could occur with honor. Treaties, it was argued, would be broken. A people would be presumed to leave what was theirs solely for the comfort and benefit of the people of the United States.

Jackson, however, stood squarely behind the congressional legislation, using the familiar language of millennialism:

> Philanthropy could not wish to see this continent restored to the condition in which it was found by our forefathers. What good man would prefer a country covered with forests, and ranged by a few thousand savages to our extensive republic, studded with cities, towns, and prosperous farms; embellished with all the improvements which art can devise, or industry execute . . . and filled with all the blessings of liberty, civilization, and religion![27]

Proremoval congressmen approached the question in the same manner as the President. They too insisted that the unquestioned higher purposes of Western civilization demanded that whites have access to all eastern lands. The United States, they argued, had never recognized Indian nations as having any of the attributes of sovereignty or inherent property rights. A half century of formal diplomacy between the United States and Indian nations was summarily dismissed by proremoval spokesmen as something meant only to flatter "[the Indians'] vanity . . . by the acknowledgement of their name and rank."[28] Congressional reports and speeches belittled Indian culture and maintained that only in the West could the "vanishing" Indians save themselves. Northern opponents of removal were mocked for wishing to deny the South what had already been accomplished in New England. Not surprisingly, members of the Georgia and Tennessee congressional delegations were prominent among those who encouraged passage of this legislation.

Opponents of the legislation, however, felt that principles of international law had consistently governed U.S. relations with the Indian nations. Aided by Evarts's arguments in the William Penn essays, they denounced the removal bill as an open and rank attempt to destroy Indian sovereignty and abrogate binding treaty obligations. Whig congressman Henry Storrs offered unsparing criticism of those who claimed that the United States had not recognized Indian sovereignty in treaties and other diplomatic actions:

> The committee [on Indian Affairs) have suggested that we should not give much weight to "the stately forms which Indian treaties have assumed, nor to the terms often employed in them," but that we should rather consider them as "mere names" and "forms of intercourse." If treating these Indian nations as proprietors of a qualified interest in the soil—as competent to enter into treaties—to contract alliance—to make war and peace—to stipulate on points involving and often qualifying the sovereignty of both parties, and possessed generally of political attributes unknown to individuals, and altogether absurd in their application to subjects, is nothing more than "mere names" and "stately forms," then this long practice of the Crown, Colonies, the States, and the Federal Government, indeed, proves nothing. Words no longer mean what words import, and things are not what they are.[29]

Storrs went on to outline the many specific and important ways in which Indian sovereignty had been recognized:

> We have not only recognized them as possessed of attributes of sovereignty, but, in some of these treaties, we have defined what these attributes are. We have taken their lands as cessions—terms totally senseless if they are citizens or individuals. We have stipulated for the right of passage through their country, and for the use of their harbors, for the restoration of prisoners, for the surrender of fugitives from justice, servants, and slaves. We have limited our own criminal jurisdiction and our own sovereignty, and have disenfranchised our citizens by subjecting them to other punishments than our own. . . . You cannot open a chapter of Vattel, or any writer on the law of nations, which does not define your duties

and explain your obligations. No municipal code reaches them. If
these acts of the Federal government do not show them to be sovereign to some extent, you cannot show that you have ever
acknowledged any nation to be so.[30]

The antiremoval cause drew the support of other prominent
members of Congress, Some, including Senator Theodore Frelinghuysen of New Jersey, had long-standing commitments to the
work of the American Board and other religious societies and
opposed the bill on behalf of those groups. Other antiremoval representatives, among them Webster and Clay, had a long history of
personal and political differences with President Jackson. These
men, like Wirt and Sergeant, were central figures in the anti-Jackson
establishment who had chosen to support the Cherokee for moral
reasons but who also knew that their opposition to removal would
discredit the President.

The intense debate surrounding the removal bill thus reflected
the larger partisan tensions of the Jackson era. The antiremoval men
opposed what they believed to be Jackson's narrow and restrictive
view of the power of the national government. They and the Jacksonian Democrats differed over the distribution of government
power, particularly as it affected the control of economic development. Removal, slavery, tariffs, and the U.S. Supreme Court's
authority to review state court decisions on constitutional questions
were among the significant political questions folded into the great
national debate over national versus state power. Ironically, the
removal bill drew most of its support from Jacksonian Democrats,
although in its requirement of central government organization and
funding it resembled the kind of Federalist National Republican
scheme they normally wished to discredit.[31]

Jackson had pledged the passage of a removal bill by the spring
of 1830. On April 26, in a straight party vote, the Senate approved
the President's legislation twenty-eight to nineteen. In the House of
Representatives, however, the measure was headed for defeat.
Democratic party congressmen from the northern states were hearing that voters did not like the bill. In an effort to save themselves,
those Democrats supported a new proposal that would delay consideration of removal for a year. When House voting on this legislation resulted in a 98–98 tally, the President knew that he needed to
act. Telling House Democrats that he "staked the success of his

administration upon this measure," he pressured and bullied, and the original removal legislation passed in the House by a vote of 102 to 97.[32] Jackson signed the reconciled Senate and House version into law in late May 1830.

A British writer visiting Washington during debate on the removal bill reflected that the legislation passed as a result of "the *fiat* of the president." Her frank reporting went on to note contradictions in the principles and practice of the Americans where the question of Indian policy was concerned: "They inveigh against the governments of Europe, because, they say, they favour the powerful and oppress the weak. . . . You will see them one hour lecturing their mob on the indefeasible rights of man and the next driving from their homes the children of the soil, whom they have bound themselves to protect by the most solemn treaties."[33]

The removal plan, entitled "An act to provide for an exchange of lands with the Indians residing in any of the states or territories, and for their removal west of the river Mississippi," spelled out the most draconian measures couched in the sanitary language of governance: Congress instructed the President to create an Indian territory on public lands west of the Mississippi River and arrange to exchange land there for Indian land in the east; convey a guaranteed legal title to these lands in place of the aboriginal title held in the east; negotiate compensation for property that could not be moved west; "cause aid and assistance to be furnished as necessary" in the move and for a year after resettlement; protect the eastern Indians enrolled in the program from western Indians and other persons already living in the territory; maintain "the same superintendence and care" of removed Indians as permitted in the east; and carry out removal without violation of existing treaties with the (small) sum of $500,000.[34]

The 1830 law officially committed the United States to a large-scale program of Indian removal. The congressional vote had been close, but in the most explicit test of Indian sovereignty before the political branches of the U.S. government, Jackson, the Democrats, and the southeastern states had prevailed. Seemingly formal principles had not been altered. The Removal Act authorized the President to carry out only a voluntary program of removal ("tribes as may choose") through lawful treaties. Nevertheless, the tenor of the proremoval debate and the very nature of the bill questioned tribal

sovereignty and aboriginal land title and attested to the unwillingness of Americans to coexist with nearby Indian nations. The United
States had adopted a national Indian removal policy that might
have appeared accommodating on paper (with its language of tribal
choice and U.S. financial aid), but representatives of the Indian
nations knew better. And so, despite questionable legal signals from
the Supreme Court in prior cases involving Indian sovereignty and
land title, in the summer months after the passage of the removal
bill John Ross encouraged William Wirt to push forward with his
legal research on behalf of the Cherokee Nation. Ross hoped that a
persuasive argument could be made to the Supreme Court so that
state laws meant to limit Indian sovereignty could be enjoined and
defeated. Ross knew that the federal courts were the Cherokee's
only hope while Jackson remained in office. Ross, a cosmopolitan
man, trusted in the law and believed that the Americans respected
the law as a source of social and commercial order. For these reasons, with some confidence, in the autumn of 1830 the Cherokee
made the final decision to challenge the legality of Georgia's jurisdiction laws before the Supreme Court of the United States.

## CHAPTER 4

# The Test of Cherokee Legal Rights Begins

No outcry was heard in the United States when, in September 1830, the judges of the Hall County Superior Court upheld Georgia's illegal seizure of the Cherokee George Tassels and sentenced him to death. The local judicial decision approving the application of state criminal jurisdiction to the Cherokee Nation certainly had the support of the Jackson White House. Curiously, however, the opinion of the local appeals court also drew on the legal theories of U.S. Supreme Court Chief Justice John Marshall, who was generally not a favorite of Jacksonian Democrats in Georgia. The theories in question were developed in *Fletcher* v. *Peck* (1810) and *Johnson* v. *M'Intosh* (1823), two cases in which the young American Supreme Court made its first efforts to apply U.S. law to Indian nations.[1]

## EARLY SUPREME COURT DOCTRINE: FLETCHER AND JOHNSON

U.S. Supreme Court involvement in federal Indian law began with *Fletcher* v. *Peck*. This famous 1810 case is best described as a squabble among thieves and is best known in law as the case first used by the high court to extol the sanctity of vested rights in property. Chief Justice John Marshall's opinion for the Court established the U.S. Constitution's contract clause (Article I, Section 10) as a shield for property rights against state action, including state legislation that would impair the obligation of contracts.[2]

The "Yazoo" case, as *Fletcher* v. *Peck* came to be known, grew out of aggressive and fraudulent speculative schemes in Native American land claimed by the state of Georgia. Indian governments were not direct parties to the case, but because the Yazoo lands originally sold by Georgia had not been transferred from the tribes properly by treaty, the Supreme Court had no choice in *Fletcher* but to address the question of the legal status of Indian land under American law.

John Marshall had been chief justice of the Supreme Court for nine years when he authored the *Fletcher* opinion. Outgoing Federalist President John Adams had appointed Marshall to the Court in 1801 to "save" the twelve-year-old U.S. Constitution from Jefferson and his followers (Jeffersonian Republicans). It was the perfect job for a jurist willing to make vigorous arguments—at a formative time in the life of the new nation—on behalf of individual liberty, property rights, and the advantages of a national economy. In colonial and revolutionary America there had been considerable regional diversity in the law. The new U.S. Constitution provided a blueprint from which spirited men such as Chief Justice Marshall could shape a unified American national law. No area was more in need of a strong jurist's touch than the national law of real property.

Much has been written of Marshall's contribution to contract law in *Fletcher*. Less often do historians note that *Fletcher* began a series of cases in which the chief justice analyzed who, according to U.S. law, had title to the lands of the continent. Marshall's discussion of land rights was brief, virtually appended to his arguments about the obligations of contract. In a few sentences the chief justice rejected the idea that Indians—who in his view "merely roamed over and hunted on" the land of the continent—could hold absolute legal title to that land. Instead, he acknowledged an Indian property right that he described as "Indian title." This designation established a general judicial protection for Indian land under American law. Specifically, in his opinion Marshall described Indian title as "certainly to be respected by all courts" until extinguished and urged only legitimate tribal consent for any extinguishment of title.[3]

It was, however, the bad luck of the Indian nations that the chief justice did not conclude his analysis with these general points. Instead, Marshall wrote on, rationalizing first that this title was *only* one of occupancy. Then Marshall turned to the question of what rights Georgia might hold under American law. Here again the chief justice spoke against Indian political and legal interests by indicating that the majority of the court believed "Indian title . . . is not such as to be absolutely repugnant to seisin in fee on the part of the state."[4] Using the ancient legal words *seisin in fee*, Marshall announced that Indian land, land to which his court had assigned the right of occupancy, might simultaneously be land in which a state such as Georgia could have a significant legal interest, including the right to hold and transfer title. The Supreme Court's reporter summed up Marshall's opinion in the introduction to *Fletcher*: "What is Indian title? It is a mere occupancy for the purpose of hunting. It is not like our tenures; they have no idea of a title to the soil itself. . . . It is not to be *transferred* but extinguished. It [is] a right regulated by treaties, not by deeds of conveyance. It depends upon the law of nations, not upon municipal right."[5]

Marshall invented the category of occupancy title and needed a legal rationalization for his confection. He found it in the concept Western jurists called the doctrine of discovery. In its most basic sense, discovery doctrine was a diplomatic rule initially used by European nations to govern their relations with one another in North and South America. To avoid the possibility of overlapping European colonial settlements, this policy dictated that the first European explorer of an area obtained the preemptive right with respect to later arrivals to acquire land from a willing Indian nation. Discovery doctrine lacked legitimacy because there had been no genuinely international agreement establishing it as a working principle of Native American–European relations. It was an "alien European theor[y] that w[as] imposed on the native population."[6] At a minimum, the doctrine attempted to limit a tribe's right to negotiate freely with the government of its choosing. Over time, the doctrine came to express the view that by their very arrival Europeans had gained certain land rights despite the presence of the original Indian occupants. If, however, John Marshall doubted the international or moral legitimacy of discovery doctrine, he did not say so in *Fletcher*. Instead, Marshall used the doctrine as a starting point for the development of an American law of continental real estate.

First, adherence to the law of discovery gave the new American nation the significant advantage of legitimizing both its domestic and its foreign policy goals in the eyes of Western law and of doing so fairly quickly. For example, the sweeping legal principle of the paramount sovereignty of the discovering nation relieved the new U.S. government of the burden of establishing its dominion over each individual tribe by means of direct action. After defeating England, the United States simply succeeded to English claims of sovereignty over the Indians. At the same time, the assertion of paramount sovereignty over Indian tribes served to preempt the competing claims of European states to Indian lands and loyalty. Discovery thus supported the assertion of American hegemony over the continent, a diplomatic stance reiterated during Marshall's time in the 1823 Monroe Doctrine.

Locally, the *Fletcher* court argued that the state of Georgia, as successor to the English colony of Georgia, had obtained fee simple title and thus, for the purposes of the *Fletcher* appeal, could grant patents to the land even though it could not eject the tribes. A host of complex practical questions arose from the *Fletcher* formula in regard to how to split the rights to and use of the land between the discoverer nation on the one hand and the Indian nations on the other hand. Marshall's opinion, however, did not address any of these questions. This was the case apparently because all the members of the Court, except Justice Johnson, feared that a more vigorous examination of the political character of Indian nations and their land rights would distract attention from the central issues of the case: the nature of the national constitution's contract clause and federal judicial review of state legislation.[7]

In addition to being a tentative and inconclusive legal statement, *Fletcher* was a confusing policy directive. The opinion instructed Congress and the President that government officials had to obtain legitimate tribal consent for the extinguishment of Indian title. This clearly imposed an obligation to make lawful treaties. At the same time, however, the Court encouraged Georgia to regard its legal rights as strong and Indian rights and property claims as tenuous.[8] The passage of Georgia's jurisdiction laws and the arrest of George Tassels cannot be regarded as incongruous in light of *Fletcher*'s ambiguity.

The members of the *Fletcher* majority, however, might have been satisfied with a decision that from their perspective simultaneously promoted the interests of the U.S. government, the states, Indian nations, and the Court itself. Tilting toward the republic, the Court had outlined a doctrine of limiting tribal land rights to occupancy, with no right of alienation (transfer of ownership to another), which was therefore considerably compromised in the context of U.S. property law. But on behalf of the tribes, Marshall's opinion asserted a legal right of occupancy that protected the residency of individual tribal members as well as the communal character of tribes. In addition, the *Fletcher* court acknowledged a tribal right of consent before any extinguishment of this occupancy title. Looking to the interests of states, the Court speculated that Georgia (*not* the United States) held fee simple title to a considerable amount of tribal land under the doctrine of discovery. This balancing of rights suggests that the judges were seeking to hand down safe, rule-driven decisions at a time when the position of the Supreme Court in the American political system was far from secure.

Supreme Court Justice William Johnson, however, sharply disagreed that the *Fletcher* majority had laid down acceptable principles of law with respect to Native American sovereignty and property rights. Johnson had been recommended for the court in 1804 by President Jefferson. He was the President's first Supreme Court nominee, someone Jefferson hoped would lead the way in building a Republican bloc of justices who would break Marshall's power. As a Jeffersonian among the Federalist-leaning justices, Johnson quickly developed a reputation as an associate who, by personality and politics, was willing to "write separately," that is, to disagree for the record. His separate opinion in *Fletcher*—marked neither as concurring nor as dissenting in accordance with the practice of the day—came at a time when Supreme Court justices felt considerable pressure from Marshall "to bend to the current," that is, to present a unified view of doctrine and one "opinion of the Court."

Johnson, however, concluded that the *Fletcher* majority had misapplied the law and misunderstood the true nature of tribal sovereignty and vested property rights. Reluctantly addressing the question and characterizing it as one of "much delicacy . . . more fitted for a diplomatic or legislative than a judicial inquiry," Johnson argued that the "national fires" of the tribes in question had not been extinguished and that they retained "absolute proprietorship of their soil."[9] Johnson also noted that "[i]nnumerable treaties . . . acknowledge [the Indians] to be an independent people, and the uniform practice of acknowledging their right to soil, by purchasing from them, and restraining all persons from encroaching upon their territory, makes it unnecessary to insist upon their right to soil."[10]

Directing his inquiry to the legal and political heart of the matter, Johnson criticized Marshall's concept of dual legal title: "Can, then, one nation be said to be seised of a fee-simple in lands, the right of soil of which is in another nation?"[11] Having stated that the tribes were "absolute proprietors," Justice Johnson argued: "Unaffected by particular treaties, [the discoverer's interest] is nothing

more than what was assumed at the first settlement of the country
. . . a right of conquest, or of purchase. . . . All the restrictions upon
the right of soil in the Indians, amount only to an exclusion of all
competitors from their markets . . . a pre-emptive right [of the dis-
coverer]." Then, in a curious twisting of politics and jurisprudence,
Justice Johnson, a southerner and a nominal supporter of states'
rights, disputed the nationalist John Marshall's conclusion that this
preemptive discovery right could be vested in a state. Rather, Johnson argued, it was a right vested only in the United States after the
cession "by the constitution, [of] both the power of pre-emption and
of conquest." Johnson's support of tribal sovereignty and absolute
ownership of tribal territory did not give comfort to Georgia, but
because it was a minority opinion, Georgia's officials paid his words
little heed.

## A Second Case: Johnson v. M'Intosh

The second Supreme Court decision cited by the *Tassels* court, *Johnson* v. *M'Intosh*, has been called one of the "most misunderstood
cases in the Anglo-American law."[12] It is also one of the most controversial cases in the field of federal Indian law.

The conflict in *Johnson* v. *M'Intosh* involved large tracts of land
claimed by two parties. The plaintiff, Johnson, asserted ownership
as a result of direct tribal grants in 1773 and 1775. The M'Intosh faction claimed possession of the lands following receipt of a U.S.
patent obtained after the same tribes had ceded those lands to the
federal government. Whether because they did not share Western
notions of ownership or for other reasons, the tribes had yielded
their title twice. Although it involved no tribal litigants, the case
required the Court to determine whether the grant of tribal land—
obtained by a non-Indian purchaser without the approval of the
federal government—conveyed a title U.S. courts could countenance. Regardless of the Court's decision, there would be no immediate tribal "losers." Either way, title would be held by non-Indians.
In a larger sense, however, tribal prerogatives were very much at
issue, as the case posed the question of whether, according to American law, Indian nations could convey legal title without interference from the United States. For this reason *Johnson* represented a
fundamental test of the sovereign powers of Indian nations.

In its *Fletcher* opinion, the Supreme Court had suggested that

Georgia—as the legatee of discovery—not the occupying tribes, held fee simple title to the land in question. Yet the opinion contained no further explanation of alienation rights. Marshall's introduction of discovery doctrine as a relevant legal authority in *Fletcher* had been a critical choice on his part, signaling his willingness to build a jurisprudence that would promote American legal title to the Indian lands of the continent. Extensive writings on the law of nations concerning the rights of non-European peoples existed at the time *Fletcher* was argued. Many of those legal theories had been presented to the Court in *Fletcher* in support of Indian sovereignty. Marshall, however, had ignored any legal ideas that might work against the national interests of the United States in favor of discovery doctrine.[13]

When the *Johnson* appeal came to the Court, the chief justice again used discovery doctrine as the centerpiece of his reasoning, applying an interpretation of discovery that was even more firmly supportive of American interests. Marshall now claimed not only that discovery doctrine gave the discoverer the "exclusive right . . . to appropriate the lands occupied by the Indians" but that discovery also led to the "considerable" impairment of the rights of those original inhabitants. The Indians, he wrote, are "the rightful occupants of the soil, with a legal as well as just claim to retain possession of it, and to use it according to their own discretion . . . [but] their rights to complete sovereignty, as independent nations, were necessarily diminished, and their power to dispose of the soil at their own will, to whomsoever they pleased, was denied by the original fundamental principle . . . discovery."[14]

While assigning the fundamental right of alienation to the United States, Marshall did reaffirm the earlier *Fletcher* principle that discovery doctrine still guaranteed to the Indian nations the right of perpetual occupancy and "use according to their own discretion."[15] Because the Court sculpted these dual political rights and property titles from discovery doctrine, *Johnson* has been judged a "brilliant compromise."[16] However, some modern scholars have characterized the *Johnson* opinion as "seiz[ing] upon this controversy to establish a judicial mythology that would rationalize the origin of land titles in the United States."[17] And even Marshall's good friend Justice Story criticized the chief justice's use of occupancy title. Five years after *Johnson*, in a speech at Salem, Massachusetts, Story argued that the Indians held their land by natural law, moral rights, and municipal law, not by some derivative principle of the discovery doctrine.[18]

*Johnson* was the first case in which the Marshall Court applied the principle of split or dual title that had been announced in *Fletcher*. The *Johnson* opinion did not satisfy anyone's hopes for a thorough definition of sovereignty or property rights. Perhaps because the stakes were so high—title to the real estate of the continent—in this skirmish, the Court again chose to be less than precise. Adding to the muddle, halfway through the opinion the Court introduced a dictum describing the American conquest of Indian nations, a discussion presumably meant to support the rights already asserted through discovery doctrine. This assertion of conquest was a curious legal maneuver because it was unnecessary for the purpose of claiming title. More important, it was not credible. The historical record shows that most of the lands gained by the United States had been acquired by purchase, not by military action. Marshall's dictum might have been aimed at appeasing General Jackson and others who believed that "Indian national fires had been extinguished." It may also have been included as a metaphor for European superiority. Certainly, the declaration of conquest permitted Marshall to offer standard stereotypes of the Indian as savage and warlike and to imply that if conquest doctrine had been used as the basis of the opinion, *Johnson*'s balancing of claims might have gone less well for the Indian nations. It is also possible that the strongly nationalist Marshall presented conquest as a prelude to the Monroe Doctrine. Tension was high in Washington over a joint French and Spanish expedition into South America and the expansionist activities of the Russians in the Northwest. While President Adams was mulling over his foreign policy options, Chief Justice Marshall might have launched the myth of conquest as an additional statement of American independence and hegemony in the "new world."

Considerable debate exists over the consequences of *Fletcher* and *Johnson* for Native Americans. Some argue that in these two opinions Marshall "lent faint color to Jackson's aggression . . . [because] Indians could be deprived by a legal fiction of their title by 'discovery.' " Others maintain, however, that the "consequences flowing to the status of Indian lands from [conquest] theory were nonexistent." While one author writes that the decision left tribes with a title of "mere occupancy and use," others have urged that the opinion should not be clouded by the conquest dictum and the otherwise minor qualification of nonalienability.[19]

Marshall's "brilliant compromise"—granting simultaneous but incomplete interests to the discoverer and to tribal nations—established the moral and political principle that Indian nations must be respected as to both occupancy rights and the requirement of consent for the extinguishment of those residential claims. Because it denied title "absolute and complete" to tribes, the decision may be viewed as corrupt. But in fact, because Indians were not direct parties to this litigation, *Johnson*, along with *Fletcher*, involved tribal rights only in the abstract. Given the political constraints on the Supreme Court and its members' optimistic belief, which ultimately proved unfounded, that tribes such as the Cherokee would voluntarily sell their land, these decisions may be regarded as efforts to impose orderly legal standards on a frontier inclined to the use of raw power. The facts of the *Tassels* litigation, however, present clear evidence that in Georgia the doctrine established in *Fletcher* and *Johnson* directly encouraged state officials to make the claim that their extension of state jurisdiction over the Cherokee was legal.

## *THE* TASSELS *CASE: FAILURE OF A LEGAL TEST OF CHEROKEE RIGHTS*

The *Tassels* case was a historical prelude that was critical to subsequent events but was little noticed by most Americans, who according to contemporary newspapers were busy debating taxes on sugar and the morality of lotteries.[20] The judges of the Georgia Superior Court who heard the appeal, however, understood its importance to Georgia and to the national debate on Indian policy. The judges began with a candid comment on the political character of the conflict: "This is a very grave and important question, which probably, never would have been submitted to judicial investigation, but for the political, party and fanatical feeling excited during the last session of Congress. When the Indians attending at Washington last winter, and their advocates, discovered that the decision of the two houses would be unfavorable to them [a reference to the passage of the Removal Bill], the idea of bringing the question before the

Supreme Court was suggested and eagerly seized upon by the deputation of the Cherokees . . . [who had gone so far as to hire a lawyer]
residing near 1000 miles from her borders"[21] (see Appendix I).

In regard to the legal issues, the court bluntly rejected Underwood's arguments on behalf of Cherokee sovereignty and ruled that
at the time of statehood Georgians had obtained sovereignty over
the Indian tribes "within their boundaries." This sovereignty, the
justices stated, had conferred full civil and criminal jurisdiction over
those tribes and their citizens. Thus, according to the superior court
judges, the arrest, trial, and conviction of Tassels had been alto-
gether legal. Their opinion, replete with the language of states'
rights, relied heavily on the *Fletcher–Johnson* sequence and on Marshall's application of discovery doctrine. The justices held that
"[w]hatever right Great Britain possessed over the Indian tribes, is
vested in the State of Georgia; and may be fully exercised . . . this
whole question is ably elucidated in the decision of the Supreme
Court, in the case of *Johnson* v. *M'Intosh* [which stated] that discovery gave to the discovering nation an exclusive right to the country
discovered, as between them and other European nations . . . and
the rights of the original inhabitants were . . . necessarily to a considerable extent impaired. . . . They were admitted to be the rightful
occupants of the soil . . . but their rights to complete sovereignty as
independent nations were necessarily diminished."[22] The court further contended that criminal jurisdiction over Indians living within
state boundaries had been assumed in the original thirteen colonies
and that this practice had been quietly followed "in a greater or less
degree," without contest, by several states, including New York.[23]

The Georgia court also argued that because there was no evidence of Congress having declared war against Indian tribes when
wars were actually fought, "it seems to be self-evident that communities which have been determined not to be objects of a declaration
of war, cannot be objects of the treaty making power."[24] Burdened
by the fact that the United States *had* signed treaties that acknowledged Cherokee sovereignty, the Georgia justices wrote that former
Presidents and Senates had been mistaken in making those
treaties.[25] Seizing on the words of its solicitor general, the Georgia
court insisted that "the relations between the Cherokee Indians and
the State of Georgia were those of pupilage. No treaty between the
United States and the Cherokees could change that relation, could

confer upon them the power of independent self-government. If there are any clauses in any of the compacts between the United States and the Cherokee Indians (mis-called treaties) which give to those Indians the right of independent self-government, they are simply void, and cannot, and ought not to be permitted to throw any obstacle in the way of the operation of the act of Georgia, extending jurisdiction over the country in the occupancy of the Cherokee Indians."[26]

The *Tassels* appeal gave the Georgia judiciary an opportunity to join forces with the state legislature and the governor in opposing Cherokee sovereignty. The judges did not hesitate to lend judicial approval to the legislature's assertion of civil and criminal jurisdiction. The impact of this decision was far-reaching. The Cherokee were ridiculed, while states' rights were fully endorsed at the expense of both the Cherokee and the United States. By holding the state jurisdiction laws valid, the Georgia court gave fresh encouragement to the state legislature and executive, which had by then made a firm commitment to a policy of denationalizing or removing the Cherokee and other southern Indian nations. Finally, the state court opinion found favor well beyond the boundaries of Georgia. For decades after 1830 the *Tassels* opinion was widely cited by state judges in support of the principle that statehood automatically conferred full jurisdiction over Indian nations.[27]

Wirt had been waiting for the outcome of *Tassels* and several other similar prosecutions. When John Ross notified him that the Georgia court had upheld the jurisdiction law, Wirt immediately appealed to the U.S. Supreme Court for a writ of error under the Court's increasingly contested Section 25 powers (federal judicial power to review state court or state legislative decisions that might violate the U.S. Constitution). On December 12, 1830, Chief Justice Marshall granted the writ and ordered Georgia to appear before the Supreme Court on "the second Monday in January next . . . to show cause . . . why judgement rendered against the said Georgia in said writ of error mentioned should not be corrected. . . ."[28] As they had years earlier in the *Chisholm* case, Georgia officials refused to be summoned to the *national* court. The state would not submit to federal judicial review of its laws. Defiant state leaders announced that "interference by the chief justice of the U. States, in the administration of the criminal laws of this state . . . [was] a flagrant violation of her rights."[29] Ten days after Marshall granted the writ, Georgia representatives voted to carry out George Tassels's sentence of death by hanging. Georgia executed Tassels on December 24, 1830.

John Ross calmly reported to Wirt on the actions of the rebellious state. The execution mooted the appeal to the Supreme Court and cost the Cherokee and the high court dearly: Tassels lost his life; for the necessary state court appeal, the Cherokee paid at least a thousand dollars in fees to Underwood and Harris; and Marshall and his court were embarrassed by Georgia's defiance and so angered states' rights supporters by granting the writ of error that they once again moved (unsuccessfully) for the repeal of the Supreme Court's Section 25 appellate jurisdiction. In contrast, for Georgia there was nothing but victory. The Tassels case gave Georgia justices the opportunity to write an opinion approving the extension of state rule over the Cherokee and gave state political officials the occasion to act on this authority in a dramatic way.

Whatever the cost, however, Ross and the rest of the Cherokee leadership stood fast in their commitment to bringing a great legal test of rights before the U.S. Supreme Court. Wirt was instructed to resume preparations for the original jurisdiction case, which by then had been planned for months. In the face of President Jackson's opposition to Indian sovereignty and steadily increasing popularity, lesser men and women might have withdrawn from the legal arena. The Cherokee did not. It is the ultimate irony that the Cherokee, only recently described by the *Tassels* court as a people "incapable of complying with the obligations which the laws of civilized society imposed," maintained their faith in the rule of law—even an enemy's law—and its promise of justice.[30]

## WIRT AND SERGEANT CHANCE: AN ORIGINAL JURISDICTION CASE: CHEROKEE NATION V. GEORGIA

Having received his instructions from John Ross after the execution of Tassels, Wirt, who was temporarily living in a Washington boardinghouse, and his co-counsel, John Sergeant, proceeded with the new test of Cherokee sovereignty. The original jurisdiction of the U.S. Supreme Court derives from the Constitution's Article III grant to hear "controversies . . . between a state, or the citizens thereof, and foreign states, citizens or subjects." On behalf of the Cherokee Nation as a foreign nation, the two attorneys petitioned the Supreme Court early in 1831 to invoke this original jurisdiction and grant an injunction barring enforcement of Georgia's jurisdiction laws within the Cherokee Nation. The request asked the Court "to restrain in the State of Georgia, the Governor, Attorney General, Judges, justices of the peace, sheriffs, deputy sheriffs, constables and others, officers, agents, and servants of that State, from executing and enforcing the laws of Georgia, or any of these laws, or serving process, or doing anything toward the execution or enforcement of those laws within the Cherokee territory. . . ."[31]

Repeating the argument made in *Tassels*, Wirt and Sergeant maintained that the Cherokee were a fully sovereign people. They contended that the state laws violated international treaties between the Cherokee Nation and the United States as well as the Constitution's supremacy clause (Article VI) barring any state law that overrides federal laws or treaties.

The Cherokee and their lawyers hoped that a favorable opinion from the Supreme Court, accepting both the Cherokee's claim of national sovereignty and the supremacy of federal law over state action, would stop Georgia from attempting to exercise jurisdiction over the Cherokee and seizing Cherokee land. Wirt and Sergeant knew that a decision favorable to the Cherokee would pit the Supreme Court squarely against a popular President and determined partisans of states' rights. Chief Justice Marshall had appeared personally sympathetic to the cause of the Cherokee the previous summer but had also taken great care not to reveal his legal views. Georgia officials had just defied the court in *Tassels*, and in the small world of Washington the savvy jurist could not ignore rumors that Jackson would refuse to execute a ruling favorable to the Cherokee if the Court issued one.

Tortured by uncertainty and possible humiliation, William Wirt appraised the problems of the litigation just before oral argument in a letter to his wife:

> I look upon the prospect still before me with some dismay—I feel rather despondent about my poor Indians—not that I have the slightest doubt of the justice of their claims on the United States, but that I fear the Supreme Court may differ with me as to the extent of *their jurisdiction* over the subject, and hold the faithful execution of treaties to belong to the Executive Branch of the Gov-

ernment (the President) and not to the Judicial. . . . [As a last hope],
Chancellor Kent, Binney, Sergeant, and Webster (I understand)
concurred with me in thinking that the Court had jurisdiction, and
that, at all events, the question must be tried, and so thought my
clients . . . I make this statement to show you that it is one of those
questions in which the wisest and best ever may differ in opinion,
that it is not I alone who have advised the course, and that if the
decision be against us you must not consider it as reflecting any
discredit on your husband.[32]

From the start of the proceedings in the case, now formally
titled *The Cherokee Nation* v. *The State of Georgia,* officials in Georgia
had refused to acknowledge the legal papers served on them by
Chief John Ross. Not surprisingly, when the time came for an attorney to speak for the state in oral arguments before Marshall and his
court, none appeared. Instead, state officials, adamant that a federal
court should not review Georgia's business, paced the halls of Congress trying to win support for the bill limiting the Supreme Court's
Section 25 powers.

In contrast, both John Sergeant and William Wirt appeared
before the court on March 11 to begin oral argument on behalf of the
Cherokee. Wirt, having just participated in the acrimonious
impeachment case against Judge Peck, was exhausted. When he
stood before the justices, Wirt managed to flourish his snuffbox, as
was his habit, using it as an "oratorical weapon." But oral argument
went on for several days, and although he was the better speaker,
the weary Wirt often had to relinquish the presentation to Sergeant.
Together, they kept to the script established years earlier in Evarts's
William Penn essays and in the various opinions Wirt had written
for the Cherokee in the summer and fall of 1830.[33] The two lawyers'
argument was forceful and eloquent, but Wirt's foreboding proved
correct: A deeply divided Supreme Court denied the centerpiece of
Wirt and Sergeant's argument that the Cherokee Nation was a foreign nation capable of suing under the Court's doctrine of original
jurisdiction.

Marshall's opinion, joined only by the recent Jackson nominee
and presidential aspirant John McLean, never addressed the question of whether Georgia had violated treaty agreements or the U.S.
Constitution (see Appendix II). Rather, in *Cherokee Nation,* as
decades before in *Marbury* v. *Madison,* Marshall extricated the court
from the rough seas of politics with procedural sleight of hand. To

shield the court from the Georgia-Cherokee conflict and the larger maelstrom of Jacksonian politics, Marshall found that he needed only to pose—and answer—a single question: "Is the Cherokee nation a foreign state in the sense in which that term is used in the constitution?"[34] Marshall's answer, much of which consisted of dictum, relied heavily on discovery doctrine and a corrupt reading of history. In spite of the dozens of international treaties agreed on by the United States and various Indian nations, Marshall concluded that the Cherokee did not constitute a foreign nation. According to the chief justice:

> Though the Indians are acknowledged to have an unquestionable
> . . . right to the lands they occupy, until that right shall be extin-
> guished by voluntary cession to our government. . . . [I]t may well
> be doubted whether those tribes which reside within the acknowl-
> edged boundaries of the United States can, with strict accuracy, be
> denominated foreign nations. They may, more correctly, perhaps,
> be denominated *domestic dependent* nations. They occupy a terri-
> tory to which we assert a title independent of their will. . . . [T]hey
> are a people in a state of pupilage. Their relation to the United
> States resembles that of a ward to his guardian.[35]

The relation of Indians to the United States was unique, Marshall declared, "perhaps unlike that of any other two people in existence."[36] A sweeping one-sided interpretation of treaties, politics, and culture led to this conclusion, a generalization necessary to support the new legal theory that tribes were something Marshall chose to call *domestic dependent*, not foreign, nations, and that Indian people were in a "state of pupilage." To build his narrative, Marshall teased apart the language of the commerce clause and manipulated history. He wrote that with respect to original jurisdiction, the framers of the Constitution could not have had Indians in mind as foreign nations because, "at the time the constitution was framed [their] habits and usages . . . in intercourse with their white neighbors" had never led them to "the idea of appealing to an American court of justice. . . ."[37] This was nothing more than a falsification of history. Since the middle of the seventeenth century Native Americans had been frequent litigants in colonial courts.[38]

Marshall sounded less like a fair-minded jurist than like a zealous politician. His discussion, not surprisingly, included no Native American perspective:

> The Indian territory is admitted to compose a part of the United
> States. In all our maps, geographical treatises, histories, and laws,
> it is so considered. In all our intercourse with foreign nations . . .
> they are considered within the jurisdictional limits of the United
> States. . . . They acknowledge themselves in their treaties to be
> under the protection of the United States. . . .[39]

By denying that the Cherokee constituted a *foreign* nation, Marshall accomplished the sleight of hand necessary to reject the Cherokee's motion for an injunction on jurisdictional grounds. Marshall
believed he was protecting the future of the Supreme Court by side-
stepping further confrontation between the judiciary and Georgia
and the Jackson administration. However, failure to grant the injunction against Georgia and judge the question of violations of treaty
rights on the merits of a legal argument denied the Cherokee the
immediate and much needed protection of the court. However, Marshall's opinion did not translate into a complete defeat for the Cherokee. Nothing in his opinion approved Georgia's attempt to extend
state jurisdiction over the Cherokee. Quite to the contrary, Marshall
repeatedly asserted that the authority to deal with Native American
nations rested solely with the government in Washington.

In designating Indian tribes "domestic dependent nations,"
Marshall had elected a very cautious strategy that while denying
the Cherokee the requested injunction reaffirmed "unquestionable"
Indian occupancy rights and formally acknowledged the national
character of Indian governments. The opinion of the court described
the Cherokee Nation as "capable of managing its own affairs and
governing itself . . . a people capable of maintaining the relations of
peace and war, of being responsible in their political character for
any violation of their engagements. . . ."[40] Marshall's opinion further
suggested that the "unique" relations between the Cherokee and the
United States—the other-than-foreign-national political status of the
Cherokee and what he further described as a relationship of "ward
to guardian"—were to be understood in terms of foreign affairs.
According to Marshall, tribes had the right to govern themselves
internally without interference from the United States or any of its
states.

According to Marshall's analysis, the United States, having
inherited discovery title from Great Britain, had a vested property
interest in Native American land and was asserting a protectorate
status over Indian nations that limited their authority indepen-

dently to make war on or negotiate with foreign nations. Marshall believed this to be consistent with international law as viewed through discovery doctrine and the eight-year-old Monroe Doctrine: "They look to our government for protection. . . . They and their country are considered by foreign nations, as well as by ourselves, as being so completely under the sovereignty and dominion of the United States, that any attempt to acquire their lands, or to form a political connexion with them, would be considered by all as an invasion of our territory, and an act of hostility."[41] For his purposes, Marshall represented Indian nations as being *domestic* in the sense that their territories were located within the exterior boundaries of the United States, *dependent* because of the limitations placed on them with respect to war and foreign negotiations, and *national* because they were distinctly separate peoples outside the American polity.[42]

The final paragraphs of Marshall's *Cherokee Nation* opinion suggest something more than caution, however. The text bespeaks an aging statesman beleaguered by those who would undo the accomplishments of his professional life. Marshall was seventy-six years old and in his thirtieth year as chief justice when he wrote *Cherokee Nation*. He had struggled long and hard to work judicial magic on behalf of a Federalist national agenda, but now his career was nearly over and political opponents stood ready to seize the Court. Colleagues of the chief justice had privately begun to think about a future without Marshall at the head of the Supreme Court. In February 1831, a few weeks before oral arguments in *Cherokee Nation*, former President John Quincy Adams fretted in a diary entry that "some shallow-pated wild-cat . . . fit for nothing but to tear the Union to rags and tatters, would be appointed in [Marshall's] place."[43] Soon after *Cherokee Nation*, in a letter to Justice Story, Marshall acknowledged these concerns, stating: "[I] cannot be insensible to the gloom that lours [sic] over us" and confiding his fears that in the future the judicial process would become "a mere inefficient pageant."[44] Marshall told Justice Story that if Jackson were defeated in the 1832 election, he would resign from the Court and hope for a worthy replacement.

Perhaps despair explains the desperate, nearly illogical balancing of interests that marks the closing paragraphs of the chief justice's opinion. In those final thoughts on the Cherokee's "bill" (their motion for an injunction against Georgia), Marshall's anguish is palpable. He questions the propriety of his court "interposing" itself into the Georgia-Cherokee conflict with the invocation of political question doctrine. (Political question doctrine holds that courts should refuse to hear certain questions because of their essentially political character or because their determination would encroach upon legislative or executive powers.)

> A serious additional objection exists to the jurisdiction of the court. Is the matter of the bill the proper subject for judicial inquiry. . . . It seeks to restrain a state from the forcible exercise of legislative power over a neighboring people, asserting their independence; their right to which the state denies. On matters . . . making it criminal to exercise the usual powers of self government in their [Cherokee] own country . . . this court cannot interpose; at least in the form in which those matters are presented.
>
> That part of the bill which respects the land occupied by the Indians, and prays the aid of the court to protect their possession, may be more doubtful. The mere question of right might perhaps be decided by this court in a proper case with proper parties. But the court is asked to do more than decide on title. The bill requires us to control the legislature of Georgia. The propriety of such an interposition by the court may well be questioned. It savours too much of the exercise of political power to be within the proper province of the judicial department. . . .
>
> If it be true that the Cherokee nation have rights, this is not the tribunal in which those rights are to be asserted. If it be true that wrongs have been inflicted, and that still greater are to be apprehended, this is not the tribunal which can redress the past or prevent the future.[45]

In this statement one can barely recognize the voice of the assertive jurist long reviled by states' rights partisans, the famed John Marshall, whose court had previously not shied from upholding the national powers of the United States in the cases *Martin* v. *Hunter's Lessee*, *McCulloch* v. *Maryland*, and *Dartmouth College* v. *Woodward*.[46] Perhaps Marshall pulled back in *Cherokee Nation* because Indian rights were at issue rather than his beloved contract clause or the national bank. Perhaps the climate of Jacksonian politics overwhelmed the usually feisty chief justice. Perhaps Marshall felt that Indian removal would occur quickly and that the Court would be foolish to invite further confrontation with members of Congress intent on limiting federal judicial authority. Certainly in

*Cherokee Nation* Marshall calculated the issues of politics and the issues of law and ruled in a manner far more protective of the interests of the Court than of those of the Cherokee Nation.

The final two paragraphs of the opinion in particular offer clear evidence of Marshall's mental exhaustion and abandonment of the Indian cause. In this text Marshall asserts that the Cherokee have asked too much of the Court. He invites more circumscribed litigation—"a proper case with proper parties"—selectively addressing the property issue of Cherokee land title. And while earlier in his opinion Marshall had not been too intimidated to express the moral support of the Court for the Cherokee Nation—"[I]f Courts were permitted to indulge their sympathies, a case better calculated to excite them can scarcely be imagined"—he did not choose to close *Cherokee Nation* with those sentiments.[47] Instead, carefully ignoring the openly hostile posture of Jackson and the majority of Congress toward the Cherokee, Marshall concluded his discussion with some of the most disheartening sentiments in American jurisprudence: "[I]f it be true that the Cherokee nation have rights, this is not the tribunal in which those rights are to be asserted . . . this is not the tribunal which can redress the past or prevent the future."

In 1831, the law set the membership of the U.S. Supreme Court at seven. Because Justice Duvall was absent during oral argument on March 12 and 14, 1831, only five associate justices had joined Marshall in hearing and deciding *Cherokee Nation*. When Marshall polled the five, only McLean—a justice whose early jurisprudence was often guided by political aspirations—indicated agreement with the analysis proposed by the chief justice. Justices Henry Baldwin and William Johnson voted with Marshall and McLean to deny the injunction, but unlike McLean, neither of those men agreed with Marshall's reasoning. Instead, Baldwin and Johnson each filed a concurring opinion.

For many years the group unity and pressure of Supreme Court boardinghouse life, along with the force of Marshall's personality, had helped maintain the custom of few seriatim opinions. In the late 1820s, however, the internal procedures of the Marshall Court began to change. Increasingly, the earlier practice of collective and often anonymous opinions was abandoned, and doctrinal differences were publicly aired more frequently in concurring and dissenting opinions.[48] In particular, on the great contemporary questions of nationalism, states' rights, and private property, Marshall failed to maintain the earlier facade of harmony. Justices Baldwin and Johnson's decision to publish concurring opinions in *Cherokee Nation* illustrates Marshall's altered relationship with the associate justices.

When Wirt and Sergeant received copies of Baldwin and Johnson's opinions, they realized that matters could have gone far worse for their client. Court newcomer Henry Baldwin had been an early supporter of President Jackson. He had joined the Supreme Court in 1830, only months before the arguments in *Cherokee Nation*. While mental illness and an inconsistent jurisprudence limited Baldwin's intellectual contributions in the course of his judicial career, his opinion in *Cherokee Nation* was not at odds with several of the themes in his later work, namely, concern for state power and the unwarranted extension of Supreme Court power. Most of all, Baldwin's *Cherokee Nation* opinion revealed him to be a Jacksonian. Justice Baldwin flatly denied that Indian tribes constituted political communities of any kind and described "mere judicial power" as inappropriate to "reverse every principle on which our government have acted for fifty-five years."[49] He considered Georgia to have full jurisdiction over the Cherokee and fee simple title to their lands. Like President Jackson, Baldwin sought to end the "Indian question" with the broadest of pronouncements:

> My view of the plaintiffs being a sovereign independent nation or foreign state, within the meaning of the constitution, applies to all the tribes with whom the United States have held treaties: for if one is a foreign nation or state, all others in like condition must be so in their aggregate capacity; and each of their subjects or citizens, aliens, capable of suing in the circuit courts. This then is the case of the countless tribes, who, in their collective and individual characters, as states or aliens, will rush to the federal courts in endless controversies, growing out of the laws of the states or of congress.[50]

The views of Justice Johnson also were awaited with interest, but not because he was new to the court. Quite the opposite. President Jefferson had urged him to break Marshall's hold on the Court, and twenty years earlier Johnson had differed with Marshall in *Fletcher*, arguing that "the state of Georgia had not a *fee-simple* in Indian lands."[51] At that time Johnson had concluded that the stage of development of Indian tribes "will be found to be various."

According to his earlier views, the Cherokee retained "limited sovereignty and the absolute proprietorship of their land," having entered into "innumerable treaties acknowledging them to be an independent people. . . ."[52] Johnson had also pointedly lectured Georgia on the nature of states' rights, writing that its "interests in the soil . . . [had been] reduced . . . when [it] ceded, to the United States, by the constitution, both the power of pre-emption and of conquest, retaining for itself only a resulting right dependent on a purchase or conquest to be made by the United States."[53]

Justice Johnson's opinion in *Cherokee Nation*, while more conciliatory than Baldwin's on the question of self-governance, cut deeply into the analysis he had presented in *Fletcher*, perhaps because of a substantial rethinking of his jurisprudential views in the 1820s. Whatever the motive, trapped by his earlier words and by the fact that the Cherokee had successfully adopted republican government in the two decades between *Fletcher* and *Cherokee Nation*, Johnson sought to justify his vote against the Cherokee with tortured and ethnocentric legal distinctions concerning the meaning of a state, a foreign state, and a member of the family of nations:

> I cannot but think that there are strong reasons for doubting the applicability of the epithet *state*, to a people so low in the grade of organized society as our Indian tribes most generally are. I would not here be understood as speaking of the Cherokees under their present form of government; which must certainly be classed among the most approved forms of civil government. Whether it can be yet said to have received the consistency which entitled that people to admission into the family of nations is, I conceive, yet to be determined by the executive of these states. Until then I must think that we cannot recognize it as an existing state, under any other character than that which it has maintained hitherto as one of the Indian tribes or nations. . . . Their condition is something like that of the Israelites, when inhabiting the deserts. I think it very clear that the constitution neither speaks of them as states or foreign states, but as just what they were, Indian tribes; an anomaly . . . which the law of nations would regard as nothing more than wandering hordes, held together only by ties of blood and habit, and having neither laws or government, beyond what is required in a savage state.[54]

Justices Story and Thompson disagreed. Voting together in dissent, the two argued "that the Cherokees compose a foreign state within the sense and meaning of the constitution, and constitute a competent party to maintain a suit against the state of Georgia."[55] It was their view, after hearing Wirt and Sergeant, that an injunction should be granted immediately.

In one sense, the dissenting votes cast by Justices Story and Thompson did not surprise Washingtonians. Both were northerners, and each was willing to speak his mind. Joseph Story had joined the court in 1811, a year after he had appeared as counsel for the land speculators in *Fletcher* v. *Peck*. A Massachusetts lawyer and scholar, Story emphasized the values of republicanism, nationalism, and the liberalism of John Locke in his jurisprudence. His vote against Georgia in *Cherokee Nation* reflected his New England roots, an unyielding commitment to the powers of the national government over those of the states, and an abiding faith in private property rights. Yet like Marshall, Story generally did not favor the practice of dissenting. In 1818 he had written court reporter Henry Wheaton that "the habit of delivering dissenting opinions on ordinary occasions weakens the authority of the Court, and is of no public benefit."[56] Clearly, however, this case was not ordinary, and Marshall did not oppose the dissent.

The second dissenter, Smith Thompson, had joined the Supreme Court in 1823 after his successful nomination by President James Monroe. Although not always supportive of the strong national powers promoted by Justice Story, Thompson willingly joined with Story in *Cherokee Nation*. Thompson had been born in New York State and educated at Princeton. He brought a northerner's perspective to the question of Indian sovereignty. In addition, as a young man Thompson had served a legal apprenticeship with the nationally prominent New York jurist and legal scholar James Kent, whose support of Indian land rights was well known.

Curiously, given the great importance of the case and the increasing practice of filing concurring and dissenting opinions, initially neither Justice Thompson nor Justice Story submitted a written opinion to be published as part of the official court record. When the spring session of the court closed a few days after the announcement of the *Cherokee Nation* decision, Chief Justice Marshall decided that the unbalanced nature of the public record would not do. Seeking to alter this and perhaps regretting his own vote, the chief justice took the unusual step of suggesting that Thompson and Story draft an opinion outlining their arguments in support of Cherokee claims. Justice Thompson honored Marshall's request with a written dissent that drew heavily on the arguments made by Wirt and Sergeant. Many historians consider it the finest opinion ever written by Thompson. Justice Story signed it, and the court reporter, Richard Peters, added it to the official published record.[57]

The Thompson dissent shows that despite their opposing votes in the case, the Marshall-McLean faction and the Thompson-Story faction did not have widely differing *legal* views. None of the four supported Georgia's assertion that statehood granted sovereignty over neighboring Indian nations, and each of these justices agreed that the Cherokee were a national political community. What separated the two groups was politics. The chief justice feared for the future of the Supreme Court and was willing to sacrifice the rights of the Cherokee people to protect the court he had served for three decades. To avoid further attacks on the powers of the Court from Jackson and states' rights forces, Marshall contrived the "domestic dependent nation" classification and then argued that the failure to meet *foreign* nation status made the Cherokee ineligible to bring an original jurisdiction case. McLean joined Marshall in this transparent ploy, but in this case neither Marshall's usual ally, Joseph Story, nor Smith Thompson feared for the Court as much as they honored the law.

Wirt had, then, been correct to anticipate a Supreme Court calculus of law and politics that would work against the Cherokee. Late in March 1831 he returned to Baltimore to ponder the possibilities of the proposed property case while he and Sergeant waited to hear from Ross whether the Cherokee wished to continue to fight Georgia in the courts and could afford to do so. Before sending an answer to Wirt, John Ross undertook a tour of the districts of the Cherokee Nation. He reported on the implications of the decision in *Cherokee Nation* as well as on the ongoing antiremoval lobby efforts of the Cherokee diplomatic delegation in the American capital. Ross was attempting to gauge the public opinion of his constituents in order to determine whether the political and legal strategies that he favored, along with their financial cost, continued to meet with popular Cherokee approval. His speeches were straightforward. In one, Ross offered his evaluation of Chief Justice Marshall's *Cherokee Nation* opinion: "Upon the whole, I view the opinion of the Court as regards our political character & the relations we sustain towards the United States, as being conclusively adverse to the pretended rights which have been asserted by Georgia over us, under the countenance of the President. I do not regret the toil & trouble . . . preparatory to the motion being made for the injunction, because I sincerely believe that a foundation is laid upon which our injured rights may be reared & made permanent."[58]

If Ross thought John Marshall had abandoned the Cherokee to protect the Supreme Court, he did not say so. Ross continued to believe that litigation, for all its limitations, was one of the few weapons available to the Cherokee in their fight for sovereign recognition, given their commitment to nonviolence. However, correspondence between Ross and Thomas Harris, one of the Cherokee's principal local attorneys, might have given Ross cause to wonder just how long the Cherokee could continue using the courts and non-Cherokee lawyers. Ross had just learned that Harris had sued William Rogers, an agent of the Cherokee Nation *in Georgia courts* for $1,500, "a balance of the sum engaged by him . . . to be paid to [Underwood, Harris] . . . as fees for professional services to defend the rights of [the Cherokee] against the laws of Georgia." An incredulous Ross wrote Harris that in having Rogers arrested by Georgia authorities, Harris had availed himself "of the *very law* against which your services have been engaged to defend the Citizens of this nation. I cannot see any consistency or propriety in the course you have taken in this matter, as I have given you every assurance consistent with honor and honesty, that the engagements made with yourself and Judge Underwood . . . would be honorably met." Ross concluded the letter with a string of taunts, saying that "surely you cannot consider your engagements as being *fulfilled* and *at an end*, nor can I believe you intend or wish to *desert our cause*, and I am certain that you can have no just grounds to suspect or believe that the authorities of the nation will turn traitors to their own Cause and *flee* from *their beloved Country to escape their Contracts*."[59]

William Wirt also was pressing Ross for payment of legal fees, although he did not bring his claims to court. In May, Ross was able to satisfy Wirt by sending a letter with $550—of borrowed money— to Baltimore. Losing no time in drawing on this new credit, in the same letter Chief Ross referred to the *Cherokee Nation* opinion and the "foundation that is laid," asking Wirt to give him advice "in regards to carrying prosecutions against such persons who are located in the Indian Territory [Cherokee lands in Georgia] under permits from the agents of Georgia, contrary to the provision of the

Intercourse law."[60] Although Wirt had been paid considerably less than his $3,000, Ross clearly expected that the attorney would stay with his Cherokee client, and he did. After receiving the $550 bank draft in July 1831, Wirt wrote to Ross that he regretted having to charge for his work and that he was ready to plunge ahead with the effort to defeat Georgia in new litigation.

A letter dated July 18, 1831, showed that Wirt was ready. The Cherokee's lawyer outlined a variety of legal possibilities in some technical detail. Here, as elsewhere in their relationship, Wirt continued to treat Ross—as Ross demanded—as a professional partner in all discussions of legal strategy. Wirt first commented that Marshall and the Supreme Court might view the Cherokee individually as aliens. If this were true, Wirt suggested that individual Cherokee might sue over various violations of their rights. However, since Cherokee land was held collectively, Wirt also suggested that Ross, as Principal Chief, could sue officials of Georgia through a federal circuit action. Wirt thought that Chief Justice Marshall favored a case "in the state courts carried through to the Supreme Court under section 25 of the Judiciary Act [1789]."[61] In the same letter, the attorney described the difficulties he anticipated with the latter strategy, namely, that he could not anticipate any success in the circuit courts. Before asking his client to decide which approach the Cherokee would have him take, Wirt offered his own "choice," along with this disheartened analysis: "[T]he only hope is a suit in the state courts . . . but the state of Georgia would never permit [this]." Wirt believed that state officials, who in *Tassels* and *Cherokee Nation* had refused to acknowledge the national power of judicial review, would block all actions and paperwork necessary for this kind of Cherokee appeal to the U.S. Supreme Court. The attorney did not need to rely on his professional judgment to reach this conclusion. Only recently Governor George Gilmer had again vowed that no federal judge would ever interfere in Georgia's business.

## CHAPTER 5

# A Decision on Indian Sovereignty

## INTRODUCTION

There had been talk of a property rights case, but the next case on behalf of Cherokee sovereignty did not involve either property or a Cherokee litigant. Instead, the contest involved two missionaries from the United States who challenged the legality of their arrest by the state of Georgia within the Cherokee Nation.

Late in 1830 the Georgia legislature passed a bill intended to prohibit the passage of "any white person" onto Cherokee Nation territory without the permission of the state.[1] The legislation was meant to harass supporters of the Cherokee and, like earlier jurisdictional measures, chase the Cherokee from their lands. The new law required that all white people living among the Cherokee apply for a residence permit from Georgia and swear an oath of allegiance to the state and its laws. In the winter of 1831, while Wirt and Sergeant were preparing to argue *Cherokee Nation,* a group of American Board missionaries sympathetic to the cause of Cherokee sovereignty defied the law, pronouncing it illegal. They were arrested by Georgia police.

Their spokesman was Samuel A. Worcester, who had worked closely with Elias Boudinot, editor of the *Cherokee Phoenix.* Worcester opposed the license and oath law both because it violated the sovereign right of the Cherokee to determine who could live in their nation and because he believed that missionary work should not be influenced by state politics. Before his arrest Worcester had corresponded with the ailing Jeremiah Evarts about the law and the proper course of action for the missionaries. Evarts, ill and en route to Havana for a cure, responded with an enthusiastic endorsement of civil disobedience and a promise of American Board help with legal costs in case of arrests. Evarts felt that civil disobedience would encourage the Cherokee to stand firm against Georgia and was "clearly the path of duty." Apparently reluctant to acknowledge the Cherokee as actors in their own right, he added that "if you leave I fear the Cherokee will make no stand whatever."[2]

The arrest of the northern missionaries gave Wirt and Sergeant an opportunity to fashion another legal challenge to Georgia's anti-Indian laws. If the men were convicted of violating state law in a Georgia court, an appeal could be taken to the U.S. Supreme Court. Wirt believed that a new test of the controversial jurisdiction laws, using the missionaries as plaintiffs, was a reasonable strategy. He had no doubt about the outcome at the Supreme Court but warned Worcester that a mandate from that body might not be heeded by Georgia officials.[3] Worcester hired Elisha W. Chester, a New England acquaintance who was practicing law in Georgia, as the missionaries' local attorney. Wirt took charge of the case from Baltimore, guiding Chester's work. The lawyers were certain that the local court would find the missionaries guilty and were preparing for an appeal to the Supreme Court. On September 15, 1831, a state court found the men guilty and sentenced all the defendants in *State v. Missionaries* to four years of hard labor at the state penitentiary. Most of the missionaries accepted pardons, but Worcester and Dr. Elizur Butler, who were committed to a test case, did not.

Samuel Worcester believed that the citizens of the United States would be aroused by Georgia's arrest of American missionaries and that the Supreme Court would rule in favor of the missionaries. However, his letters reveal a practical man who harbored no illusions about the rough and tumble world of Jacksonian politics. Months before the Supreme Court appeal, Worcester wrote to David Greene at the American Board office to tell him that a test case might be in vain because a favorable decision on "the mere question of right" could lead Georgia and Jackson to defy the Court. He was, he said, preparing himself to serve long sentence.[4]

The Cherokee leadership followed the state trial closely. John Ross worried that the Georgia legislature might repeal the law under which Worcester and Butler had been convicted, thus rendering the case moot. Georgia had prevailed in the *Tassels* appeal and had avoided direct action in *Cherokee Nation*, but those appeals had involved the Cherokee Nation. Even Georgia could not ignore the significance of imprisoning American clergy from one of the most respected missionary organizations in the nation. Ross thought that state officials might lose their nerve, but he was wrong. The missionaries were taken off to serve their sentences while Wirt began preparations for an appeal to the U.S. Supreme Court. He arranged for Chester to serve the necessary legal papers on state officials. Shortly afterward he filed for a writ of error that would allow him to bring the missionaries' case to the high court.

At the time of the new appeal the Cherokee desperately needed relief. They had been crushed in *Tassels* and blocked from meaningful action in *Cherokee Nation*. Every day more homesteaders and miners came into the Cherokee Republic from the United States. These men and women flaunted their disregard for international boundaries by camping on Cherokee land and, when gold was discovered late in the 1820s, by claiming it. The Cherokee treasury was virtually without funds because President Jackson refused to pay treaty annuities directly to the Cherokee national government. (He used a highly unusual per capita distribution to devalue the payments.) Contemporary Cherokee accounts describe a time of growing anti-Indian violence on the borders.

Yet the Cherokee and their allies in the United States were determined to maintain their opposition to the jurisdiction laws. Prominent Cherokees Elias Boudinot and John Ridge traveled north early in 1832 to lecture on Cherokee sovereignty rights and raise funds. It is likely that they were the Cherokee with whom Supreme Court Justice Joseph Story had a private meeting in Philadelphia.[5] The Cherokee leadership also was encouraged by a strong National Republican party attack on both President Jackson's Indian policy and Georgia's imprisonment of the missionaries. This was not entirely surprising, as the Republicans had just tapped Wirt's co-counsel, John Sergeant, to be vice president on Henry Clay's national ticket.

## *ARGUING* WORCESTER V. GEORGIA

The Supreme Court agreed to hear the Worcester-Butler appeal in the winter of 1832. John Marshall set February 20 as the first day for oral arguments. Technically, the issue in the case, now titled *Worcester* v. *Georgia*, was whether the missionaries had been arrested, tried, and sentenced under a state law that violated the U.S. Constitution's commerce clause. The missionaries' appeal maintained that in its assertion of states' rights Georgia had entered into an area of law reserved exclusively for the federal government under the national constitution. The appeal also asked the Court to rule whether the Cherokee Republic constituted a sovereign nation that was recognized by treaties with the United States and over which a state of the United States could have no jurisdiction.

When Wirt, John Sergeant, and Elisha Chester came to the Court on February 20, none of them knew whether Governor Lumpkin would release the prisoners if so ordered or if President Jackson would support Georgia if state officials refused to obey the Marshall Court. It was ominous that the state, again refusing to acknowledge the authority of a federal court in such appeals, had not sent counsel to participate in the oral arguments. Challenges to federal power were mounting from proponents of states' rights in the 1830s. Georgia was not alone in asserting this position, and the decision not to send state attorneys was consistent with long-standing states' rights objections to federal judicial supremacy.

On the missionaries' side, however, preparations for "the case to follow *Cherokee Nation*" had been months in the making. Since the arrests, William Wirt had been more active than John Sergeant as legal adviser to the missionaries, the American Board, Elisha Chester, and the Cherokee leadership. In the weeks before the case was called, however, Wirt found himself bedridden, and Sergeant took charge of the preparations. *The Minutes of the Supreme Court* and Sergeant's professional papers show that it was Sergeant who laid out the case for the missionaries on February 20, the first of three days of oral argument. Wirt, however, also argued on February 21 and February 23—the Court had adjourned on February 22 to attend "divine service in the Capitol" in honor of the centennial of the birth of General Washington. Justice Story reported to his wife that "both of the speeches were very able, and Wirt's, in particular, was uncommonly eloquent, forcible, and finished."[6]

Sergeant's notes for his oral argument reveal a black letter legal approach with few of the rhetorical flourishes favored by his co-counsel.[7] Standing before six justices—illness kept Justice Johnson away the entire session—Sergeant first addressed questions of jurisdiction. He was anxious that the Court would conjure up jurisdictional obstacles, as it had in *Cherokee Nation*, that would stand in the way of its considering the case on its merits. Pointedly, Sergeant reminded the justices that the Court's authority to issue writs of error in criminal cases had been a settled point of law since *Cohens v. Virginia*. In that 1821 decision the Court had rejected Virginia's claim that the judgments of state courts were final in cases involving state law. Marshall had ruled that the national court held appellate jurisdiction under Section 25 of the Judiciary Act and that the Eleventh Amendment did not bar appeals to the U.S. Supreme Court of state court decisions in which a federal question had been raised: "[T]he judicial power was extended to all cases arising under the constitution or laws of the United States, without respect to parties."[8]

When these preliminary arguments were completed, Sergeant turned to the merits of the case. He asserted that Georgia's 1830 law unconstitutionally usurped powers that rightfully belonged only to the United States and the Cherokee Republic. Next, in a strategic move that could be construed as bold, desperate, or simply logical, Sergeant told the Court that the laws and treaties affecting Cherokee–United States relations made *all* of Georgia's Indian laws, not just the one under which Worcester and Butler had been convicted, unconstitutional. The United States had repeatedly, in binding federal laws and international treaties, recognized Cherokee sovereignty and land boundaries. "This system," Sergeant said, "has made the Cherokees what they are . . . I do not deny the power of Congress to repeal their own laws—to violate and, so far as concerns themselves, to put an end to a treaty. But until repealed and annulled by Congress, they are obligatory upon every body.

> No individual can violate.
> No state can abrogate them.
> No office of this Govt can dispense with them.
> No single branch can repeal them.
> The treaty making power cannot undo them.
> Congress alone can change the system.
> If the power of Congress be thus plenary . . . there can be no
> power in the State."[9]

Sergeant's argument against Georgia proceeded on broad grounds. He insisted that Georgia's law encroached on the powers of the U.S. government protected by the U.S. Constitution instead of contending more narrowly that the 1830 state law conflicted with a federal statute, the Federal Intercourse Act of 1802.[10] Sergeant described the rights of the Cherokee government as having been violated but always spoke of Cherokee rights as secondary to the issue of federal authority. He addressed the question of Cherokee political status cautiously, employing Chief Justice Marshall's language from the previous term: "As to the Cherokees themselves. They are a State—a community. Within their territory, they possess the powers of self-government. . . . They are 'domestic, dependent nations.' "[11]

## THE COURT DECIDES

On March 3, 1832, the Marshall Court ruled, as Wirt and Worcester had predicted, against the state of Georgia. It was the judicial victory the Cherokee had sought since 1829. Writing for himself and Justices Duvall, Story, and Thompson, Chief Justice Marshall first held that there were no standing or jurisdictional issues that prohibited the Court from considering the merits of *this* appeal. The missionaries, as citizens of American states, could properly challenge their conviction under earlier Supreme Court doctrine affirming the Court's preeminent national judicial power. Marshall wrote: "It is . . . too clear for controversy, that the act of congress, by which this court is constituted, has given it the power, and . . . the duty, of exercising jurisdiction in this case."[12] The chief justice was making the most of an opportunity to remind Congress that it had conferred on the Court the controversial appellate power and the obligation to exercise it. Marshall's lecture might have sounded a false note, however, to those who remembered how willingly he had abjured any "duty" to hear *Cherokee Nation* only the year before (see Appendix III).

Any criticism was apparently muted when the chief justice turned to the merits of the missionaries' case and ruled against Georgia, announcing that the state's contested laws and actions were "repugnant to the constitution, laws, and treaties of the United States."[13] The Court concluded that Worcester and Butler had been arrested and imprisoned under an unconstitutional law and should be freed, but that was not all. Marshall's opinion declared all of Georgia's harassing legislation unconstitutional and did so in the most sweeping terms. The approach adopted by the majority condemned Georgia's laws both because they violated the authority of the United States and, as Sergeant and Wirt had argued, because they violated the political rights of the Cherokee Republic. The

Court's willingness to address and support Cherokee rights was received in Washington with surprise because of the caution Marshall had shown only a year earlier in *Cherokee Nation*. In *Worcester*, after all, the Cherokee Nation was not a direct party to the litigation. However, in an opinion that surveyed the entire history of political relations between the Cherokee, Great Britain, and the United States, the majority specifically chose to address the illegality of Georgia's actions in terms of sovereign Cherokee rights and to employ language defending the independent political status of Indian governments as it was recognized in U.S. law. Prodded by Justice Story, who wished the Court to "wash its hands clean of the iniquity of oppressing the Indians and disregarding their rights," Marshall used *Worcester* to outline the clearest, most pro-Indian doctrine of the time, refining earlier principles of federal Indian law and veering from the language of conquest used in *Johnson* v. *M'Intosh*.[14]

The influence that the Court's earlier conquest language had had on Georgia citizens and the Georgia legislature was very much on the minds of the justices who wrote the *Worcester* opinion. Concerned that dicta in *Johnson* had encouraged incursions onto Indian land as well as the passage of Georgia's jurisdiction laws, Marshall now repudiated *Johnson*'s conquest theory without, however, mentioning the earlier case by name. With this statement, Marshall intended to put to rest any notion that the Court supported nonconsensual extinguishment of Indian land title. The chief justice also qualified the exaggerated claims of his earlier establishment of discovery doctrine. "It is difficult to comprehend," Marshall wrote in *Worcester*, "that the discovery . . . should give the discoverer rights in the country discovered, which annulled the pre-existing rights of its ancient possessors."[15] He described as "extravagant and absurd" the idea that European discovery and settlement constituted conquest or conferred property title under the common law of Europe. In *Johnson*, the Court had affirmed the idea that Indians' rights in their lands were necessarily diminished by discovery. In *Worcester*, the majority turned its back on the larger implications of this theory, asserting only that the preexisting rights of the ancient possessors coupled with the European law of discovery granted no more to settlers than the exclusive right to purchase title if tribal governments consented to sell. Underscoring the importance of the principle of Indian consent articulated in *Cherokee Nation*, Marshall described European colonial charters as "grants assert[ing] a title against

Europeans only . . . [that] were considered as blank paper so far as the rights of the natives were concerned." A stern Court warned that "the power of war is given only for defense, not for conquest" and that extinguishment of property title resulting from aggression would not be recognized.

Marshall also used *Worcester* to clarify the meaning and implications of the "domestic dependent nation" designation he had invented in *Cherokee Nation* to save the Court from having a full hearing of the case. Caution ruled this new discussion. While Marshall refined the concept in *Worcester* in favor of Indian sovereignty, he again pointedly refused to describe Indian nations as foreign nations and embrace them as equal members of the Western community of nations. Nevertheless, Marshall and his colleagues did not approach the question of the political character of Indian governments in the manner of a Jacksonian. Describing them generally, Marshall wrote, "[T]he Indian nations ha[ve] always been considered as distinct, independent political communities, retaining their original natural rights, as the undisputed possessors of the soil. . . ."[16] Analyzing the legal position of the Cherokee Nation, he declared that relevant treaties, such as the Treaty of Holston and the Treaty of Hopewell, explicitly acknowledged the Cherokee's right of self-government and the national character of their government. Those treaties, Marshall wrote, guaranteed Cherokee lands and imposed on the federal government the duty to protect both land and sovereignty rights.[17] Marshall was also concerned with observations by other Court members that the ward-guardian relationship proposed in *Cherokee Nation* undermined *Worcester*'s characterization of Native American governments as national in form and fully sovereign. Marshall turned to the international law commentaries of Vattel to provide the necessary correctives, writing as follows:

> [T]he settled doctrine of the law of nations is, that a weaker power does not surrender its independence—its right to self-government, by associating with a stronger, and taking its protection. A weak state, in order to provide for its safety, may place itself under the protection of one more powerful, without stripping itself of the right of government, and ceasing to be a state.[18]

"Protection," the chief justice stated, "does not imply the destruction of the protected."[19]

The *Worcester* majority also took up the issue of interpreting treaty language, describing the United States as having "the sole and exclusive right of regulating the trade with the Indians, and *managing all their affairs.*" On behalf of the majority, Marshall argued: "To construe the expression . . . into a surrender of self-government, would be, we think, a perversion of their necessary meaning, and a departure from the construction which has been uniformly put on them. . . . It is . . . inconceivable that they could have supposed themselves, by a phrase thus slipped into an article, on another and most interesting subject [trade], to have divested themselves of the right of self-government on subjects not connected with trade."[20] Drawing on the Northwest Ordinance and the Constitution's commerce clause, Marshall further supported Cherokee claims to sovereignty by insisting that the proper construction of those phrases expressed a charge to the U.S. government, not individual states, to carry on trade and intercourse with tribal nations and to do so on the basis of tribal consent. He cautioned that documents of diplomacy that were written in English were subject to misunderstandings and to the mischief of translators.

However, consistent with *Johnson* and *Cherokee Nation*, Marshall did not concede that Indian nations had total control of foreign relations. In particular, the *Worcester* court reaffirmed that in the American view, tribal governments could only cede land to the discovering nation or its successor. The tribe is described as a "nation like any other nation" with the power of internal self-government but is asserted to be limited in certain external dealings so that the discoverer nation or its successor may protect its preemptive rights.

The concessions made in support of American interests were, however, not sufficient for two members of the Court. Justice McLean, who had been the only member of the Court to join Marshall's opinion in *Cherokee Nation*, voted with the majority in *Worcester*, agreeing in the narrowest sense that the missionaries had been imprisoned through the use of state laws that violated federal treaties and powers. He did not, however, sign Marshall's opinion. Instead, McLean criticized the opinion for its sweeping acceptance of tribal sovereignty and failure to adopt a realistic stance on the future of Indian-state relations. Georgia was in the wrong, McLean wrote, but Indian independence was doomed, a fact that Marshall and the Court would do well to recognize: "The exercise of the power of self-government by the Indians, within a state, is undoubtedly contemplated to be temporary. This is shown by the settled policy of the [U.S.] government, in the extinguishment of their title, and especially by the compact with the state of Georgia. . . . A sound national policy does require that the Indian tribes within our states should exchange their territories, upon equitable principles, or eventually, consent to become amalgamated in our political communities."[21] McLean argued that Indians could at best enjoy limited independence within the boundaries of a state and that when "either by moral degradation or a reduction in their numbers" they became incapable of self-government, the federal shield of protection should be superseded by state authority.

Justice Baldwin proved to be an even more staunch opponent of the majority position. Baldwin not only refused to sign Marshall's opinion but also refused to join the majority vote condemning Georgia's actions as a violation of federally held powers. He delivered no written opinion to the court reporter, announcing in court that his conclusions remained the same as those he had offered in *Cherokee Nation* v. *The State of Georgia*. Baldwin remained consistent in his support of Jackson and in the view that the Cherokee were properly under the jurisdiction of the state of Georgia.

Although disappointed in the positions taken by McLean and Baldwin, the Cherokee government welcomed the message from the majority. Against the backdrop of Georgia's aggression against the Cherokee and congressional and executive branch approval of the removal bill, the U.S. Supreme Court had reached out in a conciliatory manner to Native American governments. The justices held not only that the missionaries had been condemned under a law "shown to be repugnant to the constitution, laws, and treaties of the United States" but also that tribal nations had significant national political and property rights that were owed the highest respect by the United States. Although not a direct party to this round of litigation, the Cherokee Nation had finally won its case against Georgia. Marshall had abandoned his earlier strategy of self-serving judicial politics, instead supporting Indian sovereignty in opposition to the announced positions of the political branches of the federal government and ardent advocates of states' rights. It is possible to argue that the broad, forthright support of Indian sovereignty expressed in *Worcester* was abstract and occurred primarily because white men's rights and liberties were directly at issue. However, the majority might have decided *Worcester* on the narrow legal grounds proposed by Justice McLean and did not do so. At the same time, it is not possible to ignore the majority's unwillingness to accept Native American governments as full members of the international community of Western nations. They were deemed to be "distinct, independent political communities," but in Marshall's words, they were not foreign nations and were not free to cede their land to any nation but the United States.

## STUBBORN OPPOSITION: THE NONENFORCEMENT OF WORCESTER

The decision of the Court was welcomed by the Cherokee, but could it be enforced? Many people involved in the appeal expressed the opinion that Georgia and Jackson would ignore a ruling favoring the missionaries. Justice Story openly voiced his concern to a friend only days after Marshall handed down the *Worcester* v. *Georgia* decision:

> We have just decided the Cherokee case. . . . The decision produced a very strong sensation. . . . Georgia is full of anger and violence. What she will do, it is difficult to say. Probably she will resist the execution of our judgment, and if she does, I do not believe the President will interfere, unless public opinion among the religious of the Eastern and Western and Middle States, should be brought to bear strong upon him. The rumor is, that he had told the Georgians he will do nothing.[22]

Story was wise to worry, as events immediately after *Worcester* amply demonstrate the limits on the enforcement of judicial decisions. Real victory—as opposed to theoretical victory—for the missionaries and the Cherokee depended on enforcement of the Supreme Court's decision. Here they each lost, with devastating results for the Cherokee.

Two days after the justices read their opinions, the Court issued a mandate to the Georgia superior court—carried from Washington by Elisha Chester—ordering it to reverse its decision and free Worcester and Butler. Governor Lumpkin responded that he would hang the missionaries rather than "submit to this decision made by a few superannuated *life estate* Judges."[23] Officials of the Georgia superior court said that the U.S. Supreme Court had exceeded its authority and refused to reverse the conviction of the missionaries.

The two men's sentences were affirmed, and Butler and Worcester continued to be held in the state penitentiary. In the view of local officials, Georgia had to stand firm against a renegade national court that, they suggested, might soon attempt to assert its jurisdiction over *another* issue—African slavery.[24]

In Boston, David Greene knew none of this when he forwarded $500 to John Sergeant and congratulated him on the happy result at court.[25] Sergeant had returned to Philadelphia, and Wirt to Baltimore. The Cherokee delegation in Washington stayed on to monitor events while awaiting word from Chester on the actions of the superior court. A month passed with no message from the attorney. Chester already knew Governor Lumpkin and the superior court's response and, on Wirt's prior instructions, was preparing a letter asking Lumpkin to intercede and order the discharge of the prisoners.[26] The same week a messenger in Georgia, knowing of the superior court's denial, rushed to Washington to get the new Supreme Court decree needed to authorize a federal marshal to free the prisoners.[27] The Supreme Court, possibly to avoid further confrontation, had adjourned on March 17 without waiting to hear whether Georgia had obeyed its mandate and freed the missionaries.

In fact, the whole business revealed a larger unresolved legal problem in the United States. General law governing federal judicial and executive power over the states was unclear and, for some, inadequate. As a result, technical legal issues provided a smoke screen for President Jackson, who invoked them as his reason for not enforcing the Court's decision in *Worcester*. Although some historians believe that the President would have enforced the decision if the law had absolutely required it,[28] Jackson was known to be pleased by the Court's inability to "coerce Georgia."[29]

Even Wirt and Sergeant disagreed about whether a federal judge could issue the necessary writ of habeas corpus (order to produce the prisoner) after the refusal of a state court to execute a federal court decree. Responding to an inquiry from Congressman William Lewis, Wirt argued that nothing more could be done for the missionaries until Georgia put its refusal to free them in writing, something the governor's officials deliberately avoided doing until Superior Judge Charles Dougherty acquiesced and permitted the necessary affidavits to be prepared. Even after Dougherty's concession, Wirt wrote that there were legal obstacles and went on to argue the need for new federal legislation. Such a law, he said, would give federal judges the power to issue the writs necessary to free prisoners held under state laws that were declared unconstitutional by the U.S. Supreme Court. Wirt also recommended changes in the Militia Act of 1795, a statute that authorized presidential use of the militia to enforce national law. Wirt wanted the act amended to *require* that the President take action.[30]

Wirt believed that if he was correct, there was little the Supreme Court could do until Congress made these legislative changes. Two months after the Court's decision, however, he continued to counsel the possibility of resolving the problem by directly petitioning Jackson and the Congress. Wirt had not given up the fight and was displeased to hear that other Americans had advised the missionaries to admit their crime and accept a pardon. Influential "friends of the Cherokee" who only weeks before had considered the policy of Indian removal a contemptible violation of rights suddenly found the idea reasonable and necessary. Only six weeks after the *Worcester* decision, Senator Theodore Frelinghuysen, with whom Evarts had earlier worked out an antiremoval strategy, wrote David Greene at the American Board that the Cherokee ought to seek a liberal treaty of removal and leave.[31] Supreme Court Justice John McLean acted more directly. He asked the Cherokee delegation still living in the capital to meet with him and proceeded to argue the futility of continued litigation. He urged them to sign a removal treaty by which the Cherokee Nation would become a territory with a patent in fee simple and a delegate in Congress.[32] A small number of Cherokee leaders, Boudinot and John Ridge among them, had been reported to be ready to "surrender their country finding no faith is to be placed in the treaties, constitution or laws of the U. States." If all this was so, Wirt concluded to Lewis, "the state of Georgia is likely to be victorious [and] . . . the constitution, treaties, and laws of the U.S. . . . . are to be prostrated with impunity."[33]

The new supporter of removal for whom John Ross had the most biting words was Worcester's local attorney, Elisha Chester. After failing to win release of the missionaries, Chester had returned to Washington. Still in the employ of the Cherokee and the American Board, Chester nevertheless met with U.S. officials at the War Department and in mid-May let himself be hired as a special agent of that department. His job was to present the government's new proposal of removal to his client, the Cherokee National Council. In this capacity, Chester visited Wirt, Sergeant, and the officers of the American Board, urging them all to renounce their position on removal and support the government's proposal. In spite of other defections and pressure, none of these men showed any interest in Chester's message.

The missionaries also received visits from individuals who urged them to apply for pardons. David Greene heard about the visits and wrote the two prisoners that the decision on a pardon rested solely with them. He believed, however, that since they had been judged not guilty by the Supreme Court, they should not bear "the stigma of being pardoned culprits."[34] Throughout May and for the next six months, Butler and Worcester, who had long since expected to be free men, remained firmly opposed to the idea of a pardon: "If we now yield ... who will hereafter venture to place any reliance on the Supreme Court of the United States for protection against laws however unconstitutional?"[35]

Not put off by his poor reception in the North, Chester returned to the Cherokee Nation in early June, ready to outline the new removal proposition to Chief Ross. It was the first Ross knew of Chester's defection. Shortly afterward, a bitter John Ross wrote to Wirt, saying that Chester had strongly denied deserting the Cherokee for Jackson and had "boldly declared that he was acting under the special advice and influence of sincere friends of the Cherokees in Congress."[36] Chester had warned Ross that the "vulgar populace" on the Georgia frontier could not be restrained from aggression against the Cherokee and that removal was the only hope. Ross replied sarcastically that a sergeant's command under the authority of the United States would be sufficient to make that vulgar populace submit to the laws of Congress.

The Supreme Court remained out of session. Marshall's schedule did not call for the Court to reconvene for several months. Beyond some powerful new words from the justices, the only chance for "the sergeant's command" that Ross sought lay in the possibility of Henry Clay's defeat of Jackson in the presidential election. Clay, along with Daniel Webster, had been a leading supporter of a pro-Cherokee policy in Congress. While banking, economics, and opportunities for common people were the main issues in the 1832 campaign, Indian politics also figured in the debates and in voters' considerations. To the extent that the November election represented a mandate on *Worcester*, however, the Cherokee and the Marshall Court lost when Jackson trounced Clay and remained in the White House. American voters rejected Clay's candidacy and criticism of Jackson's Indian policy. The outcome of the presidential election, however, was not the only national political factor contributing to Jackson's final refusal to enforce the *Worcester* decision. In the same month, November 1832, the passage of a Nullification Ordinance in South Carolina created a significant new problem for the government in Washington. Although it could not have been predicted, the rebellion in South Carolina contributed directly to the defeat of the missionaries and the Cherokee.

The long-simmering states' rights rebellion in South Carolina exploded in the autumn of 1832. Since 1816, tension had been building between the southern states, which opposed a national tariff policy that they felt favored northern economic interests, and the federal government. Antitariff sentiment ran particularly high in South Carolina. In other southern states—Alabama, Georgia, Mississippi, and Tennessee—Jackson's support for Indian removal had lessened antipathy toward the tariff and diminished the power of the common cause involving states' rights. South Carolina, however, held firm in its opposition. On November 23, 1832, the sixth day of a state convention called to consider the legality of the tariff, South Carolina delegates declared the federal tax null and void. There was talk of civil war.

Surprising some Americans, President Jackson came out strongly against the Nullification Ordinance and those who would destroy the nation. Jackson's position might have helped the Cherokee. When South Carolina threatened military resistance to the tariff, there was talk that Jackson would ask Congress for legislation to meet state force with national force, laws that also might have been used, as Ross and Wirt had suggested, against Georgia. Few American friends of the Cherokee, however, spoke of this possibility. Indeed, many of the American politicians who had served as factotums for the Cherokee cause quickly broke ranks with Ross and the missionaries, fearing that agitation over the Cherokee would add to the danger of civil dissension in the United States. In some quarters there was a political excitement bordering on panic, with the missionaries being urged to save their country by renouncing their position and accepting a pardon. The missionaries, of course, were critical to the enforcement of the *Worcester* decision since they, not the Cherokee Nation, were the legal parties to the case. If Butler and Worcester accepted a pardon, the case would end with the legal, but not the political, affirmation of Cherokee rights. Despite *Worcester*'s text, Georgia would win, and in almost all respects the Cherokee would be no better off than before.

Initially the imprisoned men resisted the pressure put on them "to save their nation." They had their lawyers file papers to have the Supreme Court consider a new writ for their release at the January 1833 session. The attorneys maintained a reserved stance. Writing about the nullification crisis to his son-in-law in early December, William Wirt said, "I cannot help thinking it will pass off without any serious consequences."[37] Wirt's reception of Georgia Senator Forsythe just before Christmas reflected the same air of professional calm. Forsythe threatened that Butler and Worcester would have to serve out their terms if Wirt did not advise them to withdraw the new motion before the Supreme Court. Wirt responded that he had no authority to change the direction of the case unless he was instructed to do so by the two missionaries or the American Board.[38] Four days later Wirt wrote the missionary William Potter that he and Sergeant would make no decision with regard to the motion filed at the Supreme Court, since such a decision had to be made by the missionaries and the Board. His wish was "to remain merely in the professional character I have hitherto borne towards them. . . ."[39] Wirt, however, still believed, as he had in the spring, that there would be difficulties because of "deficiencies in the state of the law."[40] Wirt's letters in this period, proper in tone, seek to avoid an advisory role and are virtually devoid of any reference to the Cherokee or the effect a pardon could have on their cause. Wirt had become chiefly concerned with whether the authority of the Supreme Court would be vindicated.

Wirt and Sergeant did not have to wait long for instructions from their clients. During December, Butler and Worcester had second thoughts about the wisdom of another Supreme Court appeal: They feared its effect on the Union and doubted, for reasons that are unclear, that the Cherokee had anything more to gain from the case. Worcester wrote to the American Board to voice these concerns and asked for the view of the governing board. Its Prudential Committee, without waiting for advice from Wirt and Sergeant, met late in December 1832 and resolved "that, in view of the changes of circumstances, it is, in the opinion of the Committee, inexpedient for Messrs. Worcester & Butler to prosecute their case further before the Supreme Court of the United States."[41] Among those present, only David Greene, heir to Evarts's work, thought that there was any wisdom in carrying on with the case.

The missionaries received the text of the Prudential Committee's resolution on January 7, 1833. The next day, they wrote to Wirt and Sergeant, saying that they wished their Supreme Court appeal to be withdrawn. After a battle of wills with Governor Lumpkin over the tone of the required letter requesting pardons, the two men acknowledged the "magnanimity" of the state.[42] The governor responded with a release order

> taking into consideration the earnest solicitude for the release of these individuals . . . taking into view the triumphant ground which the state finally occupies in relation to this subject, in the eyes of the Nation, as has been sufficiently attested through various channels, especially in the recent overwhelming re-election of President Jackson . . . being assured . . . that the State is free from the menace of any pretended power whatever, to infringe upon her rights, or control her will in relation to this subject. . . . I therefore, as the organ of the State, feel bound to sustain the generous and liberal character of her people.
>
> Whatever may have been the errors of these individuals— whatever embarrassments and heart-burnings they may have been instrumental in creating—however mischievous they may have been in working evil to the State, to themselves, and the still more unfortunate Cherokees. . . . They shall go free.[43]

As directed, the warden freed Worcester and Butler on January 14, 1833. With their release, the third test case of Cherokee sovereignty had ended in a manner thoroughly at odds with Jeremiah Evarts's earlier predictions.

Early in 1831 Evarts had written to Worcester to encourage civil disobedience that would lead to a further test of Georgia's laws. He told the young missionary that standing up to Georgia would do much for the Cherokee cause. But, he said, as a race, the Cherokee did not have the heart to keep using the law as a weapon against oppression: "Courage is the thing they want . . . long continued courage or fortitude; it is the very point, in my judgment, where they will lose their country and their earthly all. . . . I have always feared for them on this point. I have often said, 'White men, in a high state of civilization, are alone competent and expect deliverance by the slow process of law.' "[44] Legal action does demand time and patience. The great irony is that Evarts was so wrong about who could stay the course: Ross and the Cherokee Council remained committed to the promise and honor of a nation under law and to the belief that American courts could be fair and neutral and that the U.S. Congress would respond favorably to memorials. For several reasons—not the least of which was to save themselves from removal—the Cherokee leadership had internalized the myths of liberal constitutionalism. It was the white man in his "high state of civilization" who could not, or would not, live by the slow process of law.

Worcester and Butler composed a long letter in February 1833 giving the reasons for their capitulation. The statement emphasized that the oath and license law had been repealed late in December 1832 but neglected to mention that all of Georgia's other anti-Indian jurisdiction laws remained in force. Thus, they could claim that the "*utmost* we could expect [were] mandates of the court . . . [to] effect our release from confinement, *without benefitting the Cherokee Nation.*" The larger notion of a test case in its fullest meaning, including enforcement, was dismissed because the "political aspect" of the United States had changed. The missionaries knew the physical and economic injury sustained daily by the Cherokee. For the two men, the possible injury to be sustained by "our public [the United States] . . . by the prosecution of our appeal" out-weighed the ongoing real abuse of the Cherokee and ultimately determined their decision.[45] Once pardoned, however, their politics took different turns. Worcester and the officers of the American Board joined Boudinot, Ridge, and others in support of a removal treaty. Butler continued to support Ross and the right of the Cherokee to remain on their own land and bitterly condemned Worcester's betrayal in joining the proremoval camp.

Wirt and Sergeant continued to be involved in the Cherokee cause. In January, commenting on the link between the missionaries' pardon and efforts to contain South Carolina, Wirt wrote that it was a "mournful" omen of the strength and durability of the Union that it could be kept together only by "means like these."[46] Nevertheless, in a short letter dated February 26, 1833, he counseled the Cherokee to delay bringing a new Supreme Court case because "as the missionaries have buried the hatchet from the patriotic desire not to involve Georgia with Carolina in a united resistance to the Union, it may be worthy of your consideration whether a better time than the present moment may not be chosen for making the question you contemplate."[47] The lawyer's loyalties were torn. He loved his country and had come to believe that the Cherokee cause could harm the Union. However, lawyers are paid to give advice. It is not unreasonable that Wirt should have advised delay out of strategic legal concern. This does not mean that either he or Sergeant had abandoned the Cherokee cause. Even as he counseled delay in his February 26 letter, Wirt wrote that he was willing to write a legal opinion on request. Several months later—after Wirt's death—Sergeant agreed to litigate several new appeals for the Cherokee.

John Ross was scornful of the missionaries' decision to withdraw the appeal to the Supreme Court in January 1833 and end the case. As an indirect party to the litigation, the Cherokee National Council was left powerless to pursue enforcement of the Court's decision as it applied to the broad question of Georgia's jurisdiction over the Cherokee. However, the irrepressible Ross was not without hope. During the nullification crisis Ross maintained that President Jackson's proclamation of the supremacy of the constitution and laws of the United States, along with new congressional legislation, might make it impossible for the President to avoid enforcing *Worcester* and relevant treaties. Ross's logic was impeccable. Unfortunately for the Cherokee, the U.S. Congress, the only body that could create the political pressure to force Jackson's hand, did not have the will to do so.

The sacrifice of the Cherokee cause to nullification politics bitterly disappointed the Cherokee, and in the opinion of many Americans, the concessions made to South Carolina failed to save the political honor of the Union. In Congress, Clay negotiated compromise legislation, the Tariff Bill of 1833, which Jackson signed into law. John Marshall's biographer later wrote, "South Carolina was mollified. For the time the storm subsided; but the net result was that Nullification triumphed—a National law had been modified at the threat of a State which was preparing to back up that threat by force."[48] South Carolina officials spared no one; they even criticized Georgia "for sneaking out of a fight."

## CONTINUING CHEROKEE FAITH IN COURTS AND LAWYERS

John Ross was a heroic and savvy leader. His character is revealed by his continuing commitment to nonviolence and to the use of the law to save his nation at a time when he and his family, along with other Cherokee opposed to removal, were being dispossessed of their houses and property by armed Georgians. It is well known that after the *Worcester* decision Ross and members of the National Council continued to lobby members of Congress and the executive branch to prevent removal. Less well known is the fact that the Cherokee people continued to believe in the possibility of receiving just treatment in American courts despite Georgia and Jackson's failure to honor *Worcester*. This continued willingness to seek redress in American courtrooms after 1832 attests to the Cherokee's faith in the rule of law and ability to hire lawyers to represent them despite their increasingly unpopular cause. This legal strategy paid off as the Cherokee won several important cases in state courts.

In his annual message of October 1833 Ross described a significant legal and political victory in the St. Clair, Alabama, circuit court. Charges against a Cherokee for the murder of another Cherokee had been discharged after the court had decided that the state law extending jurisdiction over the Cherokee (one similar to Georgia's) was unconstitutional. A few months later a similar Tennessee Indian jurisdiction law was struck down as unconstitutional after a challenge by a Cherokee defendant. Still later, in the winter of 1834, a Georgia attorney, William Underwood, who had been in the employ of the Cherokee for several years, argued a case in which the Cherokee sought an injunction to bar implementation of new state laws distributing Cherokee lands to Georgians.[49] Underwood drew on the earlier arguments of Wirt and Sergeant as well as those of John Marshall in attacking Georgia. He asserted that the Cherokee had the exclusive right to govern themselves; that they had a right to lands that had not been ceded by the tribe, subject only to the right of preemption by the United States; and that Georgia's land legislation violated treaties between the Cherokee and the United States.[50] John Cuthbert, the state's lawyer, wrote Governor Lumpkin that the Cherokee's attorney was raising political questions concerning the nature of the Cherokee Republic as well as issues of individual property rights. To the delight of the Cherokee Republic's leadership, Georgia Circuit Court Judge John W. Hooper granted the injunction on narrow grounds, and later the same year a Georgia Convention of Judges (appeals court) upheld Hooper's decision and the Cherokee's right of occupancy.

As was the case with *Worcester*, the Hooper decision did not end trespasses on Cherokee land or the criminal prosecution of Cherokees under Georgia's laws. Nevertheless, according to one government agent, "this unexpected judicial proceeding have sprang [sic] a new hope in the ignorant Cherokee, that they have recovered their country etc from the state of Georgia."[51] The governor and the legislature took what revenge they could by promising the ouster of the judges who had supported the injunction. They also swore that new legislation would undermine the court's decision.

The Cherokee, however, were sufficiently encouraged to have William Underwood make several new appeals to the U.S. Supreme Court—writ of error cases in which the Cherokee would be direct parties to the litigation. As before, the Cherokee needed lawyers practiced in supervising and arguing cases before the high court. And although the Cherokee cause no longer figured prominently in national party politics, Ross hoped his old allies among the National Republicans would continue to take an interest and be willing to represent the Cherokee. The Cherokee leader knew that William Wirt had died in February 1834, but he maintained a correspondence with John Sergeant. In early autumn 1834 Ross found that Sergeant was open to conducting further legal work for the Cherokee Nation and had Underwood forward the case transcripts needed to file for writs of error. Fees were still a delicate matter, as the Cherokee were now owed four years' worth of annuities—more than $25,000 (equivalent to a vast sum today)—by the United States. Ross wrote to Sergeant that negotiations were in progress to recover the annuities and that as soon as the United States paid, the lawyer would receive his fees.[52]

For the next several weeks letters flew back and forth between Philadelphia, Georgia, and the clerk's office at the Supreme Court in Washington. Several writs were involved. The case of *Georgia* v. *Graves* caused immediate excitement. A murder case, *Graves* was a virtual replay of the *Corn Tassels* appeal. Late in October 1834 a citation to the Supreme Court summoned Georgia officials to appear and show cause why the error shown in the writ involving James Graves, who had been tried for and convicted of murder, should not be corrected. On November 7 Governor Lumpkin notified the Georgia legislature that the Supreme Court was again attempting to interfere in the exercise of the state's criminal jurisdiction, saying that "such attempts will eventuate in the dismemberment and overthrow of our great confederacy."[53] The legislature understood its political interests and adopted a resolution refusing once again to acknowledge the Supreme Court's jurisdiction. On November 8 local counsel for the Cherokee wrote Sergeant that only the use of federal troops, which were available at the U.S. Cherokee Agency, could prevent a death sentence. Apparently no effort was made to obtain troops, and Graves, like Corn Tassels, was executed by the state.[54] Ross continued to send Sergeant records for new federal appeals, but time was running out for the Cherokee. John Marshall had died, leaving the Court without a leader for a short while. More critically, determined not to live with the effects of Judge Hooper's decision, the Georgia legislature enacted legislation intended to negate the effect of that decision and prohibit Georgia judges from granting injunctive writs in other cases involving Indians.[55]

## A TIME OF INFAMY: SHOWDOWN OVER A CHEROKEE TREATY OF REMOVAL

The pressure for Cherokee removal in Georgia in the early 1830s was matched by an equally determined effort on the part of the Jackson administration, which had already used unrelenting pressure to win removal agreements from the nearby Chickasaw, Choctaw, Creek, and Seminole. When the official elected Cherokee government held firm in its opposition to removal, Jackson's representatives sought out Cherokee dissidents with whom they could negotiate a removal treaty. They found a small group led by the Ridge family and former *Cherokee Phoenix* editor Elias Boudinot. This group was called the Treaty party.[56]

In January 1835 John Ross learned that Treaty party members had been brought to Washington for talks. With a delegation of supporters from the majority National party, Ross hurriedly set off for the American capital. The Cherokee's lawyer, William Underwood, also traveled to Washington. In the following months Ross met with countless American officials. As a matter of principle, he opposed removal and demanded that the United States honor its treaties with the Cherokee. A practical man, he also countered a $3 million offer by the United States for his nation's lands with a demand for $20 million. In March 1835 he even initiated a correspondence intended to explore the possibility of asylum for his people in Mexico. This action suggests that Ross feared that a removal treaty—

even a fraudulent one—would be approved by the U.S. Senate during 1835.

Ross found it difficult to uncover details of the treaty being worked out between Jackson and the dissidents. The Treaty party leaders rightly feared being charged as traitors under the Cherokee Republic's law of treason. Only later did Ross discover that his lawyer and adviser, William Underwood, had also secretly repudiated him and the antiremoval National party. The United States had paid for Underwood to come to the capital to negotiate for the Treaty party. Ross learned much later that U.S. officials had wooed Underwood by promising that his delinquent legal fees would be paid out of a Cherokee removal treaty settlement!

Negotiations with the dissidents were completed in March 1835. Treaty party members then left Washington for home, accompanied by an American, the Reverend John F. Schermerhorn. Schermerhorn had accepted appointment as a U.S. commissioner with responsibility for Cherokee ratification of the treaty. On March 29, 1835, at Elias Boudinot's New Echota home, the small group of dissidents secretly signed the treaty and prepared to bring it to a Cherokee council for the necessary general approval. Knowing that they were a minority faction and could be charged with treason, members of the Ridge faction urged Georgia officials to make it difficult for antitreaty meetings to take place. To aid the dissidents and the removal process, Georgia's governor kidnapped several leaders of the Cherokee government.

William Underwood had also returned to the South. Eager to ascertain whether a removal agreement would include generous set-asides for unpaid attorneys' fees, the lawyer continued to consult with John Ridge and other Treaty party leaders and to offer written advice to President Jackson. Looking to his own future and certain that removal would occur, in the summer of 1835 Underwood applied for a U.S. government appointment to appraise Cherokee property.

In October 1835 Commissioner Schermerhorn rode to the Cherokee Council to present the terms of the agreement that had been secretly approved the previous March. However, the proposal was roundly rejected by the citizens of the Cherokee Republic. In response, in one of its boldest moves, the Georgia Guard "arrested" John Ross in December and held him for thirteen days without stat-

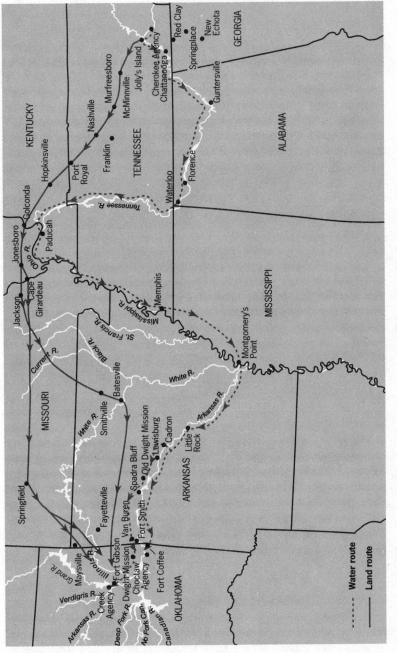

The Routes Taken by the Cherokees during Their Removal to the West, 1838–1839
Adapted from *The Cherokees* by Grace Steele Woodward, University of Oklahoma Press, 1963

ing a charge. Refusing to be silenced, Ross called for the boycott of a
new council scheduled by Schermerhorn. As soon as he was released,
Ross joined a Cherokee delegation that rode to Washington to
demand federal protection from the acts of Georgia officials. They had
barely arrived when Schermerhorn, carrying the hoax to its conclusion, obtained seventy-five Cherokee signatures—in a nation of 17,000
citizens—and declared that the Cherokee people had legally ratified a
treaty of removal. Despite earlier assurances from National Republican–Whig senators that a fraudulent treaty would not win approval,
the U.S. Senate ratified the Treaty of New Echota by one vote. Jackson
signed the document on May 23, 1836. The treaty required the
removal of all eastern Cherokee to the West by 1838.[57]

## SETTLING UP

The tale that follows is a stark and grim one that will be continued
in the Conclusion. With nearly all the Cherokee resisting, the U.S.
military organized the removal of 17,000 Cherokee to the west, a
journey the Cherokee named *Nunna daul Isunyi,* or the Trail Where
We Cried (in English, the Trail of Tears). Few families were spared
illness. Among the thousands who died during the terrible journey
was Quatie, the wife of John Ross.

The tale, however, does not end with the march west. Men such
as William Underwood had made certain that the removal treaty
would provide cash settlements with which outstanding monetary
claims against the Cherokee Nation might be paid. The ink of Jackson's signature on the treaty was barely dry when Underwood and
other lawyers who had—or claimed to have—represented the
Cherokee began to present written claims for unpaid legal fees. The
sums demanded were staggering, with several of the attorneys in
this siege of paper jousting with the government for three, five, and
even eight years. Petitions, letters, and certifications of service to
various and sundry commissioners, secretaries of war, and congressmen from several of the lawyers flowed from the summer of
1836 well into the 1840s.

A commission was established to review the claims. The Reverend Schermerhorn was among the first to submit a testimonial on
behalf of the local lawyers Underwood, Hansell, and Rockwell in
which he stated:

... and you may have heard which is the truth, that they have rendered me very special service in the Cherokee negotiations, and indeed if they had opposed me I could not have succeeded. The President in my presence said to Mr. Underwood . . . that he and his associates should [be] paid for their services to the Cherokees, and provision should be made for it in the treaty. I also as the Commissioner on the part of the U. States gave them the same assurances if they gave me their aid in effecting it; which they have faithfully done.[58]

William Underwood had first been hired in September 1830 by the Cherokee to conduct the *Corn Tassels* appeal. He later said that his legal practice had been bringing a yearly income of $4,000. Underwood professed to have rendered professional service in 315 Cherokee cases, not counting "discharges on habeas corpus and before justices of the peace," from late September 1830 through 1835. He submitted a basic bill of $30,890, added a 25 percent surcharge, and acknowledged the $2,200 already paid to him by the Cherokee. His final claim to the commission amounted to $36,402. Local attorney Samuel Rockwell submitted a request for unpaid fees in the amount of $30,970 for casework undertaken from the spring of 1834 through 1837. He listed 271 cases. Another local attorney, William Hansell, listed 281 cases in his logbook of Cherokee cases and submitted a bill for $30,075, including a 25 percent surcharge but minus the $1,000 paid him by the Cherokee Council in 1835. Hansell's bill included a sum for five months spent in Washington at the explicit request of Commissioner Schermerhorn and for his work with the treaty-making delegation opposed by Ross. Eight other attorneys, including the estate of William Wirt, entered claims.

If the lawyers had hoped for a speedy resolution of their claims, they were disappointed. Once they realized that the process would not be a simple one, they increased their letters and petitions. An 1837 letter from Underwood, Hansell, and Rockwell to the claims commissioners is particularly revealing on the question of a surcharge to which the Cherokee had never agreed and the fabrication of personal danger—never demonstrated—while litigating Cherokee cases:

> [We are presenting our accounts against the Cherokee Nation for settlement.] We have added to this account twenty-five percent except in those cases in which extra fees are charged which we consider to be fair and just from the following considerations: It

will be recollected that in reference to cases where white men are parties the fees are usually certain and most usually paid down or at least as soon as services are rendered whereas; the receipt of our fees in these cases was entirely contingent depending upon the settlement of the Cherokee difficulties with the United States, these difficulties at the time of our engagement was thought would not be closed for several years indeed they might not be settled in our lifetime. . . . Under such circumstances, we undertook the defence of the Cherokees. We know no respectable attorney who would not make a great difference between cash payment & a remote credit . . . the legal interest for the sums due us upon the performance of the service would amount to more than the twenty five percent charged.[59]

The lawyers stated that their work for the Cherokee required that they "had to measurably give up our own practice of our own circuits" and went on to claim that they had "laboured under constant expectation of personal violence in consequence of the excited state of feeling deep prejudice and odium which espousing the cause of the Cherokees created against us. These all unknown in the defence of ordinary cases where white men are parties."

The letter closed with what the attorneys trusted were appealing notices: "The importance of the principles settled, the magnitude of the questions discussed, the value of the property involved as also the rights of the Cherokee" all justified the extra charges. By the treaty, "the Cherokees are now made wealthy." In urging the treaty, the three lawyers believed they had served the "best interest of these people . . . and benefitted those by whom we were employed. Of this course the President has expressed his approbation" and said that there should be payment.

That most of the lawyers were owed fees was never in question. The issue was always, and only, the amount. In the summer of 1837 the U.S. commissioners settled on a strategy: They would ask a select committee of Cherokee to review the veracity of the lawyers' petitions. Ross and his party were still fighting the treaty under which the settlements would be made. The committee therefore had no Ross party members. After reviewing claims, the committee members concluded that many of the claims were exaggerated, a confection of double billing and work that was never done. "Read Judge Underwood's cases on which he has charged," wrote the committee members, and you have read the list of cases of the others. "Barrow & Irwin, Rockwell, Underwood, Hansell & Sims are all partners in charging in a majority of cases for the same case."[60] The committee recommended payment of $11,000 to Underwood, $5,000 each to Rockwell and Hansell, $6,000 to Barron and Irwin, $5,000 to Wirt's estate, and lesser sums to three others. The commission accepted the report and paid those lawyers the amounts certified by the Cherokee.

Underwood, Hansell, and Rockwell fumed at what they considered incomplete payments and challenged the ability of a client (the Cherokee) "ignorant of our language and all of whom were interested to preserve as much of the fund for other purposes as possible" to pass judgment on the value of their professional services.[61] New letters and memorials flew out of their offices. In March 1838 John Ross's brother, Lewis, wryly commented to Ross that Underwood and Hansell had just "decamped" from the commissioner's office "after an ineffectual application for more money."[62] Yet the attorneys did convince Schermerhorn and a few government officials that a new—proper—committee of local Georgia lawyers should review and certify their claims. This was done, with the recommendations falling between their original claims and the findings of the Indian committee. This appeal came to nothing, but still the three persisted—and after them, their heirs.

## CONCLUSION

In 1840 the chairman of the House Committee on Claims asked John Ross to submit a statement on the ongoing claims of Underwood, Hansell, and Rockwell. The response of the lawyers' onetime client provides a vivid picture of his thoughts about men who by their profession and personal willingness had allowed the Cherokee to press for justice in American courts but who, from Ross's perspective, did not stay the course. These men, Ross wrote, had indeed been in the employ of the Cherokee Nation, but that engagement had been broken by the lawyers: "They went over to a party whose encroachments they had covenanted to resist. From the moment of their change, the Cherokee Nation could no longer regard them as in their employ . . . any claims these gentlemen may have for services rendered to the Rev'd Mr. Schermerhorn & to the United States government, they rest it entirely between them and their employers. For such services, the Rev'd Mr. Schermerhorn, and the United States government are, of course, the only parties to whom these legal gentlemen can properly look for payment." The Cherokee, Ross asserted, "certainly ought not to be called upon to pay those they employ, not only for doing their duty, but for deserting it & them. If the gentlemen in question have served the United States against the 'constituted authorities' of the Cherokees, the United States, no doubt, will pay them liberally, but with their own money;—not, we trust with ours." He closed by reminding the congressman that each of the three had already been paid more than "the most faithful and effective friend of the Cherokees in the same cause, the late Mr. Wirt, who never betrayed his trust."[63]

In the shadow of other men's treachery and the haze of time, William Wirt stood as a noble figure to John Ross. In a sense, Wirt was fortunate to have died when he did. If he was tiring of the Cherokee cause, he did not have the time to reveal that, much less to indicate what his politics might have been with respect to the Treaty party or the Treaty of New Echota.

Among the American lawyers who served the Cherokee during the 1830s in Washington and in Georgia there were no martyrs. There is no evidence, flowery assertions to the contrary, that any of the lawyers ever suffered physical danger for representing the Cherokee. Unlike the Cherokee, they were not harassed and kept from their livelihoods, arrested, or driven from their homes. The national lawyers, Wirt and Sergeant, were condemned heartily by their political enemies but praised lavishly by their Whig friends. When Wirt died in the middle of the Jackson era, all Washington paused to mourn and eulogize him. Though the records in Georgia are scanty, there too men said that the question of the Cherokee was a party issue, and it is likely that Underwood, Chester, Rockwell, Hansell, and the others were praised and condemned according to individual political stances.

The Cherokee did not want for attorneys. Whether any of those lawyers felt that as a matter of justice the Cherokee *ought* to or *must* have an attorney cannot be answered. For political and economic reasons, attorneys made their services available. The writings of men such as Evarts and Wirt suggest a concern for the plight of the Indians as well as for the United States if legal instruments— covenants between honorable people—were cast aside.

The Cherokee of the preremoval period are sometimes represented as pawns in a white man's game of power and politics. Indeed, many of the events described here demonstrate the willingness, even the sense of obligation, on the part of white Americans—churchmen, politicians, attorneys, and judges—to shape the future of the Cherokee people. Despite the accuracy of that image, what emerges from a study of these Supreme Court appeals is a picture of the Cherokee as principled and practical in their affairs and determined to direct the course of their own history. They were not passive victims of the removal policy charted by Jacksonian Democrats. Instead, the citizens of the Cherokee Republic supported a leadership that chose bold navigation of the political and legal waters of the United States. Ross and his colleagues were attentive and assertive both in their dealings with the attorneys in the employ of the Cherokee Nation and in their dealings with the Cherokee's political allies in the United States. When, ultimately, the citizens of the Cherokee Republic were forced to move from their homelands, they consciously chose a policy of nonviolence and demanded as much authority for their own leaders along the removal route as officials of the United States would grant.

# Conclusion: The Life of Landmark Litigation

The Supreme Court's decision in *Worcester* did not protect the Cherokee people from the policy of removal supported by President Jackson and the Congress. At the time of its writing, however, the 1832 opinion did provide the most comprehensive federal judicial statement of its time regarding the status of Native American governments and property rights. In contrast to the earlier assertion of conquest in the *Johnson* decision, *Worcester* affirmed American recognition of Native American sovereignty and the continuing right of Indian nations to occupy their territory and control the transfer of its title. While retaining many key characteristics of the colonialist perspective, the Marshall decision theoretically equipped Native American nations with legal protection, including important procedural guarantees, that was used during the removal period and in the decades that followed. Yet the history of Cherokee removal confirms that the most fundamental procedural and substantive rights of the Cherokee were openly and knowingly violated by the government of the United States in spite of *Worcester*. President Jackson sent his commissioners to negotiate with a wholly unauthorized group of Cherokee, and the U.S. Senate supported him by ratifying the fraudulent removal treaty. Although it was thought to contain bold judicial language, the *Worcester* decision was not capable of preventing the loss of the Cherokee's homeland and their removal to foreign territory.

The Cherokee moved late in the 1830s, one of the dozens of Native American peoples forced to migrate west under the U.S. removal policy. They joined earlier Cherokee migrants as well as the Choctaw, Chickasaw, Creek, and Seminole. Shortly afterward they were followed by the Seneca, Shawnee, and Delaware from the Northeast and the Catawba and Natchez from the Southeast. People in the United States called the area where these Native Americans were resettled the "Indian Territory." In exchange for the land taken from them in the East, each nation was assigned a new homeland, with legal title, by the government of the United States. The United States continued to relocate Indian nations to this area—today known as Oklahoma—throughout the nineteenth century. The Cheyenne, Comanche, Osage, Pawnee, and Wichita were brought to the "Indian Territory" from the West before and after the Civil War. As late as 1889 Apache were resettled in the territory.

The 1835 Treaty of New Echota designated 1838 as the year for Cherokee relocation. In that year U.S. troops were sent onto Cherokee lands. Stockade forts were built for gathering and holding the unwilling migrants, who were all—men, women, and children— brought in from their homes and fields at bayonet point. Many people had no choice but to leave behind all their personal belongings and farming tools. In all, about 17,000 Cherokee were forced into these temporary stockades and subsequently marched west. Demographers speculate that as many as 8,000 deaths may have occurred among the Cherokee as a result of the 800-mile journey and the immediate effects (illness, scarcity of food, exposure, trauma) of resettlement.[1] This undoubtably reinforced the belief of many in the United States that Native Americans, who were somehow incapable of competing with whites, were doomed to extinction. However, the Americans were incorrect. Against great odds, the Cherokee rebuilt their nation in the West.

The Cherokee carried west strong leadership, a cultural heritage, and resolve. Initially, three groups competed to control the future of the republic: the Old Settler Cherokee who had emigrated west twenty years before the 1838 removal, the Ross majority party, and the Ridge-Boudinot faction. The competition between these factions led to bitter civil war marked, among other things, by the assassination of the Ridge-Boudinot leadership. Violence and nearly irreconcilable differences persisted well into the 1840s. Building on the experience of the several thousand Old Settlers in the West and the earlier economic and political accomplishments of the 1838 migrants, however, the Cherokee established a new republic on the 7-million-acre homeland that once again had a bicameral legislature, a court system, and a national newspaper. Under its 1841 public education act, the Cherokee government built a large public education system. Little more than a decade after removal, the

Cherokee had regained the stability and prosperity of their earlier life. Most Cherokee farmed, but their new economy also drew strength from the presence of successful merchants, traders, and cattle ranchers as well as timber and mining operations. The decade of the 1850s became a golden age for the Cherokee Nation.

Then came the American Civil War. The Cherokee government, still led by John Ross, attempted to maintain a neutral position. Internal politics—including support for the Confederacy among slaveholding Cherokee mixed-bloods—geography, and the early failure of Lincoln's government to lend support led Ross to sign a treaty with the Confederacy in October 1861. Many Cherokee, however, remained loyal to the Union and served in Union Army regiments. Ross was removed by Union officials to Washington, D.C., where from 1862 to 1865, with a delegation of Cherokee leaders, he worked to obtain military protection for the Cherokee Nation as well as food and clothing for Cherokee war refugees. The nature of Ross's political sympathies remains unclear; he may have cared only for the preservation of the Cherokee Republic.

The Cherokee became pawns in the American Civil War. Despite the Cherokee Nation's effort to remain neutral, in the end the Cherokee were compelled to make significant treaty concessions, including territory and the provision of a right-of-way to the railroads. Expansionist nationalism defined American diplomacy during this period. Manifest destiny, temporarily slowed by the Civil War, was again unleashed. Now more than ever, Americans dreamed of an empire stretching to the Pacific, an empire that they imagined would not be encumbered by the presence of Indian nations. Thus, after 1865, U.S. Indian policy followed several basic principles: First, the continued acquisition of Native American territory became a priority, along with the consolidation of more Indian nations within the "Indian Territory"; second, permissive tolerance of white intruders on Indian territory characterized American policy, as it had in the preremoval era; and third, the United States committed itself to assimilationist legislation, the goal of which was to force denationalization on Native Americans and end communal land holding.

These were policies that the Cherokee sought—ultimately unsuccessfully—to defeat at the close of American Civil War. In the last quarter of the nineteenth century the Cherokee government again found that *Worcester*'s legal doctrine was inadequate to sustain the Cherokee Nation against the increasingly large number of Americans who rejected the idea of Indian autonomy. To begin with, the U.S. government contrived to take lands ceded to the Cherokee under the terms of their relocation and deprive the Cherokee Nation of the grazing fees used to run schools, hospitals, and the government. The American government also defaulted on its obligation to keep squatters and profiteers—who came by the thousands, perhaps as many as 100,000—out of the Cherokee Nation. And in 1887 the U.S. Congress enacted the Dawes General Allotment Act, which committed the United States to the forcible incorporation of Native American peoples. Through the Dawes Act, the government of the United States set out to destroy Native American governments and culture, including communally held land, and to force all Indian people to accept individual land title. The Americans called this latter change "land allotment" and anticipated millions of acres of "surplus" land that would not be allocated for the new individual Indian homesteads. In a widely quoted remark, Theodore Roosevelt characterized the Dawes Act as "a mighty pulverizing engine to break up the tribal mass."

Because of its economic and political strength, the leadership of the Cherokee Republic was able to hold off implementation of these policies longer than were other Indian nations. But in 1898 the U.S. Congress passed the Curtis Act, the first of several statutes and agreements specifically designating the lands of the Cherokee and four other nearby Indian nations for allotment. Legislation in 1906 made allotment of Cherokee Nation land inescapable and provided for the admission of the Indian and Oklahoma territories into the Union as the state of Oklahoma in 1907. The destruction of the communal land base of the Cherokee Nation was quickly accomplished as the United States divided the tribal land and assigned fee simple title to Cherokee citizens who, along with Native Americans from dozens of other Indian communities in the territory—and a much larger number of non-Indians—became citizens of Oklahoma. Although theoretically *Worcester* v. *Georgia* continued to preside as the leading decision of nineteenth-century federal Indian law, the Cherokee were involuntarily annexed and absorbed into the United States of America.

## WORCESTER *THEN AND NOW*

What can be said of legal decisions that fail to accomplish their goal? What, in particular, can be said of *Worcester* v. *Georgia*, which twice failed to provide judicial protection to the people of the

Cherokee Nation in the face of an executive, legislative, and popular will to deny legally guaranteed rights of territory and sovereignty? The *Worcester* doctrine established recognition of Indian sovereignty and confirmed that legal consent was required for the extinguishment of Indian land title. Yet in both the removal and the allotment eras, this legal doctrine was ignored with impunity. In the 1830s the U.S. Supreme Court had neither the will to maintain its opposition to President Jackson and Congress nor the independent means to enforce its pro-Indian doctrine. By the late 1880s, when the legislative and executive branches of the United States had each made a commitment to the new policy of involuntary allotment and assimilation, the Supreme Court also largely turned its back on the defense of Indian political rights. Indeed, Supreme Court jurisprudence at the end of the nineteenth century and in the first years of the new century was marked more than ever by colonialist and racist assumptions. While *Worcester* was not overturned, in a new line of turn-of-the-century cases the Supreme Court reinterpreted federal Indian law doctrine in ways that favored the United States, relying on ideas of guardianship over Indians and increased congressional power in Indian affairs.

Two cases—*United States* v. *Kagama* (1886) and *Lone Wolf* v. *Hitchcock* (1903)—established the Supreme Court's new approach.[2] In *Kagama* the Court upheld the 1885 Major Crimes Act, by which Congress intended to remove seven serious crimes (murder, manslaughter, rape, assault with intent to kill, arson, burglary, and larceny) from the jurisdiction of Native American governments. The act was a direct attack on Indian sovereignty, which Americans increasingly spoke of as anachronistic. In fact, in the 1880s as in the 1830s, Americans were disinclined to share the continent with Native American nations, and the U.S. government consistently pursued policies intended to destabilize Native American governments and create dependency. Governments such as that of the Cherokee were presented popularly as "lost societies without power" that were unable to exercise sufficient government authority and therefore needed help from the United States to fill the void.[3] Thus, in *Kagama*, Justice Miller—ignoring *Cherokee Nation* and *Worcester*'s characterization of Native American societies as nations and disregarding the real political sovereignty of the Cherokee and other Indian nations in the late nineteenth century—described Indians as "within the geographic limits of the United States" and as "wards of the nation . . . *dependent* on the United States. . . . Dependent largely for their daily food. Dependent for their political rights."[4]

The American myth of the Indian's dependency and need for legal guardianship was fully asserted in the 1903 case *Lone Wolf* v. *Hitchcock,* which is often called the Indians' *Dred Scott* decision. The *Lone Wolf* court cited at length and with approval *Kagama's* wardship language and then pronounced a nearly complete, or plenary, power of Congress over Indian affairs, including property rights. The once firmly held legal requirement that Indian land could be taken only with Indian consent was not explicitly abandoned. However, the introduction of congressional plenary power and guardianship overwhelmed earlier federal Indian law doctrines emphasizing Native American autonomy and consent, leaving them shadows of their former selves. The *Kagama* and *Lone Wolf* opinions—opinions that expressed the turn-of-the-century philosophy driving American expansion—set the tone for much federal Indian policy in the twentieth century. The reasoning in these opinions was derived from neither the Constitution's Indian commerce clause nor treaties with Indian nations but instead from "blithe [assumptions of] the existence of federal authority . . . using rhetoric reminiscent of the white man's burden analysis . . . rhetoric of colonial expansion rather than the rhetoric of constitutional discourse."[5]

What, then, of *Worcester* and its doctrine? John Marshall wrote that Indian nations possess inherent sovereignty. Marshall's declaration that Indian nations were "distinct, independent political communities, retaining their original natural rights" was limited only by his conclusion that the unique relationship established by discovery limited the authority of those nations to sell their land to anyone but the discoverer.[6] *Kagama, Lone Wolf,* and the early twentieth-century cases that followed appear, however, to have made a mockery of Marshall and *Worcester* and lead one to question the status of this Indian sovereignty doctrine in the modern (post–World War II) era.

Beginning late in the 1950s, Native Americans—in part encouraged by the example of African-Americans—increased their use of litigation as a tool of redress. A survey of the legal papers filed on behalf of Indian communities shows repeated reliance by their lawyers on the principles expressed by John Marshall in *Worcester*: Indian sovereignty, federal authority in Indian affairs as a barrier to state action rather than a means of controlling Indian affairs, and the requirement of Indian consent to the extinguishment of territorial claims. The response of American courts to claims based on these principles has been mixed. While *Worcester* continues to be recognized as an important precedent, federal court opinions over the past thirty years still reflect ambivalence about whether to recognize Indian sovereignty and land rights and whether to diminish congressional oversight over Indian affairs. Federal courts have been particularly reluctant to support Indian sovereignty in disputes concerning non-Indians or to return wrongfully taken land. Moreover, the Supreme Court has shifted its position on sovereignty: Where it was viewed as an inherent right of the Indian, it is now described as a right explicitly bestowed on a dependent community by the government of the United States.

Several Supreme Court decisions in the post–World War II period stand out as modern landmarks that challenge the doctrine established in the 1830s Cherokee cases. In *Tee-Hit-Ton Indians* v. *U.S.* (1955), the Court took dead aim at the Indian property rights clearly spelled out in *Worcester* and in a strongly worded opinion argued that Indians occupied their aboriginal title land only at "the whim of the sovereign" and that the United States could take aboriginal land without granting compensation.[7] Ignoring *Worcester*, the Court attempted to support its conclusion by referring to the discredited conquest language in *Johnson* v. *M'Intosh*: "Every schoolboy knows that the savage tribes of this continent were deprived of their ancestral ranges by force and that . . . it was not a sale but the conquerors' will that deprived them of their land."[8] Twenty years after *Tee-Hit-Ton*, using a different approach, the Supreme Court defended the right of states to help themselves to Rosebud Sioux reservation land despite prior legal agreements. In *Rosebud Sioux Tribe* v. *Kneip, Governor of South Dakota* (1977), the Court employed a weight of history test that defeated the claims of the Sioux to treaty-guaranteed land because the state had long asserted (illegal) jurisdiction over the contested area.

No recent Supreme Court decision has more called into question the political rights of Native American governments recognized by the Marshall Court than *Oliphant* v. *Suquamish Indian Tribe* (1978). In this case, which stunned Indian communities, the Court denied Indian governments the right to assert criminal jurisdiction over non-Indians living on reservations. The Suquamish had argued that the right to punish the criminal acts of all residents—Indian and non-Indian—flowed automatically from the "tribe's retained inherent powers of government."[9] In rejecting this assertion, the justices ignored the distinct community doctrine outlined in *Worcester*, referring instead to the earlier line of decisions *(Fletcher, Johnson, Cherokee Nation)* that established the myth of Native American dependency. In *Oliphant* the Court demonstrated the limitations it was willing to place on Native American governments in their dealings with non-Indians, who in the Court's view should not have to contend with Indian justice. *Oliphant* bolstered U.S. policies of diminishing Indian sovereignty, destabilizing Indian communities, and creating dependency. By denying Indian governments the fundamental autonomy necessary to maintain order, the United States has forced those governments to become more dependent on the U.S. government for simple justice.

Another Supreme Court decision in 1978, however, prompted some court watchers to conclude that the federal judiciary had not turned its back entirely on the sovereignty rights of Indian communities. In *Santa Clara Pueblo* v. *Martinez*, the Court held that the Indian Civil Rights Act passed by Congress in 1968 did not extend U.S. jurisdiction to civil disputes between members and governments of Indian tribes. The decision was hailed for its support of Indian self-determination, including the right to articulate autonomous cultural values. Three years later, however, the justices voted in favor of the state of Montana and against the political and property rights of the Crow Tribe in an important treaty case that ignored both *Cherokee Nation* and *Worcester*'s principle that Indian nations have "the rights to lands they occupy, until that right shall be extinguished by a voluntary cession" and long-standing principles governing the interpretation of treaties signed with Indian nations.[10] It is not surprising that in denying the Crow civil jurisdiction over non-Indians, the Court cited *Oliphant*, which had established this principle in the area of criminal jurisdiction.

Less than a decade later the Supreme Court revisited the question of Native American sovereignty in a case involving the right of a Native American government to apply its criminal code to a nonmember Indian living on the reservation. In this case, *Duro* v. *Reina* (1990), the Court followed the rationale it had employed in *Oliphant* and explicitly stated that "Indian tribes lack jurisdiction over persons who are not tribe members [Indians not members of *this* tribe]."[11] The Court acknowledged that sovereignty "is the power to

enforce all laws against all who come within the sovereign's territory, whether citizens or aliens," but pointing to *Oliphant*, the majority also argued that "the tribes can no longer be described as sovereign in this sense."[12] Instead, the justices stated that the degree of
sovereignty given to Indians is only "that [which is] needed to control their own internal relations, and to preserve their own unique
customs and social order"—that is, sovereign powers that have not
been "implicitly lost by virtue of [the Indians'] dependent status."[13]

Finally and most recently, the fundamental right of Indians to
hold title to and govern their land has been challenged by the Vermont Supreme Court in a manner that would certainly have won
approval from Georgians of the 1830s. In *Vermont* v. *Elliot* (1992), in
a test of Missisquoi Abenaki aboriginal title, the Vermont court rad-
ically reformulated the extinguishment test established in the
Cherokee cases and found that the tribe had lost its occupancy
rights through "the increasing weight of history."[14] The Abenaki
have occupied their land for thousands of years. The land in question has neither been ceded to the U.S. government nor explicitly
diminished by an act of Congress. The Vermont jurists concluded,
however, that these legal formalities did not matter. In a pattern that
has become all too common, they failed to make *any* reference to
*Worcester*, relying instead on the earlier *Fletcher* and *Johnson* decisions and the doctrine established in the 1955 *Tee-Hit-Ton* case to
invoke the harsh language of conquest and a self-serving description of the historical record. In determining that the Abenaki had
lost their aboriginal occupancy rights not as a result of discrete and
jointly recognized historical events but because of "the cumulative
effect of many historical events,"[15] the Vermont court knowingly
contested *Worcester*. The refusal of the U.S. Supreme Court to hear
this case on appeal opens up the possibility that state and federal
courts will adopt Vermont's approach in lieu of the long-established
standards of Indian consent for extinguishment of title explicitly
stated in the Cherokee cases. The Vermont Supreme Court test
threatens to obstruct justice for Indians and further reduce their
autonomy. Without a legal standard that requires that extinguishment "spring full blown from a single telling event," arbitrary justice will be encouraged. Courts will be permitted to reconstruct historical events, using speculation and political bias to prove
extinguishment. The Vermont test, if employed widely, could have
a chilling effect on Indian communities, which will be understand-

ably concerned about the possibility of losing their aboriginal rights through litigation. The use of the "increasing weight of history" test raises the question of why a human right as fundamental as the guarantee of aboriginal land is subject to a vague legal test, lacking in clear guidelines, that allows extinguishment of aboriginal rights to occur at the whim of the sovereign.

## CONCLUSION

In the same year the Vermont Supreme Court dismissed Abenaki aboriginal occupancy rights, the High Court of Australia handed down a landmark opinion endorsing the rights of indigenous peoples. Specifically rejecting the use of legal theories from the colonial era, the high court justices argued that Australia's legal treatment of indigenous people should not "be frozen in an age of racial discrimination" and should accord with international human rights.[16] It is ironic that Australia's highest court, long influenced by colonialist jurisprudence, should confront this aspect of its past at a time when American courts are demonstrating reluctance to do the same.

That federal Indian law today is deeply flawed cannot be questioned. To a considerable extent the *Cherokee Nation* and *Worcester* decisions are to blame. The equivocating language of each decision—in particular, the assertion of an undefined ward-guardian relationship, the denial of *foreign* nation status, and the declaration of federal authority over Indian affairs—has left much room for judicial interpretation, and jurists, particularly in the *Kagama–Lone Wolf* era, did not hesitate to adapt the principles of the Cherokee cases in ways that would permit the final dispossession of Indians from their land. As a result, twentieth-century federal Indian law embraces two contradictory doctrines and contains two levels of legality. One strand of doctrine recognizes Native Americans as autonomous "domestic, dependent nations" and has established that the United States, in its dealings with Indian sovereignties, must employ legal standards of regularity, calculability, and due process—standards of fairness consistent with liberal-constitutional legal principles. Influenced by *Cherokee Nation* and *Worcester*, courts have pronounced tribes to be sovereign and have established legal rules insisting that unclear treaty language be interpreted in favor of the Indian signatories, demanding that congressional treaty abrogation be based on explicit choice and full notice, and guaranteeing compensation for the extinguishment of Indian title.[17]

However, a second line of cases supports the plenary power of the U.S. Congress as guardian over its Indian "wards." Federal courts have argued that the relationship of the federal government and Native Americans is exceptional and therefore exempt from ordinary constitutional standards and procedures. On the basis of the twin pillars of plenary power and the political question doctrine—the one granting Congress nearly absolute power over Indian affairs and the other exempting the uses of that power from the scrutiny of the courts—Indian affairs have been conducted within an extraconstitutional framework. In addition, by manipulating the ward-guardian concept introduced in *Cherokee Nation*, the American government has developed a trustee authority of sweeping dimensions over "its Indian wards," a power used to buttress the exceptional nature of federal power over Native Americans.[18]

Within this extraconstitutional framework, the most fundamental choices Congress and the executive have made over the years in regard to the rights and resources of Indian people have been exempt from external standards and immune from judicial review. Whether the political choices made entailed the protection or expropriation of Indian land, whether they entailed the forcible relocation of entire tribes or the restitution of land lawlessly taken, has been left entirely to the good grace or ill will of the United States, with neither redress nor remedy for Indians. Drawing on the competing doctrines within federal Indian law, the courts have condoned a system of rule in which the power of the U.S. government has been limited neither by a concept of the inherent rights of Indians nor by the imposition of constitutional standards or institutional restraints.

The existence of this contradiction hinders the ability of federal Indian law to be fair and just. It poses the question of why such a deeply flawed body of law can exist unchallenged today and why the exceptionalism of federal Indian law is accepted by American courts and the American people. It is difficult to determine why United States–Indian relations continue to be governed by doctrines of law that have long been rejected as unacceptable and invalid in other areas. The Supreme Court's decision in *Lone Wolf* was reached at the same time as the Court's "separate but equal" decision in *Plessy* v. *Ferguson* (1896). Yet while *Plessy* has been denounced and the principles underlying it have been rejected as reflecting unabashed racism and intolerance, *Lone Wolf* continues to be cited as a precedent, its underlying principles still unquestioned by the courts. While the law governing relations between other minorities and the American government has changed dramatically, Native Americans are still subject to legal principles that are untenable in the light of modern commitments to equality and the principles of human rights.

It would be easy to dismiss *Worcester* as important in its time but largely ineffective in protecting Indian rights over the course of history. Such a judgment is inaccurate, however, because it fails to recognize the complex nature of Native American–United States legal history. *Worcester* has been both a lifeline and a hollow hope. It has been a blessed offering both in the 1830s and today—an official federal judicial statement favoring Indian sovereignty and procedural rights. Although it failed to protect the Cherokee people, *Worcester* has been a bulwark for other Indian governments in more circumscribed matters of internal sovereignty and treaty rights. It has, however, also been a curse whose indefinite language haunts us. The Marshall Court refused to acknowledge Native American governments as full partners in the Western community of nations, leaving generations of jurists a malleable text that can be easily interpreted to the advantage of the United States. The Court's decision must be praised for providing a disenfranchised and dominated people something better than the language of conquest and wardship and must be condemned for betraying Native American communities.

It is significant that Indian communities have relied on the law and have articulated their grievances in terms of rights thought to be promised or owed by law. That the United States has largely betrayed Native Americans should not detract from the Cherokee's faith in the power of law or the possibility that the United States might still, like Australia, begin to decolonize its federal Indian law in the twenty-first century.

# Appendix I:
# The State v. George Tassels, 1 Dud. 229 (1830): Indictment for Murder

This was an indictment against the prisoner, a native Cherokee Indian, for the murder of another native Cherokee Indian, within the territory in the occupancy of the Cherokee tribe of Indians. The indictment has been found under a statute of this State, passed in the year 1829, for extending the laws of this State over the Cherokee country and for the purpose of giving the Superior Courts of certain counties jurisdiction of offenses committed in the said Cherokee territory, annexes the whole of said territory to certain counties of the State bordering on the same. A part of said territory was attached to the county of Hall, and it was in the part so attached, that the offense described in the indictment was charged to have been committed. To this indictment a plea to the jurisdiction of the court was filed, and the judge presiding in Hall county has reserved the question for the opinion of the judges in convention.

*Underwood*, who was counsel for defendant, contended in support of the plea, that the act of 1829, of the State of Georgia, extending the criminal jurisdiction of the State over the Cherokee country was unconstitutional, and therefore void. That by various treaties negotiated between the United States and the Cherokee Indians, beginning with the treaty of Hopewell, and ending with the year 1819, the Cherokee *nation* had been treated with, and considered an independent sovereign State, and therefore could not be subjected to the laws of a State—that in those several treaties the right of self-government had been expressly recognized and distinctly maintained by the Cherokee tribe or nation—that extending the criminal jurisdiction of the laws of Georgia over the Cherokee nation, was an infringement of the right of self-government secured to the Cherokee Indians by the treaties with the United States, which treaties were by the constitution of the United

States, declared to be the supreme law of the land. The constitution declares all treaties made, or to be made, the supreme law of the land. The treaty of Hopewell is of anterior date to the constitution, and is therefore expressly recognized by it, and consequently entitled to more weight in the decision of this question. That treaty contains an article acknowledging the right to declare war against the United States, which by counsel was relied upon as unequivocal evidence that the United States acknowledged the Cherokee Indians to be a sovereign, foreign State, possessing at least the sovereign attribute of declaring war.

Mr. *Trippe,* solicitor general of the western circuit, in reply, cited Kent's Commentaries, vol. 3. to show that Indian tribes had been considered inferior, dependent, and in a state of pupilage to the whites. He placed much stress upon that part of the articles of cession and agreement of 1802, between the State of Georgia and the United States, by which the United States relinquishes to the State of Georgia all her rights to the land lying east of the tract ceded by the State of Georgia to the United States. He denied the inference drawn by adverse counsel from the article in the treaty of Hopewell, which regulates the manner in which future wars should be commenced between the two people.—And he contended that the treaties were void, because the general government had no right to treat with Indians within the limits of the State, but upon the single subject of commerce, that being the only power granted them in the constitution.

*By the Convention of Judges.* This is a very grave and important question, which probably never would have been submitted to judicial investigation, but for the political, party and fanatical feeling excited during the last session of Congress. When the Indians attending at Washington last winter, and their advocates, discovered that the decision of the two houses would be unfavorable to them, the idea of bringing the question before the Supreme Court was suggested and eagerly seized upon by the deputation of the Cherokees.

In consequence of that determination, it is presumed that the plea now under consideration has been interposed. The manner however in which this plea has been interposed ought not, and it is presumed will have no influence upon its decision. The relations which have existed between the Indian tribes of the American continent and the different European nations who have established colonies in America, and with the colonies themselves, are to be collected from the histories and public acts of those nations, and for the space of about two hundred years. During that time, many changes of public opinion and of public conduct towards the Indian tribes have taken place; which changes are strongly marked in the records and proceedings of the different European nations who had colonial establishments in America. Those changes have, however, introduced some uncertainty as to the actual relations which ought to exist, and do actually exist, between the governments formed by European descendants and the aboriginal tribes. But the conduct of the crown of Great Britain to the Indian tribes has been less variant. The relation between this State and the Cherokee Indians depends upon the principles established by England towards the Indian tribes occupying that part of North America which that power colonized. Whatever right Great Britain possessed over the Indian tribes, is vested in the State of Georgia, and may be rightfully exercised. It is not the duty, nor is it the intention of this convention to enter into a vindication of the rights exercised by the British Crown over the Indian tribes; but if the question is considered open to investigation, no doubt is entertained that the policy adopted by the British Crown towards the Indian tribes might be vindicated by reason, sound morality and religion. But this whole question is ably elucidated in the decision of the Supreme Court, in the case of Johnson *v.* McIntosh, 8 Wheat. Repts. 543. part of which, this convention will transcribe in this decision. After stating that discovery gave to the discovering nation an exclusive right to the country discovered, as between them and other European nations, the decision proceeds—"Those relations which were to exist between the discoverer and the natives were to be regulated by themselves. The right thus acquired being exclusive, no other power could interpose between them. In the establishment of these relations, the rights of the original inhabitants were in no instance entirely disregarded, but were necessarily to a considerable extent impaired. They were admitted to be the rightful occupants of the soil; with a legal as well as just claim to retain possession of it, and to use it according to their own discretion; but their rights to complete sovereignty as independent nations were necessarily diminished, and their power to dispose of the soil to whomsoever they pleased, was denied by the original fundamental principle, that discovery gave exclusive title to those who made it. While the different nations of Europe respected the right of the natives as occupants, they asserted and claimed the ultimate dominion in themselves, and claimed and exercised as a consequence of this ultimate dominion, a power to grant the soil, while yet in possession of the natives. These grants have been considered by all, to convey a title to the grantees, subject only to the Indian right of occupancy. The history of America from its discovery to the present day, proves, we think, the universal recognition of these principles."

After giving the history of various grants by Great Britain, France and Spain, to lands in the occupancy of Indian tribes, it adds, "Thus all the nations of Europe, who have acquired territory in America, have asserted in themselves, and have recognized in others, the exclusive right of the discoverer to appropriate the lands occupied by the Indians." Have the American States rejected or adopted this principle? The decision then proceeds to show that the United States have adopted the principle, and acted upon it as far as they have acted. The opinion adds "The United States then have unequivocally assented to that great and broad rule, by which its civilized inhabitants now hold this country. They hold and assert in themselves the title by which it was acquired. They maintain, as all others have maintained, that discovery gave an exclusive right to extinguish the Indian title to occupancy, either by purchase or by conquest, and gave also a right to such a degree of sovereignty as the people would allow them to exercise." Again, on page 591, the decision proceeds,—"However extravagant the pretension of converting the discovery of an inhabited country into conquest may appear; if the principle has been asserted in the first instance, and afterwards sustained; if a country has been held and acquired under it; if the property of the great mass of the community originates in it, it becomes the law of the land, and cannot be questioned. The Indian inhabitants are to be considered merely as occupants, to be protected, indeed, while in peace, in the possession of their lands, but to be deemed incapable of transferring the absolute title to others. However this restriction may be opposed to natural right and to the usages of civilized nations, yet if it be indispensable to that system under which the country has been settled, and be adapted to the actual condition of the two people, it may perhaps be supported by reason, and certainly cannot be rejected by courts of justice. This question is not new to this court. The case of Fletcher *v.* Peck, 5 Cranch. 87, grew out of a sale made by the State of Georgia, of a large tract of country within the limits of that State, the grant of which was afterwards resumed. The action was brought by a subpurchaser on the contract of sale, and one of the covenants in the deed was, that the State of Georgia was at the time of sale, seized in fee of the premises. The real question presented by the issue was, whether the seizin in fee was in the State of Georgia or in the United States. After stating that this controversy between the several States had been compromised, the court thought it necessary to notice the Indian title, which, although entitled to the respect of all courts until it should be legitimately extinguished, was declared not to be such as to be absolutely repugnant to a seizin in fee in the State."

In addition to the preceding authorities, tending to show that the Indian tribes found in America, when it was discovered by the Europeans, were not, and could not be considered sovereign States, two other facts resulting from the legislation of the United States, will be brought into view.—1st. The Constitution of the United States gives to Congress power to regulate commerce with foreign nations, among the several States, and with the Indian tribes. In exercising the first part of this grant, Congress has prescribed rules and regulations, with which foreigners must comply when they come to the ports and are within the jurisdiction of the United States. All sovereign States have exercised the same power in the same way. But when Congress exercises the latter power, viz., the power of regulating trade with the Indian tribes, the law directs how the citizens of the United States shall conduct towards the Indians, and how the Indians shall behave to them. Whence this difference of conduct under the same grant of power? Because the subjects of European kingdoms, who come into American ports to trade, are component parts of sovereign and independent States, and the Indian, whose trade is so differently regulated, are members of communities that are not sovereign States.

2d. The Constitution of the United States gives to Congress the right of declaring war. Presidents Washington, Jefferson, Madison and Monroe, each waged war with Indian tribes; yet the statute book of the United States contains not a single declaration against an Indian tribe. Is it conceivable that the two houses of Congress would have silently acquiesced in the usurpation of their rights by the executive department, if the Indian tribes had been supposed to be the proper objects of a declaration of war? They must have been judged improper objects of declaration of war, only because they were held not to be sovereign States. Indeed it is difficult to conceive how any person, who has a definite idea of what constitutes a sovereign State, can have come to the conclusion that the *Cherokee Nation* is a sovereign and independent State. By the cases of Johnson *v.* M'Intosh, and Fletcher *v.* Peck, it has been determined by the Supreme Court of the United States, that no title to land can be derived from them immediately to an individual, and that a State is seized in fee of all lands within its chartered limits, notwithstanding the land may be in the occupancy of the Indians, and that such grants are good and valid, and cannot be questioned in courts of law. Counsel in support of the plea to the jurisdiction, admitted that the Cherokee Indians could not alien or transfer their lands to any but the State of Georgia or to the United States for her use, but seemed to suppose this limitation of their sovereignty was the result of treaty stipulations. This is a mistake. No treaty can be found, in which any Indian tribe has agreed that another government should be authorized to alien and transfer its territory. The decision, that the State of Georgia was seized in fee of the Yazoo lands, was not the result of any treaty, but the legal consequence of the right acquired by the European nations, upon their first discovery of any port of the American continent. Vattel, p. 101 says, "We do not therefore deviate from the views of nature, in confining the Indians within narrower limits. However, we cannot help praising the moderation of the English Puritans, who first settled in New England, who, notwithstanding their being furnished by a charter from their sovereign, purchased of the Indians the land of which they intended to take possession. This laudable example was followed by William Penn and the colony of Quakers that he conducted to Pennsylvania." From this quotation, it is manifest that Vattel held that they had a legal right to the land within their charter, without any purchase from the Indians. Other passages from the same author support the same doctrine. The State of New York, as late as the year 1822, vested in their courts exclusive criminal jurisdiction of all offenses committed by Indians within their reservations; other States have followed the example in a greater or less degree, and every thing has gone on quietly; but so soon as the State of Georgia pursues the same course, a hue and cry is raised against her, and a lawyer residing near 1000 miles from her borders has been employed to controvert her rights and obstruct her laws, and who has not been ashamed to say that he has been able to find no authority which justifies a denial to the *Cherokee Nation* of the right of a *sovereign, independent State.* Yet by the decision of the Supreme Court, which cannot be unknown to that gentleman, every acre of land in the occupancy of his *sovereign, independent Cherokee Nation,* is vested in fee in the State of Georgia. It is presumed to be the *first sovereign independent State* which did not hold an acre of land in fee, but which was admitted to hold every acre of land only by occupancy, while the title in fee was held by a foreign sovereign State. The Convention, from the view which authorities previously presented furnish, can discover no legal obstacle to the extension of the laws over the territory now in the possession of the Cherokee Indians. If any obstacle to that extension exist, it must be sought for in those treaties which have been negotiated between the Cherokee Indians and the United States. But here a preliminary question is presented. Are the Indian tribes within the limits of the United States, legal objects of the treaty making power? It has been shown in the preceding part of this decision, that they have not been considered legal objects of a declaration of war. It has also been shown that by all the departments of the government, they have not been treated as a sovereign, independent State, in the regulation of its commerce. Can any further evidence be required, that the Indian tribes are not the constitutional objects of the treaty making power? It is presumed not. It seems to be self-evident that communities which have been determined not to be objects of a declaration of war, cannot be the objects of the treaty making power. But it may be answered, that the President and Senate have determined that the Indian tribes are the proper objects of the treaty making power, and that treaties have actually been made with them. This is admitted. But it may be safely contended that a construction put by the President and Senate on that part of the Constitution, which grants the treaty making power, is not entitled to as much weight as a construction placed upon other parts of the Constitution by all the departments of the government, entirely inconsistent with that placed upon the treaty making power, by only two of the departments which had concurred in that construction.

But for the purpose of investigating the subject more fully, let it be for the present taken for granted, that the Indian tribes are the proper objects of the treaty making powers. The rights and the relations of those tribes had been unalterably fixed long before the treaty making power created by the

Constitution of the United States existed, and it was not competent for that power, when rightfully exerted, to alter or change those rights and relations. The rights of the Indians to the soil upon which they lived, was that of occupancy only, the fee being vested in the State of Georgia. Any attempt to change the right of occupancy into a fee, would have invaded the seizin in fee declared to be vested in Georgia by the Supreme Court of the United States, and would have been null and void. Again, the relations existing between the Cherokee Indians and the State of Georgia were those of pupilage. No treaty between the United States and the Cherokees could change that relation, could confer upon them the power of independent self-government. If there are any clauses in any of the compacts between the United States and the Cherokee Indians (miscalled treaties) which give to those Indians the right of independent self-government, they are simply void, and cannot, and ought not to be permitted to throw any obstacle in the way of the operation of the act of Georgia, extending jurisdiction over the country in the occupancy of the Cherokee Indians. But it may be urged, that the State of Georgia having neglected for about fifty years to exercise this jurisdiction over the Cherokee Indians, is barred by the lapse of time, from exercising it now. It might be deemed a sufficient reply to this objection to cite the maxim "nullum tempus," which has been determined by the courts of this State, and are as far as is known to this Convention, by all the States to apply to the State governments, with the same force as it applied to the British King. But this Convention will not rest the reply upon this maxim, because a more intelligible and satisfactory reason can be readily given. When America was first discovered, as has been shown in the decision of Johnson *v.* M'Intosh, discovery was considered equivalent to conquest. It became therefore the duty of the discovering, or conquering nation, to make some provision for the aborigines, who were a savage race, and of imbecile intellect. In ordinary conquest, one of two modes was adopted. Either the conquered people were amalgamated with their vanquishers, and became one people; or they were governed as a separate but dependent State. The habits, manners, and imbecile intellect of the Indians, opposed impracticable barriers to either of these modes of procedure. They could neither sink into the common mass of their discoverer or conquerors, or be governed as a separate dependent people. They were judged incapable of complying with the obligations which the laws of civilized society imposed, or of being subjected to any code of laws which could be sanctioned by any christian community. Humanity therefore required that they should be permitted to live according to their customs and manners; and that they should be protected in their existence, under these customs and usages, as long as they chose to adhere to them. But the Cherokees now say, they have advanced in civilization, and have formed for themselves a regular government. Admit the fact, they are there in a situation to be brought under the influence of the laws of a civilized State—of the State of Georgia. The obstacle which induced the State of Georgia to forbear the exercise of the rights which Great Britain, as the discovering nation had authority to exercise over them, and which, vested in Georgia, no longer exists, if the Cherokees or their counsel are to be believed. The State of Georgia is imperiously called upon to exercise its legitimate powers over the Cherokee territory. Indeed, it seems strange that an objection should now be made to that jurisdiction. That a government should be seized in fee of a territory, and yet have no jurisdiction over that country, is an anomaly in the science of jurisprudence; but it may be contended that, although the State of Georgia may have the jurisdiction over the Cherokee territory, yet it has no right to exercise jurisdiction over the persons of the Cherokee Indians who reside upon the territory of which the State of Georgia is seized in fee. Such distinction would present a more strange anomaly, than that of a government having no jurisdiction over territory of which it was seized in fee. This convention holds it to be well established, that where a sovereign state is seized in fee of territory, it has exclusive jurisdiction over that territory, not only on the surface and every thing that is to be found in that surface, but as Sir William Blackstone defines, a title in fee simple to lands, that it extends not only over the surface, but *"usque ad coelum"* & c. Now the right of the tenant in fee could not be less extensive than that of the *power* granting the fee. The seizin in fee, therefore, vests not only the surface, but the bowels of the earth, and through the air about the earth, as far as the air can be appropriated to the use of man, or even *"usque ad colem"* as the maxim has it. If seizin in fee vests in the tenant not only the surface, but extends to the centre downwards, and to heaven upwards, what, this convention would respectfully inquire, is to limit the right of jurisdiction?

In conclusion, it may be proper to notice some of the arguments and positions assumed by counsel in support of the plea. It was contended that the article in the treaty of Hopewell which required the Indians, in case of real or supposed wrongs, to demand satisfaction for the injury, and if it was refused to give notice of intention to make war. This was considered by counsel as unequivocal evidence of the recognition by the United States of the Cherokee Indians as a sovereign State. It does not appear so to this convention. The Indian tribes in North America were as ferocious as barbarous. They had been immemorially in the habit of making secret and bloody attacks upon the white settlements. These attacks usually struck the white settlers with panic terror by the secrecy and rapidity with which they were perpetrated. To guard against a mischief so terrific and appalling, the treaty imposes upon the Cherokee Indians the obligation of giving notice of their intention to make their bloody incursions into the white settlements. It was a salutary restriction which was the origin of, at least, one approach towards the habits and usages of civilized man. To have omitted the restriction for fear of the admission which it is contended is given to the Cherokee Indians of making war upon the United States, would have been weak. For it was matter of universal notoriety, that the various Indian tribes within the United States were immemorially in the habit of making war in the manner above described, and the restriction was a salutary one, and has had the desired effect. Counsel for the Cherokee Indians contended that by the articles of treaty and cession between the State of Georgia and the United States, the former had given the latter a right to hold treaties with the Cherokee Indians, and that the State of Georgia was bound to abstain from all efforts to extinguish the Indian right to lands within her own limits. This convention conceives both positions to be erroneous.

1st. The articles of treaty and cession conferred no right upon the United States to hold treaties with the Cherokee Indians. Those articles impose upon the United States the duty of extinguishing the Indian title, but confer no political power on the federal government. If there be such a thing as a political axiom it is certainly one that the federal government can derive no political power from a compact with an individual state. That government had at the time of entering into those articles the right of holding treaties with the Indians or it had not. If it be true, as intimated by counsel, that the title to Indian lands could be extinguished only by treaty, and the federal government had no right to make such treaties, then the federal government in entering into the articles of treaty and cession took upon itself an impossible condition. But it is not true that the Indian title cannot be extinguished but by treaty. That title can be extinguished by bargain and sale or by deed as well without the form of a treaty as with it. Indian treaties for extinguishing their right to their lands are in fact, though not in form, nothing but contracts for the purchase and sale of Indian lands. But secondly, the state of Georgia in imposing the obligation upon the United States to extinguish the Indian title to lands within her limits did not relinquish any right she possessed of extinguishing that right herself. Having given a valuable consideration to another power to induce that power to assume the obligation of extinguishing the Indian title, it was natural that she should rely upon the good faith of that power in discharging its engagements, and should cease for a reasonable time any directs efforts to effect the same object. But if the contracting power should act with bad faith or should from any other cause disappoint the just expectations of the state; Georgia might rightfully resume her suspended right of extinguishing the Indian title, and demand payment from the United States of whatever sum the extinguishment cost her. It may be proper before closing this opinion to state, that the United States in their practice under the constitution, consider all Indian tribes within or without the United States improper objects of a declaration of war. The Seminole Indians were resident in Florida, then a province of Spain; yet the President prosecuted a war against them, without a declaration of war. The wants of that war produced a deep sensation in the nation, and were discussed with animation in the two houses of congress; yet during the whole of that discussion, no intimation was thrown out on any side of either house calling in question the right of the President to prosecute a war with an Indian tribe, even resident out of the limits of the United States. This convention deems it a waste of time to pursue this examination. It has satisfied itself, and it is hoped the community, that independent of the provision of the state constitution claiming jurisdiction over its chartered limits, that the State of Georgia had the right in the year 1829, to extend its laws over the territory inhabited by the Cherokee Indians, and over the Indians themselves; that said act of 1829, is neither unconstitutional, nor inconsistent with the rights of the Cherokee Indians. The plea to the jurisdiction of the court submitted to this convention is therefore overruled.

# Appendix II:
# The Cherokee Nation v.
# The State of Georgia,
# 30 U.S. (5 Peters) 1 (1831)

Mr. Chief Justice Marshall delivered the opinion of the Court.

This bill is brought by the Cherokee nation, praying an injunction to restrain the state of Georgia from the execution of certain laws of that state, which, as is alleged, go directly to annihilate the Cherokee as a political society, and to seize, for the use of Georgia, the lands of the nation which have been assured to them by the United States in solemn treaties repeatedly made and still in force.

If courts were permitted to indulge their sympathies, a case better calculated to excite them can scarcely be imagined. A people once numerous, powerful, and truly independent, found by our ancestors in the quiet and uncontrolled possession of an ample domain, gradually sinking beneath our superior policy, our arts and our arms, have yielded their lands by successive treaties, each of which contains a solemn guarantee of the residue, until they retain no more of their formerly extensive territory than is deemed necessary to their comfortable subsistence. To preserve this remnant, the present application is made.

Before we can look into the merits of the case, a preliminary inquiry presents itself. Has this court jurisdiction of the cause?

The third article of the constitution describes the extent of the judicial power. The second section closes an enumeration of the cases to which it is extended, with "controversies" "between a state or the citizens thereof, and foreign states, citizens, or subjects." A subsequent clause of the same section gives the supreme court original jurisdiction in all cases in which a state shall be a party. The party defendant may then unquestionably be sued in this court. May the plaintiff sue in it? Is the Cherokee nation a foreign state in the sense in which that term is used in the constitution?

The counsel for the plaintiffs have maintained the affirmative of this proposition with great earnestness and ability. So much of the argument as was intended to prove the character of the Cherokee as a state, as a distinct political society, separated from others, capable of managing its own affairs and governing itself, has, in the opinion of a majority of the judges, been completely successful. They have been uniformly treated as a state from the settlement of our country. The numerous treaties made with them by the United States recognize them as a people capable of maintaining the relations of peace and war, of being responsible in their political character for any violation of their engagements, or for any aggression committed on the citizens of the United States by any individual of their community. Laws have been enacted in the spirit of these treaties. The acts of our government plainly recognize the Cherokee nation as a state, and the courts are bound by those acts.

A question of much more difficulty remains. Do the Cherokees constitute a foreign state in the sense of the constitution?

The counsel have shown conclusively that they are not a state of the union, and have insisted that individually they are aliens, not owing allegiance to the United States. An aggregate of aliens composing a state must, they say, be a foreign state. Each individual being foreign, the whole must be foreign.

This argument is imposing, but we must examine it more closely before we yield to it. The condition of the Indians in relation to the United States is perhaps unlike that of any other two people in existence. In general, nations not owing a common allegiance are foreign to each other. The term *foreign nation* is, with strict propriety, applicable by either to the other. But the relation of the Indians to the United States is marked by peculiar and cardinal distinctions which exist no where else.

The Indian territory is admitted to compose a part of the United States. In all our maps, geographical treatises, histories, and laws, it is so considered. In all our intercourse with foreign nations, in our commercial regulations, in any attempt at intercourse between Indians and foreign nations, they are considered as within the jurisdictional limits of the United States, subject to many of those restraints which are imposed upon our own citizens. They acknowledge themselves in their treaties to be under the protection of the United States; they admit that the United States shall have the sole and exclusive right of regulating the trade with them, and managing all their affairs as they think proper; and the Cherokees in particular were allowed by the treaty of Hopewell, which preceded the constitution, "to send a deputy of their choice, whenever they think fit, to congress." Treaties were made with some tribes by the state of New York, under a then unsettled construction of the confederation, by which they ceded all their lands to that state, taking back a limited grant to themselves, in which they admit their dependence.

Though the Indians are acknowledged to have an unquestionable, and, heretofore, unquestioned right to the lands they occupy, until that right shall be extinguished by a voluntary cession to our government; yet it may well be doubted whether those tribes which reside within the acknowledged boundaries of the United States can, with strict accuracy, be denominated foreign nations. They may, more correctly, perhaps, be denominated domestic dependent nations. They occupy a territory to which we assert a title independent of their will, which must take effect in point of possession when their right of possession ceases. Meanwhile they are in a state of pupilage. Their relation to the United States resembles that of a ward to his guardian.

They look to our government for protection; rely upon its kindness and its power; appeal to it for relief to their wants; and address the president as their great father. They and their country are considered by foreign nations, as well as by ourselves, as being so completely under the sovereignty and dominion of the United States, that any attempt to acquire their lands, or to form a political connexion with them, would be considered by all as an invasion of our territory, and an act of hostility.

These considerations go far to support the opinion, that the framers of our constitution had not the Indian tribes in view, when they opened the courts of the union to controversies between a state or the citizens thereof, and foreign states.

In considering this subject, the habits and usages of the Indians, in their intercourse with their white neighbours, ought not to be entirely disregarded. At the time the constitution was framed, the idea of appealing to an American court of justice for an assertion of right or a redress of wrong, had perhaps never entered the mind of an Indian or of his tribe. Their appeal was to the tomahawk, or to the government. This was well understood by the statesmen who framed the constitution of the United States, and might furnish some reason for omitting to enumerate them among the parties who might sue in the courts of the union. Be this as it may, the peculiar relations between the United States and the Indians occupying our territory are such, that we should feel much difficulty in considering them as designated by the term *foreign state*, were there no other part of the constitution which might shed light on the meaning of these words. But we think that in construing them, considerable aid is furnished by that clause in the eighth section of the third article; which empowers congress to "regulate commerce with foreign nations, and among the several states, and with the Indian tribes."

In this clause they are as clearly contradistinguished by a name appropriate to themselves, from foreign nations, as from the several states composing the union. They are designated by a distinct appellation; and as this appellation can be applied to neither of the others, neither can the appellation distinguishing either of the others be in fair construction applied to them. The objects, to which the power of regulating commerce might be directed, are divided into three distinct classes—foreign nations, the several states, and Indian tribes. When forming this article, the convention considered them as entirely distinct. We cannot assume that the distinction was lost in framing a subsequent article, unless there be something in its language to authorize the assumption.

The counsel for the plaintiffs contend that the words "Indian tribes" were introduced into the article, empowering congress to regulate commerce, for the purpose of removing those doubts in which the management of Indian affairs was involved by the language of the ninth article of the confederation. Intending to give the whole power of managing those affairs to the government about to be instituted, the convention conferred it explicitly; and omitted those qualifications which embarrassed the exercise of it as granted in the confederation. This may be admitted without weakening the construction which has been intimated. Had the Indian tribes been foreign nations, in the view of the convention; this exclusive power of regulating intercourse with them might have been, and most probably would have been, specifically given, in language indicating that idea, not in language contradistinguishing them from foreign nations. Congress might have been empowered "to regulate commerce with foreign nations, including the Indian tribes, and among the several states." This language would have suggested itself to statesmen who considered the Indian tribes as foreign nations, and were yet desirous of mentioning them particularly.

It has been also said, that the same words have not necessarily the same meaning attached to them when found in different parts of the same instrument: their meaning is controlled by the context. This is undoubtably true. In common language the same word has various meanings, and the peculiar sense in which it is used in any sentence is to be determined by the context. This may not be equally true with respect to proper names. *Foreign nations* is a general term, the application of which to Indian tribes, when used in the American constitution, is at best extremely questionable. In one article in which a power is given to be exercised in regard to foreign nations generally, and to the Indian tribes particularly, they are mentioned as separate in terms clearly contradistinguishing them from each other. We perceive plainly that the constitution in this article does not comprehend Indian tribes in the general term "foreign nations;" not we presume because a tribe may not be a nation, but because it is not foreign to the United States. When, afterwards, the term "foreign state" is introduced, we cannot impute to the convention the intention to desert its former meaning, and to comprehend Indian tribes within it, unless the context force that construction on us. We find nothing in the context, and nothing in the subject of the article, which leads to it.

The court has bestowed its best attention on this question, and, after mature deliberation, the majority is of opinion that an Indian tribe or nation within the United States is not a foreign state in the sense of the constitution, and cannot maintain an action in the courts of the United States.

A serious additional objection exists to the jurisdiction of the court. Is the matter of the bill the proper subject for judicial inquiry and decision? It seeks to restrain a state from the forcible exercise of legislative power over a neighbouring people, asserting their independence; their right to which the state denies. On several of the matters alleged in the bill, for example on the laws making it criminal to exercise the usual powers of self government in their own country by the Cherokee nation, this court cannot interpose; at least in the form in which those matters are presented.

That part of the bill which respects the land occupied by the Indians, and prays the aid of the court to protect their possession, may be more doubtful. The mere question of right might perhaps be decided by this court in a proper case with proper parties. But the court is asked to do more than decide on the title. The bill requires us to control the legislature of Georgia, and to restrain the exertion of its physical force. The propriety of such an interposition by the court may be well questioned. It savours too much of the exercise of political power to be within the proper province of the judicial department. But the opinion on the point respecting parties makes it unnecessary to decide this question.

If it be true that the Cherokee nation have rights, this is not the tribunal in which those rights are to be asserted. If it be true that wrongs have been inflicted, and that still greater are to be apprehended, this is not the tribunal which can redress the past or prevent the future.

The motion for an injunction is denied.

# Appendix III:
# Samuel A. Worcester v. The State of Georgia, 31 U.S. (6 Pet.) 515 (1832)

Mr. Chief Justice Marshall delivered the opinion of the Court.

This cause, in every point of view in which it can be placed, is of the deepest interest.

The defendant is a state, a member of the union, which has exercised the powers of government over a people who deny its jurisdiction, and are under the protection of the United States.

The plaintiff is a citizen of the state of Vermont, condemned to hard labour for four years in the penitentiary of Georgia; under colour of an act which he alleged to be repugnant to the constitution, laws, and treaties of the United States.

The legislative power of a state, the controlling power of the constitution and laws of the United States, the rights, if they have any, the political existence of a once numerous and powerful people, the personal liberty of a citizen, are all involved in the subject now to be considered.

It behoves this court, in every case, more especially in this, to examine into its jurisdiction with scrutinizing eyes; before it proceeds to the exercise of a power which is controverted.

The first step in the performance of this duty is the inquiry whether the record is properly before the court. . . .

It is, then, we think, too clear for controversy, that the act of congress, by which this court is constituted, has given it the power, and of course imposed on it the duty, of exercising jurisdiction in this case. This duty, however unpleasant, cannot be avoided. Those who fill the judicial department have no discretion in selecting the subjects to be brought before them. We must examine the defense set up in this plea. We must inquire and decide whether the act of the legislature of Georgia, under which the plaintiff in error has been prosecuted and condemned, be consistent with, or repugnant to, the constitution, laws and treaties of the United States.

It has been said at the bar, that the acts of the legislature of Georgia seize on the whole Cherokee country, parcel it out among the neighbouring counties of the state, extend her code over the whole country, abolish its institutions and its laws, and annihilate its political existence.

If this be the general effect of the system, let us inquire into the effect of the particular statute and section on which the indictment is founded.

It enacts that "all white persons, residing within the limits of the Cherokee nation on the 1st day of March next, or at any time thereafter, with out a license or permit from his excellency the governor, or from such agent as his excellency the governor shall authorise to grant such permit or license, and who shall not have taken an oath hereinafter required, shall be guilty of a high misdemeanour, and, upon conviction thereof, shall be punished by confinement to the penitentiary, at hard labour, for a term not less than four years."

The eleventh section authorises the governor, should he deem it necessary for . . . the enforcement of the laws in force within the Cherokee nation, to raise and organize a guard, & c.

The thirteenth section enacts, "that the said guard or any member of them, shall be, and they are hereby authorised and empowered to arrest any person legally charged with or detected in a violation of the laws of this state, and to convey, as soon as practicable, the person so arrested, before a justice of the peace, judge of superior, or justice of inferior court of this state, to be dealt with according to law."

The extra-territorial power of every legislature being limited in its action, to its own citizens or subjects, the very passage of this act is an assertion of jurisdiction over the Cherokee nation, and of the rights and powers consequent on jurisdiction.

The first step, then, in the inquiry, which the constitution and laws impose on this court, is an examination of the rightfulness of this claim.

America, separated from Europe by a wide ocean, was inhabited by a distinct people, divided into separate nations, independent of each other and of the rest of the world, having institutions of their own, and governing themselves by their own laws. It is difficult to comprehend the proposition, that the inhabitants of either quarter of the globe could have rightful original claims of dominion over the inhabitants of the other, or over the lands they occupied; or that the discovery of either by the other should give the discoverer rights in the country discovered, which annulled the pre-existing rights of its ancient possessors.

After lying concealed for a series of ages, the enterprise of Europe, guided by nautical science, conducted some of her adventurous sons into this western world. They found it in possession of a people who had made small progress in agriculture or manufactures, and whose general employment was war, hunting, and fishing.

Did these adventurers, by sailing along the coast, and occasionally landing on it, acquire for the several governments to whom they belonged, or by whom they were commissioned, a rightful property in the soil, from the Atlantic to the Pacific; or rightful dominion over the numerous people who occupied it? Or has nature, or the great Creator of all things, conferred these rights over hunters and fishermen, on agriculturists and manufacturers?

But power, war, conquest, give rights, which, after possession, are conceded by the world; and which can never be controverted by those on whom they descend. We proceed, then, to the actual state of things, having glanced at their origin; because holding it in our recollection might shed some light on existing pretensions.

The great maritime powers of Europe discovered and visited different parts of this continent at nearly the same time. The object was too immense for any one of them to grasp the whole; and the claimants were too powerful to submit to the exclusive or unreasonable pretensions of any single potentate. To avoid bloody conflicts, which might terminate disastrously to all, it was necessary for the nations of Europe to establish some principle which all would acknowledge, and which should decide their respective rights as between themselves. This principle, suggested by the actual state of things, was, "that discovery gave title to the government by whose subjects or by whose authority it was made, against all other European governments, which title might be consummated by possession."

This principle, acknowledged by all Europeans, because it was the interest of all to acknowledge it, gave to the nation making the discovery, as its inevitable consequence, the sole right of acquiring the soil and of making settlements on it. It was an exclusive principle which shut out the right of competition among those who had agreed to it; not one which could annul the previous rights of those who had not agreed to it. It regulated the right given by discovery among the European discoverers; but could not affect the rights of those already in possession, either as aboriginal occupants, or as occupants by virtue of a discovery made before the memory of man. It gave the exclusive right to purchase, but did not found that right on a denial of the right of the possessor to sell.

The relation between the Europeans and the natives was determined in each case by the particular government which asserted and could maintain this pre-emptive privilege in the particular place. The United States succeeded to all the claims of Great Britain, both territorial and political; but no attempt, so far as is known, has been made to enlarge them. So far as they existed merely in theory, or were in their nature only exclusive of the claims of other European nations, they still retain their original character, and remain dormant. So far as they have been practically exerted, they exist in fact, are understood by both parties, are asserted by the one, and admitted by the other.

Soon after Great Britain determined on planting colonies in America, the king granted charters to companies of his subjects who associated for the purpose of carrying the views of the crown into effect, and of enriching themselves. The first of these charters was made before possession was taken of any part of the country. They purport, generally, to convey the soil, from the Atlantic to the South Sea. This soil was occupied by numerous and warlike nations, equally willing and able to defend their possessions. The extravagant and absurd idea, that the feeble settlements made on the sea coast, or the companies under whom they were made, acquired legitimate power by them to govern the people, or occupy the lands from sea to sea, did not enter the mind of any man. They were well understood to convey the title which, according to the common law of European sovereigns respecting America, they might rightfully convey, and no more. This was the exclusive right of purchasing such lands as the natives were willing to sell. The crown could not be understood to grant what the crown did not affect to claim; nor was it so understood.

The power of making war is conferred by these charters on the colonies, but *defensive* war alone seems to have been contemplated. In the first charter to the first and second colonies, they are empowered, "for their several *defences*, to encounter, expulse, repel, and resist, all persons who shall, without license," attempt to inhabit "within the said precincts and limits of the said several colonies, or that shall enterprise or attempt at any time hereafter the least detriment or annoyance of the said several colonies or plantations."

. . . This power to repel invasion, and, upon just cause, to invade and destroy the natives, authorizes offensive as well as defensive war, but only "on just cause." The very terms imply the existence of a country to be invaded, and of an enemy who has given just cause of war.

. . . The charter to Georgia professes to be granted for the charitable purpose of enabling poor subjects to gain a comfortable subsistence by cultivating lands in the American provinces, "at present waste and desolate." It recites; "and whereas our provinces in North America have been frequently ravaged by Indian enemies, more especially that of South Carolina, which, in the late war by the neighbouring savages, was laid waste by fire and sword, and great numbers of the English inhabitants miserably massacred; and our loving subjects, who now inhabit there, by reason of the smallness of their numbers, will, in case of any new war, be exposed to the like calamities, inasmuch as their whole southern frontier continueth unsettled, and lieth open to the said savages."

These motives for planting the new colony are incompatible with the lofty ideas of granting the soil, and all its inhabitants from sea to sea. They demonstrate the truth, that these grants asserted a title against Europeans only, and were considered as blank paper so far as the rights of the natives were concerned. The power of war is given only for defense, not for conquest.

The charters contain passages showing one of their objects to be the civilization of the Indians, and their conversion to Christianity—objects to be accomplished by conciliatory conduct and good example; not by extermination.

The actual state of things, and the practice of European nations, on so much of the American continent as lies between the Mississippi and the Atlantic, explain their claims, and the charters they granted. Their pretensions unavoidably interfered with each other; though the discovery of one was admitted by all to exclude the claim of any other, the extent of that discovery was the subject of unceasing contest. Bloody conflicts arose between them, which gave importance and security to the neighbouring nations. Fierce and warlike in their character, they might be formidable enemies, or effective friends. Instead of rousing their resentments, by asserting claims to their lands, or to dominion over their persons, their alliance was sought by flattering professions, and purchased by rich presents. The English, the French, and the Spaniards, were equally competitors for their friendship and their aid. Not well acquainted with the exact meaning of words, nor supposing it to be material whether they were called the subjects, or the children of their father in Europe; lavish in professions of duty and affection, in return for the rich presents they received; so long as actual independence was untouched, and their right to self government acknowledged, they were willing to profess dependence on the power which furnished supplies of which they were in absolute need, and restrained dangerous intruders from entering their country: and this was probably the sense in which the term was understood by them.

Certain it is, that our history furnishes no example, from the first settlement of our country, or any attempt on the part of the crown to interfere with the internal affairs of the Indians, farther than to keep out the agents of foreign powers, who, as traders or otherwise, might seduce them into foreign alliances. The king purchased their lands when they were willing to sell, at a price they were willing to take; but never coerced a surrender of them. He also purchased their alliance and dependence by subsidies; but never intruded into the interior of their affairs, or interfered with their self government, so far as respected themselves only.

The general views of Great Britain, with regard to the Indians, were detailed by Mr. Stuart, superintendent of Indian affairs, in a speech delivered at Mobile, in presence of several persons of distinction, soon after the peace of 1763. Towards the conclusion he says, "lastly, I inform you that it is the king's order to all his governors and subjects, to treat Indians with justice and humanity, and to forbear all encroachments on the territories allotted to them; accordingly, all individuals are prohibited from purchasing any of your lands; but, as you know that, as your white brethren cannot feed you when you visit them unless you give them ground to plant, it is expected that you will cede lands to the king for that purpose. But, whenever you shall be pleased to surrender any of your territories to his majesty, it must be done, for the future, at a public meeting of your nation, when the governors of the provinces, or the superintendent shall be present, and obtain the consent of all your people. The boundaries of your hunting grounds will be accurately fixed, and no settlement permitted to be made upon them. As you may be assured that all treaties with your people will be faithfully kept, so it is expected that you, also, will be careful strictly to observe them."

The proclamation issued by the king of Great Britain, in 1763, soon after the ratification of the articles of peace, forbids the governors of any of the colonies to grant warrants of survey, or pass patents upon any lands whatever, which, not having been ceded to, or purchased by, us (the king), as aforesaid, are reserved to the said Indians, or any of them.

"And we do further strictly enjoin and require all persons whatever, who have, either willfully or inadvertently, seated themselves upon any lands within the countries above described, or upon any other lands which, not having been ceded to, or purchased by us, are still reserved to the said Indians, as aforesaid, forthwith to remove themselves from such settlements."

... A proclamation, issued by Governor Gage, in 1772, contains the following passage: "whereas many persons, contrary to the positive orders of the king, upon this subject, have undertaken to make settlements beyond the boundaries fixed by the treaties made with the Indian nations, which boundaries ought to serve as a barrier between the whites and the said nations; particularly on the Ouabache." The proclamation orders such persons to quit those countries without delay.

Such was the policy of Great Britain towards the Indian nations inhabiting the territory from which she excluded all other Europeans; such her claims, and such her practical exposition of the charters she had granted: she considered them as nations capable of maintaining the relations of peace and war; of governing themselves, under her protection; and she made treaties with them, the obligation of which she acknowledged.

This was the settled state of things when the war of our revolution commenced. The influence of our enemy was established; her resources enabled her to keep up that influence; and the colonists had much cause for the apprehension that the Indian nations would, as the allies of Great Britain, add their arms to hers. This, as was to be expected, became an object of great solicitude to congress. Far from advancing a claim to their lands, or asserting any right of dominion over them, congress resolved "that the securing and preserving the friendship of the Indian nations appears to be a subject of the utmost moment to these colonies."

The early journals of congress exhibit the most anxious desire to conciliate the Indian nations. Three Indian departments were established; and commissioners appointed in each, "to treat with the Indians in their respective departments, in the name and on the behalf of the United Colonies, in order to preserve peace and friendship with the said Indians, and to prevent their taking any part in the present commotions."

The most strenuous exertions were made to procure those supplies on which Indian friendships were supposed to depend; and every thing which might excite hostility was avoided.

The first treaty was made with the Delawares, in September 1778.

The language of equality in which it is drawn, evinces the temper with which the negotiation was undertaken, and the opinion which then prevailed in the United States.

"1. That all offences or acts of hostilities, by one or either of the contracting parties against the other, be mutually forgiven, and buried in the depth of oblivion, never more to be had in remembrance."

"2. That a perpetual peace and friendship shall, from henceforth, take place and subsist between the contracting parties aforesaid, through all succeeding generations: and if either of the parties are engaged in a just and necessary war, with any other nation or nations, that then each shall assist the other, in due proportion to their abilities, till their enemies are brought to reasonable terms of accommodation," & c.

"3. The third article stipulates, among other things, a free passage for the American troops through the Delaware nation; and engages that they shall be furnished with provisions and other necessaries at their value.

"4. For the better security of the peace and friendship now entered into by the contracting parties against all infractions of the same by the citizens of either party, to the prejudice of the other, neither party shall proceed to the infliction of punishments on the citizens of the other, otherwise than by securing the offender or offenders, by imprisonment, or any other competent means, till a fair and impartial trial can be had by judges or juries of both parties, as near as can be to the laws, customs and usages of the contracting parties, and natural justice," & c.

5. The fifth article regulates the trade between the contracting parties, in a manner entirely equal.

6. The sixth article is entitled to peculiar attention, as it contains a disclaimer of designs which were, at the time, ascribed to the United States, by their enemies, and from the imputation of which congress was then peculiarly anxious to free the government. It is in these words: "Whereas the

enemies of the United States have endeavoured, by every artifice in their power, to possess the Indians in general with an opinion that it is the design of the states aforesaid to extirpate the Indians, and take possession of their country: to obviate such false suggestion the United States do engage to guaranty to the aforesaid nation of Delawares, and their heirs, all their territorial rights, in the fullest and most ample manner, as it hath been bounded by former treaties, as long as the said Delaware nation shall abide by, and hold fast the chain of friendship now entered into."

The parties further agree, that other tribes, friendly to the interest of the United States, may be invited to form a state, whereof the Delaware nation shall be the heads, and have a representation in congress.

This treaty, in its language, and in its provisions, is formed, as near as may be, on the model of treaties between the crowned heads of Europe.

The sixth article shows how congress then treated the injurious calumny of cherishing designs unfriendly to the political and civil rights of the Indians.

During the war of the revolution, the Cherokees took part with the British. After its termination, the United States, though desirous of peace, did not feel its necessity so strongly as while the war continued. Their political situation being changed, they might very well think it advisable to assume a higher tone, and to impress on the Cherokees the same respect for congress which was before felt for the king of Great Britain. This may account for the language of the treaty of Hopewell. There is the more reason for supposing that the Cherokee chiefs were not very critical judges of the language, from the fact that every one makes his mark; no chief was capable of signing his name. It is probable the treaty was interpreted to them.

The treaty is introduced with the declaration, that "the commissioners plenipotentiary of the United States give peace to all the Cherokees, and receive them into favour and protection of the United States of America, on the following conditions."

When the United States gave peace, did they not also receive it? Were not both parties desirous of it? If we consult the history of the day, does it not inform us that the United States were at least as anxious to obtain it as the Cherokees? We may ask, further: did the Cherokees come to the seat of the American government to solicit peace; or, did the American commissioners go to them to obtain it? The treaty was made at Hopewell, not at New York. The word "give," then, has no real importance attached to it.

The first and second articles stipulate for the mutual restoration of prisoners, and are of course equal.

The third article acknowledges the Cherokees to be under the protection of the United States of America, and of no other power.

This stipulation is found in Indian treaties, generally. It was introduced into their treaties with Great Britain; and may probably be found in those with other European powers. Its origin may be traced to the nature of their connexion with those powers; and its true meaning is discerned in their relative situation.

The general law of European sovereigns, respecting their claims in America, limited the intercourse of Indians, in a great degree, to the particular potentate whose ultimate right of domain was acknowledged by the others. This was the general state of things in time of peace. It was sometimes changed in war. The consequence was, that their supplies were derived chiefly from that nation, and their trade confined to it. Goods, indispensable to their comfort, in the shape of presents, were received from the same hand. What was of still more importance, the strong hand of government was interposed to restrain the disorderly and licentious from intrusions into their country, from encroachments on their lands, and from those acts of violence which were often attended by reciprocal murder. The Indians perceived in this protection only what was beneficial to themselves—an engagement to punish aggressions on them. It involved, practically, no claim to their lands, no dominion over their persons. It merely bound the nation to the British crown, as a dependent ally, claiming the protection of a powerful friend and neighbour, and receiving the advantages of that protection, without involving a surrender of their national character.

This is the true meaning of the stipulation, and is undoubtedly the sense in which it was made. Neither the British government, nor the Cherokee, ever understood it otherwise.

The same stipulation entered into with the United States, is undoubtedly to be construed in the same manner. They receive the Cherokee nation into their favour and protection. The Cherokees acknowledge themselves to be under the protections of the United States, and of no other power. Protection does not imply the destruction of the protected. The manner in which this stipulation was understood by the American government, is explained by the language and acts of our first president.

The fourth article draws the boundary between the Indians and the citizens of the United States. But, in describing this boundary, the term "allotted" and the term "hunting ground" are used.

It is reasonable to suppose, that the Indians, who could not write, and most probably could not read, who certainly were not critical judges of our language, should distinguish the word "allotted" from the words "marked out." The actual subject of contract was the dividing line between the two nations; and their attention may very well be supposed to have been confined to that subject. When, in fact, they were ceding lands to the United States, and describing the extent of their cession, it may very well be supposed that they might not understand the term employed, as indicating that, instead of granting, they were receiving lands. If the term would admit of no other signification, which is not conceded, its being misunderstood is so apparent, results so necessarily from the whole transaction; that it must, we think, be taken in the sense in which it was most obviously used.

So with respect to the words "hunting grounds." Hunting was at that time the principal occupation of the Indians, and their land was more used for that purpose than for any other. It could not, however, be supposed, that any intention existed of restricting the full use of the lands they reserved.

To the United States, it could be a matter of no concern, whether their whole territory was devoted to hunting grounds, or whether an occasional village, and an occasional corn field, interrupted, and gave some variety to the scene.

The fifth article withdraws the protection of the United States from any citizen who has settled, or shall settle, on the lands allotted to the Indians, for their hunting grounds; and stipulates that, if he shall not remove within six months the Indians may punish him.

The sixth and seventh articles stipulate for the punishment of the citizens of either country, who may commit offences on or against the citizens of the other. The only inference to be drawn from them is, that the United States considered the Cherokees a nation.

The ninth article is in these words: "for the benefit and comfort of the Indians, and for the prevention of injuries or oppressions on the part of the citizens or Indians, the United States, in congress assembled, shall have the sole and exclusive right of regulating the trade with the Indians, and *managing all their affairs*, as they think proper."

To construe the expression "managing all their affairs," into a surrender of self-government, would be, we think, a perversion of their necessary meaning, and a departure from the construction which has been uniformly put on them. The great subject of the article is the Indian tribe. The influence it gave, made it desirable that congress should possess it. The commissioners brought forward the claim, with the profession that their motive was "the benefit and comfort of the Indians, and the prevention of injuries or oppressions." This may be true, as respects the regulation of their trade, and as respects the regulation of all affairs connected with their trade, but cannot be true, as respects the management of all their affairs. The most important of these, are the cession of their lands, and security against intruders on them. Is it credible, that they should have considered themselves as surrendering to the United States the right to dictate their future cessions, and the terms on which they should be made? or to compel their submission to the violence of disorderly and licentious intruders? It is equally inconceivable that they could have supposed themselves, by a phrase thus slipped into an article, on another and most interesting subject, to have divested themselves of the right of self-government on subjects not connected with trade. Such a measure could not be "for their benefit and comfort," or for "the prevention of injuries and oppression." Such a construction would be inconsistent with the spirit of this and of all subsequent treaties; especially of those articles which recognise the right of the Cherokees to declare hostilities, and to make war. It would convert a treaty of peace covertly into an act, annihilating the political existence of one of the parties. Had such a result been intended, it would have been openly avowed.

This treaty contains a few terms capable of being used in a sense which could not have been intended at the time, and which is inconsistent with the practical construction which has always been put on them; but its essential articles treat the Cherokees as a nation capable of maintaining the relations of peace and war; and ascertain the boundaries between them and the United States.

The treaty of Hopewell seems not to have established a solid peace. To accommodate the differences still existing between the state of Georgia and the Cherokee nation, the treaty of Holston was negotiated in July 1791. The existing constitution of the United States had been then adopted, and the government, having more intrinsic capacity to enforce its just claims, was perhaps less mindful of high sounding expressions, denoting superiority. We hear no more of giving peace to the Cherokees. The mutual desire of establishing permanent peace and friendship, and of removing all causes of war, is honestly avowed, and, in pursuance of this desire, the first article declared, that there shall be perpetual peace and friendship between all the citizens of the United States of America and all the individuals composing the Cherokee nation.

The second article repeats the important acknowledgement, that the Cherokee nation is under the protection of the United States of America, and of no other sovereign whosoever.

The meaning of this has been already explained. The Indian nations were, from their situation, necessarily dependent on some foreign potentate for the supply of their essential wants, and for their protection from lawless and injurious intrusions into their country. That power was naturally termed protector. They had been arranged under the protection of Great Britain: but the extinguishment of the British power in their neighbourhood, and the establishment of that of the United States in its place, led naturally to the declaration, on the part of the Cherokees, that they were under the protection of the United States, and of no other power. They assumed the relation with the United States, which had before subsisted with Great Britain.

This relation was that of a nation claiming and receiving the protection of one more powerful: not that of individuals abandoning their national character, and submitting as subjects to the laws of a master.

The third article contains a perfectly equal stipulation for the surrender of prisoners.

The fourth article declares, that "the boundary between the United States and the Cherokee nation shall be as follows: beginning" & c. We hear no more of "allotments" or of "hunting grounds." A boundary is described, between nation and nation, by mutual consent. The national character of each; the ability of each to establish this boundary, is acknowledged by the other. To preclude for ever all disputes, it is agreed that it shall be plainly marked by commissioners, to be appointed by each party; and, in order to extinguish for ever all claim of the Cherokees to the ceded lands, an additional consideration is to be paid by the United States. For this additional consideration the Cherokees release the right to the ceded land, for ever.

By the fifth article, the Cherokees allow the United States a road through their country, and the navigation of the Tennessee river. The acceptance of these cessions is an acknowledgement of the right of the Cherokees to make or withhold them.

By the sixth article, it is agreed, on the part of the Cherokees, that the United States shall have the sole and exclusive right of regulating their trade. No claim is made to the management of all their affairs. This stipulation has already been explained. The observation may be repeated, that the stipulation is itself an admission of their right to make or refuse it.

By the seventh article the United States solemnly guaranty to the Cherokee nation all their lands not hereby ceded.

The eighth article relinquishes to the Cherokees any citizens of the United States who may settle on their lands; and the ninth forbids any citizen of the United States to hunt on their lands, or to enter their country without a passport.

The remaining articles are equal, and contain stipulations which could be made only with a nation admitted to be capable of governing itself.

This treaty, thus explicitly recognizing the national character of the Cherokees, and their right of self government; thus guarantying their lands; assuming the duty of protection, and of course pledging the faith of the United States for that protection; has been frequently renewed, and is now in full force.

To the general pledge of protection have been added several specific pledges, deemed valuable by the Indians. Some of these restrain the citizens of the United States from encroachments on the Cherokee country, and provide for the punishment of intruders.

From the commencement of our government, congress has passed acts to regulate trade and intercourse with the Indians; which treat them as nations, respect their rights, and manifest a firm purpose to afford that protection which treaties stipulate. All these acts, and especially that of 1802, which is still in force, manifestly consider the several Indian nations as distinct political communities, having territorial boundaries, within which their authority is exclusive, and having a right to all the lands within those boundaries, which is not only acknowledged, but guarantied by the United States.

In 1819, congress passed an act for promoting those humane designs of civilizing the neighbouring Indians, which had long been cherished by the executive. It enacts, "that, for the purpose of providing against the further decline and final extinction of the Indian tribes adjoining to the frontier settlements of the United States, and for introducing among them the habits and arts of civilization, the president of the United States shall be, and he is hereby authorized, in every case where he shall judge improvement in the habits and condition of such Indians practicable, and that the means of instruction can be introduced *with their own consent,* to employ capable persons, of good moral character, to instruct them in the mode of agriculture suited to their situation; and for teaching their children in reading, writing and arithmetic; and for performing such other duties as may be enjoined, according to such instructions and rules as the president may give and prescribe for the regulation of their conduct in the discharge of their duties."

This act avowedly contemplates the preservation of the Indian nations as an object sought by the United States, and proposes to effect this object by civilizing and converting them from hunters into agriculturists. Though the Cherokees had already made considerable progress in this improvement, it cannot be doubted that the general words of the act comprehend them. Their advance in the "habits and arts of civilization," rather encouraged perseverance in the laudable exertions still farther to meliorate their condition. This act furnishes strong additional evidence of a settled purpose to fix the Indians in their country by giving them security at home.

The treaties and laws of the United States contemplate the Indian territory as completely separated from that of the states; and provide that all intercourse with them shall be carried on exclusively by the government of the union.

Is this the rightful exercise of power, or is it usurpation?

While these states were colonies, this power, in its utmost extent, was admitted to reside in the crown. When our revolutionary struggle commenced, congress was composed of an assemblage of deputies acting under specific powers granted by the legislatures, or conventions of the several colonies. It was a great popular movement, not perfectly organized; nor were the respective powers of those who were entrusted with the management of affairs accurately defined. The necessities of our situation produced a general conviction that those measures which concerned all, must be transacted by a body in which the representatives of all were assembled, and which could command the confidence of all: congress, therefore, was considered as invested with all the powers of war and peace, and congress dissolved our connexion with the mother country, and declared these

United Colonies to be independent states. Without any written definition of powers, they employed diplomatic agents to represent the United States at the several courts in Europe; offered to negotiate treaties with them, and did actually negotiate treaties with France. From the same necessity, and on the same principles, congress assumed the management of Indian affairs; first in the name of the United Colonies; and, afterwards, in the name of the United States. Early attempts were made at negotiation, and to regulate trade with them. These not providing successful, war was carried on under the direction, and with the forces of the United States, and the efforts to make peace, by treaty, were earnest and incessant. The confederation found congress in the exercise of the same powers of peace and war, in our relations with Indian nations, as with those of Europe.

Such was the state of things when the confederation was adopted. That instrument surrendered the powers of peace and war to congress, and prohibited them to the states, respectively, unless a state be actually invaded, "or shall have received certain advice of a resolution being formed by some nation of Indians to invade such a state, and the danger is so imminent as not to admit of delay till the United States is congress assembled can be consulted." This instrument also gave the United States in congress assembled the sole and exclusive right of "regulating the trade and managing all the affairs with the Indians, not members of any of the states: provided, that the legislative power of any state within its own limits be not infringed or violated."

. . . The Indian nations had always been considered as distinct, independent political communities, retaining their original natural rights, as the undisputed possessors of the soil, from time immemorial, with the single exception of that imposed by irresistible power, which excluded them from intercourse with any other European potentate than the first discoverer of the coast of the particular region claimed: and this was a restriction which those European potentates imposed on themselves, as well as on the Indians. The very term "nation," so generally applied to them, means "a people distinct from others." The constitution, by declaring treaties already made, as well as those to be made, to be the supreme law of the land, has adopted and sanctioned the previous treaties with the Indian nations, and consequently admits their rank among those powers who are capable of making treaties. The words "treaty" and "nation" are words of our own language, selected in our diplomatic and legislative proceedings, by ourselves, having each a definite and well understood meaning. We have applied them to Indians, as we have applied them to the other nations of the earth. They are applied to all in the same sense.

Georgia, herself, has furnished conclusive evidence that her former opinions on this subject concurred with those entertained by her sister states, and by the government of the United States. Various acts of her legislature have been cited in the argument, including the contract of cession made in the year 1802, all tending to prove her acquiescence in the universal conviction that the Indian nations possessed a full right to the lands they occupied, until that right should be extinguished by the United States, with their consent: that their territory was separated from that of any state within whose chartered limits they might reside, by a boundary line, established by treaties: that, within their boundary, they possessed rights with which no state could interfere: and that the whole power of regulating the intercourse with them, was vested in the United States. A review of these acts, on the part of Georgia, would occupy too much time, and is the less necessary, because they have been accurately detailed in the argument at the bar. Her new series of laws, manifesting her abandonment of these opinions, appears to have commenced in December 1828.

In opposition to this original right, possessed by the undisputed occupants of every country; to this recognition of that right, which is evidenced by our history, in every change through which we have passed; is placed the charters granted by the monarch of a distant and distinct region, parcelling out a territory in possession of others whom he could not remove and did not attempt to remove, and the cession made of his claims by the treaty of peace.

The actual state of things at the time, and all history since, explain these charters; and the king of Great Britain, at the treaty of peace, could cede only what belonged to his crown. These newly asserted titles can derive no aid from the articles so often repeated in Indian treaties; extending to them, first, the protection of Great Britain, and afterwards that of the United States. These articles are associated with others, recognizing their title to self government. The very fact of repeated treaties with them recognizes it; and the settled doctrine of the law of nations is, that a weaker power does not surrender its independence—its right to self government, by associating with a stronger, and taking its position. A weak state, in order to provide for its safety, may place itself under the protection of one more powerful, without stripping itself of the right of government, and ceasing to be a state. Examples of this kind are not wanting in Europe, "Tributary and feudatory states," says Vattel, "do not thereby cease to be sovereign and independent states, so long as self government and sovereign and independent authority are left in the administration of the state." At the present day, more than one state may be considered as holding its right of self government under the guarantee and protection of one or more allies.

The Cherokee nation, then, is a distinct community occupying its own territory, with boundaries accurately described, in which the laws of Georgia can have no force, and which the citizens of Georgia have no right to enter, but with the assent of the Cherokees themselves, or in conformity with treaties, and with the acts of congress. The whole intercourse between the United States and this nation, is, by our constitution and laws, vested in the government of the United States.

The act of the state of Georgia, under which the plaintiff in error was prosecuted, is consequently void, and the judgment a nullity. Can this court revise, and reverse it?

If the objection to the system of legislation, lately adopted by the legislature of Georgia, in relation to the Cherokee nation, was confined to its extra-territorial operation, the objection, though complete, so far as respected mere right, would give this court no power over the subject. But it goes much further. If the review which has been taken be correct, and we think it is, the acts of Georgia are repugnant to the constitution, laws, and treaties of the United States.

They interfere forcibly with the relations established between the United States and the Cherokee nation, the regulation of which, according to the settled principles of our constitution, are committed exclusively to the government of the union.

They are in direct hostility with treaties, repeated in a succession of years, which mark out the boundary that separates the Cherokee country from Georgia; guaranty to them all the land within their boundary; solemnly pledge the faith of the United States to restrain their citizens from trespassing on it; and recognize the pre-existing power of the nation to govern itself.

They are in equal hostility with the acts of congress for regulating this intercourse, and giving effect to the treaties.

The forcible seizure and abduction of the plaintiff in error, who was residing in the nation with its permission, and by authority of the president of the United States, is also a violation of the acts which authorise the chief magistrate to exercise this authority.

Will these powerful considerations avail the plaintiff in error? We think they will. He was seized, and forcibly carried away, while under guardianship of treaties guarantying the country in which he resided, and taking it under the protection of the United States. He was seized while performing, under the sanction of the chief magistrate of the union, those duties which the humane policy adopted by congress had recommended. He was apprehended, tried, and condemned, under colour of a law which has been shown to be repugnant to the constitution, laws, and treaties of the United States. Had a judgment, liable to the same objections, been rendered for property, none would question the jurisdiction of this court. It cannot be less clear when the judgment affects personal liberty, and inflicts disgraceful punishment, if punishment could disgrace when inflicted on innocence. The plaintiff in error is not less interested in the operation of this unconstitutional law than if it affected his property. He is not less entitled to the protection of the constitution, laws, and treaties of his country.

This point has been elaborately argued and, after deliberate consideration, decided, in the case of Cohens v. The Commonwealth of Virginia. . . .

It is the opinion of this court that the judgment of the superior court for the county of Gwinnet, in the state of Georgia, condemning Samuel A. Worcester to hard labour, in the penitentiary of the state of Georgia, for four years, was pronounced by that court under colour of law which is void, as being repugnant to the constitution, treaties, and laws of the United States, and ought, therefore, to be reversed and annulled.

# Endnotes

## Introduction

1. Office of the Governor of the State of Georgia, Press Advisory, November 24, 1992.
2. G. Edward White, *The Marshall Court & Cultural Change 1815–1835*, abridged ed. New York: Oxford University Press, 1991, p. 676.
3. David M. Engel, "Law in the Domains of Everyday Life: The Construction of Community and Difference," in Austin Sarat and Thomas Kearns (eds.): *Law in Everyday Life*. Ann Arbor: University of Michigan Press, 1993, pp. 169–70.

## Chapter 1

1. Richard Erdoes and Alfonso Ortiz, *American Indian Myths and Legends*. New York: Pantheon, 1984, pp. 106–107.
2. Russell Thornton, *The Cherokees: A Population History*. Lincoln: University of Nebraska Press, 1990, p. 5.
3. "Introduction," in Charles Hudson and Carmen Chaves Tesser (eds.): *The Forgotten Centuries: Indians and Europeans in the American South, 1521–1704*. Athens: University of Georgia Press, 1994, pp. 6–7.
4. For a discussion of terminology and a full description of southeastern chiefdoms, see Charles Hudson, *The Juan Pardo Expeditions: Explorations of the Carolinas and Tennessee, 1566–1568*. Washington, D.C.: Smithsonian Institution Press, 1990, pp. 54–66.
5. Hudson and Tesser, op. cit., p. 271.
6. Ibid., p. 268.

7. Hudson, op. cit., pp. 54–55.
8. Hudson and Tesser, op. cit., p. 12.
9. Ibid., pp. 41–43.
10. Ibid., p. 99.
11. Interview with Charles Hudson, January 19, 1993.
12. Charles Hudson, "The Genesis of Georgia's Indians," in Harvey H. Jackson and Phinizy Spalding (eds.): *Forty Years of Diversity: Essays on Colonial Georgia*. Athens: University of Georgia Press, 1984, p. 31.
13. Hudson and Tesser, op. cit., p. 259.
14. A subsequent church enumeration in 1676 found that only 5,000 Apalachees had survived. Ibid., p. 259. For further discussion of Native American population decline, see the work of Peter Wood, Russell Thornton, and Henry Dobyns.
15. Hudson and Tesser, op. cit., p. 272.
16. Ibid.
17. Several sources maintain that the Cherokee originated somewhere to the northwest above the Ohio River. Other scholars accept a northeastern origin, in part because of the linguistic affinities of the Cherokee to Iroquoian peoples. See Gary C. Goodwin, *Cherokees in Transition: A Study of Changing Culture and Environment Prior to 1775*. Chicago, Ill.: University of Chicago Press, 1977, pp. 32–33.
18. Ibid., p. 36.
19. James Mooney originated this figure a century ago in *Myths of the Cherokee*. Washington, D.C.: Smithsonian Institution. Bureau of American Ethnology. Nineteenth Annual Report, 1900, p. 14. His data have been employed by modern scholars, including Russell Thornton, Gary Goodwin, John Reid, and William Anderson.
20. John Reid, *A Law of Blood: The Primitive Law of the Cherokee Nation*. New York: New York University Press, 1970, p. 36.
21. This paragraph draws from data in ibid., pp. 12–16, and John Reid, *A Better Kind of Hatchet: Law, Trade and Diplomacy in the Cherokee Nation during the Early Years of European Contact*. University Park, Pa.: Pennsylvania State University Press, 1976, pp. 2–3.
22. See Reid, *A Law of Blood*, and Rennard Strickland, *Fire and the Spirits: Cherokee Law from Clan to Court*. Norman: University of Oklahoma Press, 1975.
23. Reid, *A Better Kind of Hatchet*, pp. 14–15.
24. Hudson and Tesser, op. cit., p. 586.
25. Ibid., p. 320.
26. Phinizy Spalding, *Oglethorpe in America*. Chicago, Ill.: University of Chicago Press, 1977, pp. 4, 20.
27. Kenneth Coleman, N. Bartley, W. Holmes, F. Boney, R. Spalding, and

C. Wynes, *A History of Georgia,* 2d ed. Athens: University of Georgia Press, 1991, pp. 15–17.

28. Spalding, op. cit., pp. 48–51, 60–61, 72.
29. Reid, *A Better Kind of Hatchet,* p. 190.
30. Coleman et al., op. cit., p. 44. In contrast, the Cherokee numbered 10,000 to 20,000 in this period, and the Creek considerably more.
31. Spalding, op. cit., p. 88.
32. Ibid., pp. 96–97.
33. Ibid., p. 51.
34. Ibid., p. 156. The legislation failed because of the jealousy of competing trading firms and colonies, including Carolina. See Michael D. Green, *The Politics of Indian Removal: Creek Government and Society in Crisis.* Lincoln: University of Nebraska Press, 1982, pp. 23–24.
35. Strickland, op. cit., chap. 3.
36. Edward J. Cashin, " 'But Brothers, It Is Our Land We Are Talking About': Winners and Losers in the Georgia Backcountry," in Ronald Hoffman, Thad W. Tate, and Peter J. Albert (eds.): *An Uncivil War: The Southern Backcountry during the American Revolution.* Charlottesville: University Press of Virginia, 1985, pp. 241–242; Green, op. cit., pp. 30–31.
37. Hoffman et al., op. cit., p. 241. By 1789 there were 100,000 non-Indians in the state of Georgia. Ibid., p. 321. Historians also attribute the increase in the non-Indian population to changes resulting from the 1763 British victory over France in the Seven Years' War. Green, op. cit., p. 28.
38. Hoffman, op. cit., pp. 244–245.
39. Ulrich Bonnell Phillips, *Georgia and State Rights.* Macon, Ga.: Mercer University Press, 1984, reproduction of the 1902 edition, p. 29.
40. See Charles J. Kappler (ed.): *Indian Affairs: Laws and Treaties.* Washington, D.C.: U.S. Government Printing Office, 1904, vol. 2, pp. 8–11.
41. Renee Jacobs, "Iroquois Great Law of Peace and the United States Constitution: How the Founding Fathers Ignored the Clan Mothers," *American Indian Law Review,* no. 2, p. 497 (no date).
42. Petra T. Shattuck and Jill Norgren, *Partial Justice: Federal Indian Law in a Liberal Constitutional System.* New York: Berg, 1991; Vine DeLoria and Clifford M. Lytle, *American Indians, American Justice.* Austin: University of Texas Press, 1983; Rennard Strickland, "Genocide-at-Law: An Historic and Contemporary View of the Native American Experience," *University of Kansas Law Review,* 1986, vol. 34, p. 713.
43. See Robert A. Williams, Jr., *The American Indian in Western Legal Thought: The Discourses of Conquest.* New York: Oxford University Press, 1990.
44. Hugo Grotius, *On the Law of War and Peace* (Classics of International

Law ed., 1925); Emmerich von Vattel, *The Law of Nations or the Principles of Natural Law* (Classics of International Law ed., 1916).

45. F. Cohen, *Handbook of Federal Indian Law*. U.S. Government Printing Office, Washington, D.C.: 1942, p. 47.
46. R. Clinton, "The Proclamation of 1763: Colonial Prelude to Two Centuries of Federal-State Conflict over the Management of Indian Affairs," *Boston University Law Review*, 1989, vol. 69, pp. 329, 362.
47. Northwest Ordinance, July 13, 1787, ch. 8, 1 Stat. 50. It is notable that a 1537 papal bull was almost word for word the source of the part of the ordinance dealing with Native American relations. Article IX of the Articles of Confederation provided that "[T]he United States, in Congress assembled, shall . . . have the sole and exclusive right and power of . . . regulating the trade and managing all affairs with the Indians not members of any of the states, provided that the legislative right of any state within its own limits be not infringed or violated." Articles of Confederation, Art. IX (1777), reprinted in *Journals of the Continental Congress, 1774–1789*, 1907, vol. 9, p. 919. The confusing reservation of state authority was subsequently deleted from the U.S. Constitution.
48. Clinton, op. cit., p. 371, quoting from *Journals of the Continental Congress, 1774–1789*, 1936, pp. 457–459. The paragraph draws on Clinton, pp. 370–374.
49. Phillips, op. cit., p. 22.
50. Green, op. cit., p. 35.
51. George R. Lamplugh, *Politics on the Periphery: Factions and Parties in Georgia, 1783–1806*. Newark: University of Delaware Press, 1986, pp. 64–65.
52. See William G. McLoughlin, *Cherokees and Missionaries, 1789–1839*. New Haven, Conn.: Yale University Press, 1984, p. 6, summarizing the work of Raymond Fogelson and Charles Hudson.
53. Ibid., pp. 3–8; Strickland, op. cit., chap. 3.
54. Phillips, op. cit., p. 15.
55. 2 Dall. 419, 1 L.Ed. 440 (1793). The litigation arose when a citizen of South Carolina sued to recover a debt owed by the state. The Supreme Court's unpopular decision in *Chisholm*, permitting a citizen of one state to sue another state in federal court, led to the adoption of the Eleventh Amendment to the U.S. Constitution.
56. Mary Young, "Racism in Red and Black: Indians and Other Free People of Color in Georgia Law, Politics, and Removal Policy," *Georgia Historical Quarterly*, Fall 1989, vol. 73, p. 492.
57. Title offices were among the most important institutions on the frontier. See ibid., pp. 516–517.
58. McLoughlin, op. cit., p. 2.

59. Ronald N. Satz, "The Cherokee Trail of Tears," *Georgia Historical Quarterly*, Fall 1989, vol. 73, p. 437.
60. *American State Papers, Public Lands*, 8 vols. Washington, D.C.: Gales and Seaton, 1832–1861, vol. 1, p. 126.
61. U.S. agent Return J. Meigs made the proposition. The Cherokee, however, expressed no interest. See William G. McLoughlin, *Cherokee Renascence in the New Republic*. Princeton, N.J.: Princeton University Press, 1986, pp. 129–130. In the early nineteenth century, even when a particular President came out strongly in favor of an Indian policy of removal or acculturation, other Indian policies were pursued.
62. William L. Anderson (ed.): *Cherokee Removal: Before and After*. Athens: University of Georgia Press, 1992, pp. viii–ix.
63. Green, op. cit., pp. 45–46.
64. Ibid., p. 50.
65. Mary Young, "The Exercise of Sovereignty in Cherokee Georgia," *Journal of the Early Republic*, Spring 1990, vol. 10, p. 44.
66. McLoughlin, op. cit., pp. xv–xvii.

## *Chapter 2*

1. October 23, 1822, "Resolution of the Cherokee National Legislature," Washington, D.C.: National Archives, Microfilm M-208, reel 1.
2. William G. McLoughlin, *Cherokee Renascence in the New Republic*. Princeton: Princeton University Press, 1986, p. 225, and Rennard Strickland, *Fire and the Spirits: Cherokee Law from Clan to Court*. Norman: University of Oklahoma Press, 1975, chap. 4.
3. Article IV, Section 1. A copy of the Cherokee Constitution of 1827 is most easily found in Strickland, op. cit., app. 3.
4. Ronald N. Satz, "The Cherokee Trail of Tears: A Sesquicentennial Perspective," *Georgia Historical Quarterly*, Fall 1989, vol. 431, p. 443.
5. Ibid., p. 443.
6. Benedict Anderson, *Imagining Community: Reflections on the Origin and Spread of Nationalism*. London: Verso, 1991.
7. McLoughlin, op. cit., and Theda Perdue (ed.), *Cherokee Editor: The Writings of Elias Boudinot*. Knoxville: University of Tennessee Press, 1983.
8. Ulrich Bonnell Phillips, *Georgia and State Rights*. Macon: Mercer University Press, 1984 (reprint of 1902 edition), p. 113.
9. *Acts of the General Assembly of the State of Georgia*, 1828, pp. 88–89.
10. Act of December 19, 1829, *Acts of the General Assembly of the State of Georgia*, pp. 98–101.
11. Michael D. Green, *The Politics of Indian Removal*. Lincoln: University of Nebraska Press, 1982, p. 156.

12. Gary E. Moulton, *The Papers of Chief John Ross,* 2 vols. Norman: University of Oklahoma Press, 1985, vol. 1, p. 3.

13. Ibid., vol. 1, p. 166.

14. Ibid., vol. 1, pp. 154–157.

15. Ibid., pp. 164–165; Frances Paul Prucha (ed.): *Cherokee Removal: The "William Penn" Essays and Other Writings.* Knoxville: University of Tennessee Press, 1981, p. 4.

16. Green, op. cit., pp. 48–49.

17. The "William Penn" essays are most easily read in Prucha, op. cit.

18. Clifford S. Griffin, *Their Brothers' Keepers: Moral Stewardship in the United States, 1800–1865* New Brunswick, N.J.: Rutgers University Press, 1960, p. 5.

19. Evarts to Rev. Dr. Worcester, February 3 and 16, in E. C. Tracy, *Memoir of the Life of Jeremiah Evarts, Esq.* Boston: Crocker and Brewster, 1845, pp. 128–129.

20. Ibid., pp. 129–130.

21. Prucha, op. cit., p. 53.

22. Ibid., p. 52.

23. Tracy, op. cit., p. 339.

24. Ross to Evarts, April 6, 1830, in Moulton, op. cit., vol. 1, p. 187.

25. Wilson Lumpkin, *The Removal of the Cherokee Indians from Georgia.* New York: Arno Press and the New York Times, 1969, p. 173.

26. Prucha, op. cit., p. 12; Evarts to Eleazar Lord, October 13, 1830, in Tracy, op. cit., pp. 400–401.

27. Evarts to Eleazar Lord, December 31, 1829, in ibid., p. 353.

28. Joseph C. Burke, "The Cherokee Cases: A Study in Law, Politics, and Morality," *Stanford Law Review,* February 1969, vol. 500, p. 506.

29. *Jackson* v. *Goodell,* 20 Johns. 188, 189–94 (N.Y. Sup. Ct. 1822). James Kent overturned Spenser's decision. See *Jackson* v. *Goddell,* 20 Johns. 693, 713–17 (N.Y. 1822).

30. U.S. Department of Justice, *Official Opinions of the Attorneys Generals of the United States,* 1 Op. Atty. Gen. 645 (1824) (Washington, 1852).

31. Worcester to D. Greene, November 25, 1829. Houghton Library, Harvard University, ABCFM, 18.3.1, vol. 5.

32. 2 Op. Atty. Gen. 110, 133 (1828).

33. Stanley Kutler (ed.): *John Marshall.* Englewood Cliffs, N.J.: Prentice-Hall, 1972, p. 92.

34. Wirt to Carr, June 21, 1830, in John Pendleton Kennedy, *Memoirs of the Life of William Wirt,* 2 vols. Philadelphia: Lea and Blanchard, 1849, vol. 2, pp. 291–293. Wirt was under pressure from his family "not to oppose the settled policy and wishes of [his] own government." He responded with a tirade about his right to defend the Cherokee. Maryland Historical Society, William Wirt Papers. Library of Congress, Reel 13.

35. Wirt to Ross, June 4, 1830. Moulton, op. cit., vol. 1, pp. 189–190.
36. Wirt, *Opinion on the Right of the State of Georgia* (Baltimore, Md., F. Lucas, Jr., 1830), p. 3.
37. Ibid., p. 14.
38. Wirt to Gov. George R. Gilmer, June 4, 1830. Georgia Department of Archives and History, *Cherokee Indian Letters, Talks, and Treaties.* WPA Project, AH-1252, reel 1, 211; Moulton, op. cit., vol. 1, p. 190.
39. Wirt to Carr, June 4, 1830, in Kennedy, *Life of William Wirt,* 294. Wirt presumably thought Georgia would resist a Section 25 case by failing to create the record necessary for the writ of error because of the course of action pursued by Virginia in *Martin* v. *Hunter's Lessee,* 1 Wheat. 304 (1816).
40. Kennedy, op. cit., pp. 295–296.
41. Wirt to Ross, August 9, 1830. Moulton, op. cit., vol. 1, p. 196.
42. Wirt to Ross, September 22, 1830. Moulton, op. cit., vol. 1, p. 199.
43. Burke, op. cit., p. 512.
44. Wirt to Swain, October 4, 1830. Maryland Historical Society, William Wirt Papers, reel 13. Wirt to James Madison, Oct. 5, 1830, ibid.
45. Wirt to Ross, November 15, 1830. Moulton, op. cit., vol. 1, p. 206 and Ross response, vol. 1, p. 210.
46. *State* v. *Tassels,* 1 Dud. 229, 230 (1830).

## *Chapter 3*

1. William G. McLoughlin, *Cherokees and Missionaries, 1789–1839.* New Haven, Conn.: Yale University Press, 1984, p. 4.
2. William G. McLoughlin, *Cherokee Renascence in the New Republic.* Princeton, N.J.: Princeton University Press, p. 136.
3. This discussion of Washington, D.C., and its architecture draws on Pamela Scott and Antoinette J. Lee, *Buildings of the District of Columbia.* New York: Oxford University Press, 1993.
4. Ibid., p. 113.
5. All quotes in this paragraph are from The United States Senate Commission on Art and Antiquities, *The Supreme Court Chamber, 1810–1860.* Washington, D.C.: U.S. Government Printing Office, 1981, pp. 1 and 9.
6. Ibid., pp. 4–5.
7. U.S. Senate Commission on Art and Antiquities, op. cit., p. 6.
8. Here and in subsequent paragraphs I draw on Vivien Green Fryd, *Art and Empire: The Politics of Ethnicity in the United States Capitol, 1815–1860.* New Haven, Conn.: Yale University Press, 1992, pp. 1–41.
9. Gordon S. Wood, *The Radicalism of the American Revolution.* New York: Vintage, 1991, p. 96.
10. George M. Fredrickson, *The Black Image in the White Mind: The Debate on*

*Afro-American Character and Destiny, 1817–1914*. New York: Harper & Row, 1971, vol. 1, pp. 46–47.

11. Robert V. Remini, *The Legacy of Andrew Jackson: Essays on Democracy, Indian Removal, and Slavery*. Baton Rouge: Louisiana State University Press, 1988, p. 39.

12. Charles Sellers, *The Market Economy: Jacksonian America, 1815–1846*. New York: Oxford University Press, 1991, pp. 32, 43.

13. Robert V. Remini, *Andrew Jackson and the Course of American Empire, 1767–1821*. New York: Harper & Row, 1977, p. 71.

14. Remini, *Andrew Jackson and the Course of American Empire*, p. 327.

15. Michael D. Green, *The Politics of Indian Removal*. Norman: University of Nebraska Press, 1982, p. 48.

16. Remini, *Andrew Jackson and the Course of American Empire*, p. 335.

17. For a discussion of the idea of expansion with honor, see Robert F. Berkhofer, *The White Man's Indian: Images of the American Indian from Columbus to the Present*. New York: Vintage, 1978, pp. 143–145.

18. Perry Miller, *Errand into the Wilderness*. Cambridge, Mass.: Harvard University Press, 1956.

19. *Oxford Annotated Bible*. New York: Oxford University Press, 1962, p. 1509.

20. Fryd, op. cit., p. 86.

21. Wood, op. cit., p. 332.

22. McLoughlin, *Cherokee Renascence in the New Republic*, pp. xvi–xvii.

23. Fredrickson, op. cit., p. 9. Chapter 1 contains a summary of the intellectual rationalizations behind the early colonization movement. For a comparative discussion of race politics in this period in Georgia, see Mary Young, "Racism in Red and Black: Indians and Other Free People of Color in Georgia Law, Politics and Removal Policy," *Georgia Historical Quarterly*, Fall 1989, vol. 73, p. 492.

24. Remini, *The Legacy of Andrew Jackson*, p. 48.

25. Remini, *Andrew Jackson and the Course of American Empire*, chaps. 24 and 384.

26. James D. Richardson, *A Compilation of the Messages and Papers of the Presidents, 1782–1892*, "Annual Address to Congress, December 8, 1829." Washington, D.C.: 1908, vol. 2, p. 1021.

27. 7 Cong. Deb. app. x (1830).

28. House Committee on Indian Affairs, H.R. Rep. No. 227 (1830), 11.

29. 6 Cong. Deb. (1830).

30. 6 Cong. Deb. 1010 (1830).

31. Fredrickson, op. cit., p. 25. Historian Mary Young notes that President Jackson sought to block government funds for the African colonization movement at the same time that he gave full support to the national financing of removal. She considers the acquisition of land to be the

critical factor in Jackson's approval of federal removal funds. See Young, op. cit.

32. Remini, *The Legacy of Andrew Jackson*, p. 66.
33. Mrs. Frances Trollope, *The Domestic Manners of the Americans*, II, 3d ed. London: Whittaker, Treacher, 1832, p. 12.
34. Removal Act, ch. 148, 4 Stat. 411 (1830) (codified as amended at 25 U.S.C. Sect. 174) (1982).

## Chapter 4

1. *Fletcher* v. *Peck*, 10 U.S. (6 Cranch) 87 (1810); *Johnson* v. *M'Intosh*, 21 U.S. (8 Wheat.) 543 (1823).
2. *Fletcher*, 10 U.S. (6 Cranch) at 142.
3. Ibid., pp. 142–143.
4. Ibid.
5. Ibid., p. 121.
6. United States Commission on Civil Rights, *Indian Tribes: A Continuing Question for Survival*. Washington, D.C.: 1981, p. 16.
7. Berman, "The Concept of Aboriginal Rights in the Early History of the United States," *Buffalo Law Review*, 1978, vol. 27, pp. 637, 642.
8. American Indian Policy Review Commission: *Task Force One: Trust Responsibilities and the Federal-Indian Relationship*. Washington, D.C.: U.S. Government Printing Office, 1976, p. 75.
9. *Fletcher*, 10 U.S. (6 Cranch), 146.
10. Ibid., pp. 146–147.
11. All quotes in this paragraph are found in ibid., p. 147.
12. Berman, "The Concept of Aboriginal Rights," p. 655.
13. Berman, op. cit., p. 646.
14. *Johnson*, 21 U.S. (8 Wheat.), 584 and 574.
15. Ibid., p. 574.
16. Newton, "At the Whim of the Sovereign: Aboriginal Title Reconsidered," *Hastings Law Journal*, 1980, vol. 31, pp. 1215, 1223.
17. Berman, op. cit., p. 646.
18. R. Kent Newmyer, *Supreme Court Justice Joseph Story: Statesman of the Old Republic*. Chapel Hill: University of North Carolina Press, 1985, p. 213.
19. See W. Veeder, *Suppression of Indian Tribal Sovereignty*, unpublished manuscript, 1973, p. 17, and Berman, op. cit., pp. 647–649.
20. *State* v. *George Tassels*, 1 Dud. 229 (1830) (Georgia), which appears as Appendix 1.
21. Ibid., pp. 230, 234.
22. Ibid., p. 231.
23. *Tassels*, 1 Dud. 229, p. 234.

24. Ibid., p. 234.
25. Ibid., p. 235.
26. Ibid.
27. Sidney Harring, *Crow Dog's Case: American Indian Sovereignty, Tribal Law, and United States Law in the Nineteenth Century.* New York: Cambridge University Press, 1994, p. 34.
28. *Niles Daily Register,* January 8, 1831, pp. 338–339.
29. T. Wilkins, *Cherokee Tragedy: The Story of the Ridge Family and the Decimation of a People.* Norman: University of Oklahoma Press, 1970, p. 209.
30. *Tassels,* 1 Dud. 229, 236.
31. Harring, op. cit., p. 30.
32. Wirt, to his wife, February 10, 1831. Maryland Historical Society, William Wirt Papers, reel 13.
33. See R. Peters, *The Case of the Cherokee Nation against the State of Georgia: Argued and Determined at the Supreme Court of the United States, January Term, 1831* (1831). The importance of *Cherokee Nation* led the court reporter to give the case particular attention and to publish the arguments made before the court.
34. *Cherokee Nation* v. *Georgia,* 30 U.S. (5 Pet.) 1, 16 (1831).
35. Ibid., p. 17. Italics added.
36. Ibid., p. 16.
37. Ibid., p. 18.
38. See, for example, Yasuhide Kawashima, *Puritan Justice and the Indian: 1630–1763.* Middletown, Ohio: Wesleyan University Press, 1986; Robert Williams, Jr., "The Algebra of Federal Indian Law: The Hard Trail of Decolonizing and Americanizing the White Man's Indian Jurisprudence," *Wisconsin Law Review* 1986, p. 219, note 134.
39. *Cherokee Nation,* 30 U.S. (5 Pet.), 17.
40. Ibid., p. 17.
41. Ibid., pp. 17–18.
42. Clinton, "Tribal Courts and the Federal Union," *1989 Harvard Indian Law Symposium.* Cambridge, Mass.: Harvard Law School Publications Center, 1989, p. 19.
43. Swindler, "Politics as Law: The Cherokee Cases," *American Indian Law Review,* 1975, vol. 7, p. 14, citing *Memoirs of John Quincy Adams,* C. F. Adams (ed.): Philadelphia, 1836, p. 315.
44. Swindler, op. cit., p. 14, citing *Massachusetts Historical Society Proceedings* (2d series), XIV (Oct. 12, 1831).
45. *Cherokee Nation,* 30 U.S. (5 Pet.), 20.
46. See, for example, *Martin* v. *Hunter's Lessee,* 1 Wheat. 304 (1816); *McCulloch* v. *Maryland,* 4 Wheat. 316 (1819); *Dartmouth College* v. *Woodward,* 4 Wheat. 518 (1819); *Sturges* v. *Crowninshield,* 4 Wheat. 122 (1819); and *Cohens* v. *Virginia,* 6 Wheat. 264 (1821).

47. *Cherokee Nation*, 30 U.S. (5 Pet.), 15.
48. See G. Edward White, *The Marshall Court & Cultural Change 1815–1835*, abridged ed. New York: Oxford University Press, 1991.
49. *Cherokee Nation*, 30 U.S. (5 Pet.), 49.
50. Ibid., p. 32.
51. *Fletcher*, 10 U.S. (6 Cranch), 146.
52. Ibid., pp. 146–147.
53. Ibid., p. 147.
54. *Cherokee Nation*, 30 U.S. (5 Pet.), 21–22, 27.
55. Ibid., p. 80.
56. White, op. cit., p. 187.
57. Burke, "The Cherokee Cases: A Study in Law, Politics, and Morality," *Stanford Law Review*, February 1969, pp. 500, 516–518.
58. Ross to the Cherokees, April 14, 1831. Moulton, op. cit., vol. 1, p. 217.
59. Ross to Harris, April 27, 1831, ibid., vol. 1, pp. 219–220.
60. Ross to Wirt, May 10, 1831, ibid., vol. 1, pp. 220–221.
61. Wirt to Ross, July 18, 1831, ibid., vol. 1, pp. 221–222.

## *Chapter 5*

1. Act of December 22, 1830. *Acts of the General Assembly of the State of Georgia*, 1831, pp. 114–117.
2. Evarts to Worcester, February 1, 1831. Harvard University, Houghton Library, ABCFM; Worcester to David Greene, March 14, 1831, Houghton Library, ABCFM.
3. Wirt to Worcester, July 19, 1831, cited in Edward A. Miles, "After John Marshall's Decision: Worcester v. Georgia and the Nullification Crisis," *Journal of Southern History*, November 1973, vol. 39, p. 525. The missionaries were U.S. postmasters from whom the Jackson Administration had withdrawn federal immunity.
4. Worcester to Greene, June 2, 1831. Houghton Library, ABCFM.
5. Letter of Joseph Story to his wife, January 13, 1832, in William W. Story (ed.): *Life and Letters of Joseph Story*, II (reprint of 1851 ed., Freeport, N.Y.: Books for Libraries Press, no date), p. 79.
6. Joseph Story to Mrs. Joseph Story, February 26, 1832, in ibid., p. 84.
7. See untitled and undated manuscript at the Historical Society of Pennsylvania, Sergeant Papers, box 5, file 18.
8. 6 Wheaton 264, 412 (1821).
9. Untitled, undated Sergeant manuscript, Sergeant Papers, pp. 21–22.
10. Burke, "The Cherokee Cases," *Stanford Law Review*, February 1969, p. 521.
11. Untitled, undated, Sergeant manuscript, Sergeant Papers, pp. 16, 19.
12. *Worcester* v. *Georgia*, 31 U.S. (6 Pet.), 541.

13. Ibid., 562.
14. Joseph Story to Sara Story, March 4, 1832, in Story, op. cit., vol. 2, pp. 83–84; *Johnson* v. *M'Intosh*, 21 U.S. (8 Wheat.) 543, 587–590 (1823).
15. All quotations in this paragraph are from *Worcester* 31 U.S. (6 Pet.), 543–546.
16. Ibid., p. 559.
17. Treaty of Holston, July 2, 1791, United States-Cherokee Indians, 7 Stat. 39; Treaty of Hopewell, November 28, 1785, United States-Cherokee Indians, 7 Stat. 18; *Worcester*, 31 U.S. (6 Pet.), 551–556.
18. *Worcester*, 31 U.S. (6 Pet.), 561.
19. Ibid., p. 552.
20. *Worcester*, 31 U.S. (6 Pet.), 553–554.
21. Ibid., p. 593.
22. Joseph Story to Professor Ticknor, March 8, 1832, in Story, op. cit., p. 83.
23. Coody to Wirt, March 28, 1832. Maryland Historical Society, William Wirt Papers, reel 15.
24. William McLoughlin has suggested that at the time of this appeal southerners were beginning to link Indian antiremoval and antislavery agitation as, to them, twin evils. See William McLoughlin *Cherokees and Missionaries, 1789–1839*. New Haven, Conn.: Yale University Press, 1984, p. 264.
25. Greene to Sergeant, March 9, 1832. Historical Society of Pennsylvania, Sergeant Papers.
26. Wirt to Lewis, April 28, 1832, pp. 10–11. The Papers of William Wirt, Collection of the Library of Congress, Manuscript Division, reel 4; Chester to Lumpkin, April 4, 1832, Georgia Department of Archives and History, Indians: Cherokees, File II, box 75.
27. Burke, op. cit., p. 525.
28. Charles Warren, *The Supreme Court in United States History*, 2 vols. (new revised ed., Boston: Little, Brown, 1926), vol. I, pp. 758–769.
29. Jackson to Brigadier General John Coffee, April 7, 1832, in John Spencer Bassett (ed.): *Correspondence of Andrew Jackson*. Washington, D.C.: Carnegie Institution of Washington, 1929, p. 247.
30. Wirt to Lewis, April 28, 1832. The Papers of William Wirt, Collection of the Library of Congress, Manuscript Division, reel 4.
31. Frelinghuysen to Greene, April 23, 1832. Quoted in Miles, "After John Marshall's Decision," *Journal of Southern History*, November 1973, p. 530.
32. Ross to Wirt, June 8, 1832. Gary E. Moulton, *The Papers of Chief John Ross*, 2 vols. Norman: University of Oklahoma Press, 1985, vol. 1, p. 245.
33. Ibid.
34. Ibid., p. 531.
35. Ibid., p. 532.

36. Ross to Wirt, June 8, 1832. Moulton, op. cit., vol. 1, pp. 245–246.

37. Wirt to Randall, Maryland Historical Society, William Wirt Papers, reel 25.

38. Wirt to Sergeant, December 22, 1832, in ibid., reel 23. In this letter Wirt asks if Sergeant is in agreement that on the one hand the authority of the Supreme Court is at stake but that on the other hand, as attorneys, they should obey the instructions of their clients.

39. Wirt to Potter, Dec. 26, 1832. Maryland Historical Society, William Wirt Papers, reel 23.

40. B. B. Wisner to Wirt, December 28, 1832. Maryland Historical Society, William Wirt Papers, reel 15.

41. Wisner to Wirt, December 28, 1832. Maryland Historical Society, William Wirt Papers, reel 15; Miles, op. cit., pp. 539, 543. Wisner reports that the resolution was unanimous.

42. Jack F. Kilpatrick and Anna G. Kilpatrick, *New Echota Letters: Contributions of Samuel A. Worcester to the Cherokee Phoenix.* Dallas: Southern Methodist University Press, 1968, pp. 116–129. See also Worcester to Sergeant, Jan. 22. 1833. Sergeant Collection, box 4, file 8.

43. Release order for Samuel A. Worcester and Elizur Butler. Governor Wilson Lumpkin to Charles C. Mills, Esq., Principal Keeper of the Penitentiary. January 14, 1833. State of Georgia Archives.

44. McLoughlin, op. cit., p. 259.

45. *Cherokee Phoenix,* July 27 and August 3, 1833. Reprinted in Kilpatrick, op. cit., pp. 121–128.

46. Wirt to William Drayton, January 15, 1833. Historical Society of Pennsylvania, Drayton Collection: Col. Wm. Drayton Papers.

47. Wirt to John Williams, February 26, 1833. Maryland Historical Society, William Wirt Papers.

48. Albert J. Beveridge, *The Life of John Marshall.* Boston: Houghton Mifflin, 1916–1919, vol. 4, p. 574.

49. Act of November 29, 1833, and Act of December 20, 1833, *Acts of the General Assembly of the State of Georgia, 1833,* pp. 126–127 and 114–118.

50. John A. Cuthbert to Governor Lumpkin, April 8, 1834. Georgia Department of Archives and History, *Cherokee Indian Letters,* reel 2, p. 477.

51. Letter of William Hardin to Governor Lumpkin, March 3, 1834, in ibid., reel 2, p. 439.

52. Ross to Sergeant, October 7, 1834. Sergeant Papers, box 4, file 11.

53. Ulrich Bonnell Phillips, *Georgia and State Rights.* Macon: Mercer University Press, 1984 (reprint of 1902 ed.), p. 84.

54. Rockwell and Hansell to Sergeant. Sergeant Papers, box 4, file 12.

55. Act of December 20, 1834, *Acts of the General Assembly of the State of Georgia, 1834,* pp. 152–156.

56. See generally, Theda Perdue, "The Conflict Within: Cherokees and Removal," in William L. Anderson, *Cherokee Removal: Before and After.* Athens: University of Georgia Press, 1991.
57. Charles J. Kappler, *Indian Affairs: Laws and Treaties.* Washington, D.C.: U.S. Government Printing Office, 1904, vol. 2, pp. 439–448, 448–449.
58. Schermerhorn to Commissioners Lumpkin and Carroll, July 11, 1836. National Archives, RG 75, M574, roll 18.
59. Underwood, Hansell, and Rockwell to Commissioners Lumpkin and Kennedy, February 20, 1837. National Archives, RG 75, M574, roll 18. Quotes in the following two paragraphs are also taken from this letter.
60. Report of the Indian Committee, July 17, 1837. National Archives, RG 75, M574, roll 1.
61. Underwood, Hansell, and Rockwell to "Our friends and representatives," September 14, 1837, National Archives, RG 75, M574, roll 18.
62. Lewis Ross to John Ross, March 22, 1838. Moulton, op. cit., vol. 1, p. 615.
63. Ross to D. Russell, July 13, 1840. National Archives, RG 75, M574, roll 1, frames 469–473.

## Conclusion

1. Russell Thornton, "The Demography of the Trail of Tears Period: A New Estimate of Cherokee Population Losses," in William L. Anderson (ed.): *Cherokee Removal: Before and After.* Athens: University of Georgia Press, 1991, p. 93.
2. 118 U.S. 375 (1886) and 187 U.S. 553 (1903).
3. Charles F. Wilkinson, *American Indians, Time, and the Law.* New Haven, Conn.: Yale University Press, 1987, p. 24.
4. *United States* v. *Kagama*, 118 U.S. 379, 383–4. For a full discussion of the late nineteenth-century transformation of federal Indian law, see Petra T. Shattuck and Jill Norgren, *Partial Justice.* New York: Berg, 1991, in particular chaps. 2 and 3.
5. Robert N. Clinton, "Tribal Courts and the Federal Union," *1989 Harvard Indian Law Symposium,* 1990, vol. 15, pp. 27–28.
6. *Worcester* v. *Georgia*, 31 U.S. (6 Pet.), 559 (1832).
7. *Tee-Hit-Ton Indians* v. *U.S.*, 348 U.S. 272, 289 (1955).
8. Ibid., p. 290.
9. *Oliphant* v. *The Suquamish Indian Tribe*, 98 S. Ct. 1014 (1978).
10. *Montana* v. *United States*, 450 U.S. 544, 554–55 (1981).
11. *Duro* v. *Reina*, 110 S. Ct. 2053, 2059 (1990).
12. Ibid., p. 2060.
13. Ibid.
14. 616 Atlantic Reporter, 2d Series 210 (1992).

15. Ibid., p. 218.
16. *Mabo* v. *Queensland,* 66 High Ct. of Australia 408 (1992) 409, 422, and 451.
17. Wilkinson and Volkman, "Judicial Review of Indian Treaty Abrogation," *California Law Review,* 1975, vol. 63, p. 601.
18. I draw here on Shattuck and Norgren, op. cit., pp. 190–192.

# Suggested Readings

Abel, Annie Heloise. "The History of Events Resulting in Indian Consolidation West of the Mississippi," *Annual Report of the American Historical Association for the Year 1906,* 2 vols. Washington, D.C.: American Historical Association, 1908, vol. I, pp. 233–450.

Anderson, William L. (ed.). *Cherokee Removal: Before and After.* Athens: University of Georgia Press, 1992.

Ball, Milner. "Constitution, Court, Indian Tribes," *American Bar Foundation Research Journal,* Winter 1987.

Bassett, John Spencer (ed.). *The Correspondence of Andrew Jackson,* 6 vols. Washington, D.C.: Carnegie Institution of Washington, 1926–1933.

Berkhofer, Robert F. *The White Man's Indian: Images of the American Indian from Columbus to the Present.* New York: Random House, 1978.

Burke, Joseph C. "The Cherokee Cases: A Study in Law, Politics, and Morality," *Stanford Law Review,* February 1969, vol. 21.

Champagne, Duane. *Social Order and Political Change: Constitutional Governments among the Cherokee, the Choctow, the Chickasaw, and the Creek.* Stanford, Ca.: Stanford University Press, 1992.

Clinton, Robert N., Nell Jessup Newton, and Monroe E. Price. *American Indian Law: Cases and Materials,* 3d ed. Charlottesville, Va.: Michie, 1991.

Coleman, Kenneth, N. Bartley, W. Holmes, F. Boney, R. Spalding, and C. Wynes. *A History of Georgia,* 2d ed. Athens: University of Georgia Press, 1991.

Conser, Walter H., Jr. "John Ross and the Cherokee Resistance Campaign, 1833–1838," *Journal of Southern History,* May 1978, vol. 44.

Corkran, David H. *The Cherokee Frontier: Conflict and Survival, 1740–62.* Norman: University of Oklahoma Press, 1962.

Corry, John Pitts. *Indian Affairs in Georgia, 1732–1756.* Ph.D. dissertation, Philadelphia: University of Pennsylvania, 1936.

Dale, Edward E., and Gaston Little (eds.). *Cherokee Cavaliers: Forty Years of Cherokee History as Told in the Correspondence of the Ridge-Watie-Boudinot Family.* Norman: University of Oklahoma Press, 1939.

Debo, Angie. *And Still the Waters Run: The Betrayal of the Five Civilized Tribes,* 1940 (revised ed., Princeton: Princeton University Press, 1972).

Deloria, Vine. *American Indian Policy in the Twentieth Century.* Norman: University of Oklahoma Press, 1985.

―――― and Clifford M. Lytle. *American Indians, American Justice.* Austin: University of Texas Press, 1983.

Dippie, Brian W. *The Vanishing American: White Attitudes and U.S. Indian Policy.* Middletown, Conn.: Wesleyan University Press, 1982.

Eaton, Rachel. *John Ross and the Cherokee Indians.* Chicago: 1921.

Ehle, John. *Trail of Tears: The Rise and Fall of the Cherokee Nation.* New York: Doubleday, 1988.

Erdoes, Richard, and Alfonso Ortiz. *American Indian Myths and Legends.* New York: Pantheon, 1984.

Evarts, Jeremiah. *Essays on the Present Crisis.* Boston: Thomas Kite, 1829.

Foreman, Grant. *Indian Removal: The Emigration of the Five Civilized Tribes.* Norman: University of Oklahoma Press, 1932, 1972.

Frickey, Philip P. "Marshalling Past and Present: Colonialism, Constitutionalism, and Interpretation in Federal Indian Law." *Harvard Law Review,* December 1993, vol. 107.

Gabriel, Ralph H. *Elias Boudinot, Cherokee and His America.* Norman: University of Oklahoma Press, 1941.

Goodwin, Gary C. *Cherokees in Transition: A Study of Changing Culture and Environment Prior to 1775.* Chicago: University of Chicago Press, 1977.

Green, Michael D. *The Politics of Indian Removal: Creek Government and Society in Crisis.* Lincoln: University of Nebraska Press, 1982.

Harring, Sidney. *Crow Dog's Case: American Indian Sovereignty, Tribal Law, and United States Law in the Nineteenth Century.* New York: Cambridge University Press, 1994.

Hatch, Nathan O. *The Democratization of American Christianity.* New Haven, Conn.: Yale University Press, 1989.

Hatley, Tom. *The Dividing Paths: Cherokees and South Carolinians Through the Era of Revolution.* New York: Oxford University Press, 1993.

Hoffman, Ronald, Thad W. Tate, and Peter J. Albert. *An Uncivil War: The Southern Backcountry during the American Revolution.* Charlottesville: University Press of Virginia, 1985.

Horsman, Reginald. *Race and Manifest Destiny: The Origins of American Racial Anglo-Saxonism.* Cambridge, Mass.: Harvard University Press, 1981.

Hudson, Charles. *The Juan Pardo Expeditions: Explorations of the Carolinas and*

*Tennessee, 1566–1568*. Washington, D.C.: Smithsonian Institution Press, 1990.

———. *The Southeastern Indians*. Knoxville: University of Tennessee Press, 1977.

Hudson, Charles, and Carmen Chaves Tesser (eds.). *The Forgotten Centuries: Indians and Europeans in the American South, 1521–1704*. Athens: University of Georgia Press, 1994.

Kappler, Charles J. *Indian Affairs: Laws and Treaties*. Washington, D.C.: U.S. Government Printing Office, 1904.

Kennedy, John P. *Memoirs of the Life of William Wirt*. Philadelphia: Lea Blanchard, 1849.

Kilpatrick, Jack F., and Anna G. Kilpatrick. *New Echota Letters: Contributions of Samuel A. Worcester to the Cherokee Phoenix*. Dallas: Southern Methodist University Press, 1968.

King, Duane (ed.). *The Cherokee Indian Nation*. Knoxville: University of Tennessee Press, 1979.

Lamplugh, George R. *Politics on the Periphery: Factions and Parties in Georgia, 1783–1806*. Newark: University of Delaware Press, 1986.

Lumpkin, Wilson. *The Removal of the Cherokee Indians from Georgia*, 2 vols. New York: Dodd Mead, 1907.

Lyons, Oren R., and John C. Mohawk (eds.). *Exiled in the Land of the Free*. Santa Fe, N. M.: Clear Water Press, 1992.

McLoughlin, William G. *After the Trail of Tears: The Cherokees' Struggle for Sovereignty, 1839–1880*. Chapel Hill: University of North Carolina Press, 1993.

———. *Cherokee Renascence in the New Republic*. Princeton, N. J.: Princeton University Press, 1986.

———. *Cherokees and Missionaries, 1789–1839*. New Haven, Conn.: Yale University Press, 1984.

——— with Walter H. Conser, Jr., and Virginia Duffy McLoughlin. *The Cherokee Ghost Dance: Essays on the Southeastern Indians, 1789–1861*. Macon, Ga.: Mercer University Press, 1984.

Magrath, C. Peter. *Yazoo: Law and Politics in the New Republic*. New York: Norton, 1966.

Malone, Henry. *Cherokees of the Old South: A People in Transition*. Athens: University of Georgia Press, 1956.

Merrell, James H. *The Indians' New World: Catawbas and Their Neighbors from European Contact through the Era of Removal*. Chapel Hill: University of North Carolina Press, 1989.

Miles, Edwin A. "After John Marshall's Decision," *Journal of Southern History*, 1973, vol. 39.

Mooney, James. *Historical Sketch of the Cherokee*. Chicago: Aldine, 1975.

Moulton, Gary E. *John Ross: Cherokee Chief*. Athens: University of Georgia Press, 1978.

———. *The Papers of Chief John Ross*, 2 vols. Norman: University of Oklahoma Press, 1985.

Neely, Sharlotte. *Snowbird Cherokees: People of Persistence*. Athens: University of Georgia Press, 1991.

Newton, Nell Jessup. "Federal Power over Indians: Its Sources, Scope and Limitations," *University of Pennsylvania Law Review*, 1984, vol. 132.

Parrington, Vernon Louis. *Main Currents in American Thought*. New York: Harcourt Brace, 1927–1930.

Perdue, Theda (ed.). *Cherokee Editor: The Writings of Elias Boudinot*. Knoxville: University of Tennessee Press, 1983.

———. *Slavery and the Evolution of Cherokee Society, 1540–1866*. Knoxville, University of Tennessee Press, 1979.

Peters, Richard. *The Case of the Cherokee Nation against the State of Georgia*. Philadelphia, 1831.

Phillips, Ulrich Bonnell. *Georgia and State Rights*. Macon, Ga.: Mercer University Press, 1984 (reprint of 1902 ed.).

Prucha, Francis Paul. *American Indian Policy in the Formative Years: The Indian Trade and Intercourse Acts, 1790–1834*. Cambridge, Mass.: Harvard University Press, 1962.

———. *Cherokee Removal: The 'William Penn' Essays and Other Writings by Jeremiah Evarts*. Lincoln: University of Nebraska Press, 1981.

———. *The Great Father: The United States Government and the American Indians*, 2 vols. Lincoln: University of Nebraska Press, 1984.

Reid, John Phillip. *A Better Kind of Hatchet: Law, Trade and Diplomacy in the Cherokee Nation during the Early Years of European Contact*. University Park, Pa.: Pennsylvania State University Press, 1976.

———. *A Law of Blood: The Primitive Law of the Cherokee Nation*. New York: New York University Press, 1970.

Remini, Robert V. *Andrew Jackson and the Course of American Empire, 1767–1821*. New York: Harper & Row, 1977.

———. *Andrew Jackson and the Course of American Freedom, 1822–1832*. New York: Harper & Row, 1981.

———. *The Legacy of Andrew Jackson: Essays on Democracy, Indian Removal, and Slavery*. Baton Rouge: Louisiana State University Press, 1988.

Rogin, Michael. *Fathers and Children: Andrew Jackson and the Subjugation of the American Indians*. New York: Knopf, 1975.

Royce, Charles C. *The Cherokee Nation of Indians* (1887). Reprint, Chicago: Aldine, 1975.

Satz, Ronald N. *American Indian Policy in the Jacksonian Era*. Lincoln: University of Nebraska Press, 1975.

Schlesinger, Arthur M., Jr. *The Age of Jackson.* Boston: Little, Brown, 1945.

Sellers, Charles. *The Market Economy: Jacksonian America, 1815–1846.* New York: Oxford University Press, 1991.

Shattuck, Petra T., and Jill Norgren. *Partial Justice: Federal Indian Law in a Liberal Constitutional System.* Providence, R. I.: Berg, 1991.

Sheehan, Bernard. *Seeds of Extinction.* Chapel Hill: University of North Carolina Press, 1973.

Spalding, Phinizy. *Oglethorpe in America.* Chicago: University of Chicago Press, 1977.

Starkey, Marion L. *The Cherokee Nation.* New York: Knopf, 1946.

Starr, Emmet. *History of the Cherokee Indians and Their Legends and Folk Lore* (1921). Reissued, New York: Kraus Reprint Co., 1969.

Strickland, Rennard. *Fire and the Spirits: Cherokee Law from Clan to Court.* Norman: University of Oklahoma Press, 1975.

Thornton, Russell. *The Cherokees: A Population History.* Lincoln: University of Nebraska Press, 1990.

Tocqueville, Alexis de. *Democracy in America,* 2 vols. New York: Knopf, 1945. See in particular, vol. I, chap. 18.

Tracy, E. C. *Memoir of the Life of Jeremiah Evarts, Esq.* Boston: Crocker and Brewster, 1845.

Van Every, Dale. *The Disinherited: The Lost Birthright of the American Indian.* New York: Morrow, 1966.

Wallace, Anthony F. C. *The Long, Bitter Trail: Andrew Jackson and the Indians.* New York: Hill & Wang, 1993.

Wardell, Morris L. *A Political History of the Cherokee Nation* (reprint). Norman: University of Oklahoma Press, 1977.

White, G. Edward. *The Marshall Court & Cultural Change* (abridged ed.). New York: Oxford University Press, 1991.

Wilkins, Thurmond. *Cherokee Tragedy: The Story of the Ridge Family and the Decimation of a People.* New York: Macmillan, 1970.

Wilkinson, Charles F. *American Indians, Time, and the Law.* New Haven, Conn.: Yale University Press, 1987.

Williams, Robert A. *The American Indian in Western Legal Thought: The Discourses of Conquest.* New York: Oxford University Press, 1990.

Wood, Gordon S. *The Radicalism of the American Revolution.* New York: Vintage, 1991.

Young, Mary. "The Exercise of Sovereignty in Cherokee Georgia," *Journal of the Early Republic,* Spring 1990, vol. 10.

———. "Racism in Red and Black: Indians and Other Free People of Color in Georgia Law, Politics, and Removal Policy," *Georgia Historical Quarterly,* Fall 1989, vol. 73.

———*Redskins, Ruffleshirts and Rednecks.* Norman: University of Nebraska Press, 1961.

# Index